D0735334

Words of Praise for
Home at the Tree of Life

"This remarkable book takes you on an incredible journey into the spiritual dimension where you'll discover life-altering answers to universal questions of life and existence. It will change your perceptions of reality!"

-Dan Lux, Executive Producer

"In her book *Home at the Tree of Life* Dr. Gabor gives us first person account of events as they happened with her clients, opening up our understanding of where we're really from. This book answers the tough questions the mind yearns to validate and gives a glimpse beyond the limited physical, putting us back into the land of all possibilities."

-Theodoros Kousouli, D.C., C.Ht.
www.DrKousouli.com

"Dr. Elena Gabor's pioneering work *Home at the Tree of Life* provides readers with a rare glimpse into the fascinating and mysterious journey of the human soul. The mastery of her work creates a bridge from the physical world to the ethereal and celestial realms. Her exploration of the subconscious and superconscious mind through hypnosis creates a synthesis of divine incarnation, guiding clients and readers alike to the roots of our eternal Home.

Dr. Gabor's hypnotherapy bares rich fruit as she takes her readers on a journey through the mysteries of unconscious wisdom. Based on the clinical histories of her clients, *Home at the Tree of Life* reveals the personal journey of four people's exploration of their subconscious universe and their soul's journey back to Source, the inevitable healing that comes from courageously exploring the inner life and the wisdom gained through exploration-hypnosis. Her engaging book has the ability to deliver readers to the gateway of eternity and divinity that lies deep within of each one of us."

-John Sanders, Psy.D.t., C.Ht.

HOME

at the

TREE of LIFE

AN INTRODUCTION TO SUBCONSCIOUS,
ETHEREAL SCIENCE

Life Transforming Journeys through the Exploration of
the Subconscious Universe and the Soul's Reconnection
with The Source of Life

Dr. Elena Gabor

Home at the Tree of Life: An Introduction to Subconscious, Ethereal Science
Copyright © 2013 Dr. Elena Gabor, www.drgabor.com

This book is based on Dr. Elena Gabor's research with her clients from the United States and Europe. The names and some of the personal information of the people in this book have been changed to protect their identity.

The information contained in this book is intended for educational purpose, and not for diagnosis, prescription or treatment of any health disorders. In no way is this book intended to replace, countermand or conflict with the advice given to you by your own physician. The author of this book does not offer medical advice or prescribe the use of any techniques as a form of treatment for medical or psychological problems without the advice of a physician, either directly or indirectly. The intent of the author is only to provide information of general nature that can be used as an adjunct to healthcare programs prescribed by healthcare professionals. The author and publisher disclaim all liability in connection with the use of this book.

Special thanks to the editorial team: Ana Valentine, Crystal Reed, Kayla Leung, Ilene Segalove, Jennifer Champion, Lisa Gizara, Carolina Solano, Deborah Edler and Sam Stone, and to Ari Gabor and Alessandra Yanes for transcribing the sessions.

Cover design by Laura Wright LaRoche, LLPix Photography, www.llpix.com

Library of Congress Control Number: 2012923804
IBSN 13: 978-0-9883114-0-4
IBSN 10: 0988311402

Publisher Elena Gabor drelenagabor@yahoo.com

Printed in the United States of America.

Home at the Tree of Life is dedicated

To all of you who have the desire to understand the mysteries of the mind, life and death, and have asked questions this book addresses.

To all of my clients who have agreed to have their stories published in this book, to empower you in your journey of self-discovery and well-being.

To all of the amazing people who have invested their time and talent to contribute to the creation of this book.

To my son Ari who fills my life with love, to my family and friends for their love and support, and to the memory of my grandparents Lena and Pavel who brought so much love and happiness into my life.

To all of my friends and colleagues who have dedicated their lives to the progress of medicine and to help elevate the human condition.

And last, but not least,
to the Love forces of the Universe that inspire and accompany us throughout our lives.

Contents

Foreword

by Marilyn Gordon,
the best–selling author of
Realize your Greatness

Dr. Elena Gabor's book *Home at the Tree of Life* is an enlightening book that will open the doors of your consciousness and will certainly transform the way you see life. If you are looking for a book that is panoramic in scope and that answers your deepest questions on the nature of reality, you have found it in this book.

Dr. Gabor is a talented practitioner of medical hypnotherapy and past life regression. In her book, she takes her clients on journeys not only into the lives that have significantly impacted the problems they're concerned with now, but she takes them into the universe. From here, they channel their wisdom about the life of the soul.

This book answers the burning questions of existence: What is the purpose of life? Why is there suffering on Earth? What kind of energy are we made of? How do we reach a higher level of existence? Do we really create our reality? What happens when we sleep? What is it like to die? What is it like to be in the Light after we die? What's the difference between a beginner soul and an advanced one? Who are our Spiritual Guides? Who are the angels? And much more!

Not only is Dr. Gabor a talented practitioner, but she has also drawn gifted clients to her. In deep relaxation, they are able to reach advanced states of consciousness in which they contact Guides and bring forth astounding information. They also find information about their own former lifetimes that have contributed to the problems they're grappling with in this one.

When the clients first came to her, they were in states of profound distress. Through the process of regression and through the guidance of Dr. Gabor, they proceeded to rise out of states of dire depression and suffering into a radiance and happiness greater than they had known before.

If you want to be uplifted, open the pages of this book and travel on the journey of self-understanding that graces its pages. A powerful and mind-opening journey, indeed.

Marilyn Gordon
Director of The Life Transformation Company, Author,
Transformational Teacher, Board Certified Hypnotherapist

Introduction

I have always been fascinated by the mysteries of the mind and wondered whether our consciousness survives physical death. The innovative process of self-discovery and healing known as hypnotherapy or subconscious mind therapy is an effective method for uncovering the mysteries of the subconscious universe.

The real-life stories of four of my clients from Europe and the United States described in this book reveal how the exploration of their subconscious transformed their lives. Our work took the clients with health challenges from severe depression, suicidal thoughts, anxiety, fear, fatigue, alcohol dependency, precancerous lesions, excess weight and lack of self-confidence into healing and successful recovery.

In a state of profound relaxation and focused concentration (hypnosis), these explorers connected with their subconscious awareness and discovered that some of the real root causes of their current challenges originated in past lives. By connecting with other facets of their own multi-dimensional selves—their past life identities that experienced the original traumas—they not only gained deep insights into their current plights, but they also learned powerful lessons about love and positivity that helped them overcome their current challenges.

Past life explorations enabled my clients to realize that death is not real, that when the physical body dies, the soul emerges from the body like a Phoenix from its ashes. They understood that the soul is eternal and can live countless physical and nonphysical lifetimes. They also discovered the Light that people usually see in near-death experiences, where they felt wonderful sentiments which are difficult to describe in words. They continued their journey by exploring the magnificent universe that exists beyond the Light (referred to as *Home* in this book), the place where all souls come into existence and where they return after physical death. There my clients connected to the universal mind and accessed an inestimable wealth of information about the nature of our existence. I have coined the term "Subconscious, Ethereal Science" to refer to this body of knowledge for which we, as human beings, have always longed. This knowledge reveals who we really are, what our purpose on Earth is, what diseases truly are, how they form and how we can heal ourselves and live happy and balanced lives.

As a result of these profound experiences, my clients' symptoms subsided and their health improved substantially in a short period of time. In just a few sessions their health was restored.

It is astonishing to watch people recover from such serious disorders with absolutely no medication. This process of self-exploration made my clients realize that our own consciousness is in all accounts responsible for our physiological and emotional experiences, and ultimately our life. This epiphany combined with their new understanding of the essential role positive thinking plays in healing helped them change their life perspectives, form new neural pathways of thinking, and ultimately to heal.

My journey toward the specific findings presented in this book began when I stumbled across the remarkable results achieved by a medical doctor using subconscious mind therapy to treat severe mental and physical disorders. (Subconscious mind therapy includes hypnotherapy and is a generic term for all therapeutic approaches that address the subconscious mind. It is an alternative approach to healing.) After much research, I discovered that many well-known doctors of different medical specialties, as well as many therapists around the world achieved wonderful results in utilizing this therapeutic approach with their patients without using prescription medication. I even met people who were not part of the medical community using these techniques with great success. It seemed too good to be true. I was very interested in this *new* science but I needed to be sure it was real. At the time I had been practicing as a Medical Doctor of Stomatology (the equivalent of a Doctor of Dental Medicine) for ten years in Europe, but I decided to embark on an exciting journey to pursue my calling on finding out more about the subconscious universe.

I continued to research everything I could find about this field, and after completing an in-depth training in the United States I began applying my new knowledge. As a scientist, I started to observe and document all of the concordances and patterns. I began to see how vital the exploration of the subconscious mind is for understanding diseases and the mechanisms of healing, and how crucial it is for understanding the complexity of the mind. The similarities of my clients' experiences, discoveries and testimonies were impressive, as well as the improvements in their health. These discoveries are not only profound and reproducible, but they also generate amazing therapeutic results.

I feel strongly that a new field of medicine needs to be researched and implemented: Subconscious Medicine—the study of the subconscious mind. The science of the subconscious universe should no longer be absent from the medical books.

So now let us begin the story of my journey of exploring the mysteries of the mind. After living for a few years in Santa Monica, a beautiful city located on the coast of the Pacific Ocean in sunny California and working with more than a thousand hypnotherapy clients, I found some of the answers I was seeking. Then one day, as I was back in Europe for a few months, one of my psychiatrist colleagues asked me if I could see one of her patients named Mia who was suffering from severe depression and was not responding well to medication. Mia actually began having suicidal thoughts after taking the prescribed medicines. She confessed to her psychiatrist that she felt overwhelmed and was losing control over her life. At the time, I had no idea that this young woman would bring forth the answers to many of my unanswered questions, and our work would reveal many of the profound mysteries of life and death.

Introduction

CHAPTER ONE

Memories Erased by the Waves of Time

"Turn your face to the sun and the shadows will fall behind you."
Maori proverb

MIA' S CASE

When Mia, a beautiful woman in her late twenties walked into the office, her face was marred by sadness and worry. I invited her to sit down and as she began speaking I could sense her suffering. This would be her first experience with hypnotherapy. She insisted she had tried everything to overcome her depression, anxiety, and suicidal thoughts, yet nothing had worked. She believed that this therapeutic approach was her last resort, and if this process did not help, she felt she would die.

A few months prior to our initial meeting, Mia had learned from her psychiatrist about the benefits of hypnotherapy, but when she was told that accessing her subconscious mind would require getting into a deeply relaxed state called hypnosis (where the brain reaches the Alpha, Theta and REM states) Mia was hesitant to proceed. She had preconceived beliefs about hypnosis mostly based on the religious teachings of her childhood when she actually had no idea what hypnosis entailed. Mia finally agreed to come to an appointment with me only when she became desperate because her condition was getting worse and her prescribed medication was not helpful.

By that time, I was exclusively using hypnotherapy with my clients, which had proven to have a much stronger and more successful impact than any other method I had studied and used.

My earlier university training had ingrained in me a scientific way of thinking, one that was limited to the beliefs of modern medicine and dentistry. However, armed with a multitude of questions along with the determination to free my mind of any preconceived and limiting ideas or assumptions I had adopted from science, I embarked upon the journey that would open doors I never even knew existed. It gave me access to often unexplored areas and to a path down where few doctors had ever ventured. The investigation of the techniques that address the subconscious mind and an understanding of the subsequent healing process quickly became my priority.

We have all heard the sayings, "Everything is in your mind" and "You create your own reality." Some even argue that we create our diseases and that by changing the way we think, we can actually change our lives and improve our health. Does our way of thinking really have such a big impact on our reality that it truly defines our health and our experiences? And if it can influence our health so powerfully, why isn't the importance of positive thinking emphasized in medicine?

Many of the major issues that challenge us (depression, anxiety, fears, addictions, weight problems, certain cases of infertility and so on) seem to be deeply rooted in the subconscious mind. Hypnotherapy addresses three aspects of our mind, our consciousness. First, there is the conscious aspect of the mind that we use when we are awake. It begins forming in early childhood and serves as our logic, analytic center. The second aspect is the subconscious mind itself. It coordinates activities related to the normal functioning of the physical body and is constantly present throughout our entire lives. The third aspect of the mind is called the superconscious mind, the higher self. It is that higher state of awareness that can be accessed in very deep states of meditation or hypnosis. The cooperation of these three aspects of the mind ensures the normal functioning of the human being. During hypnotherapy the client connects with the subconscious, and often even with the superconscious state of awareness.

As my clients' cases reveal, both the subconscious and the superconscious aspects of the mind hold the keys to overcoming most undesirable conditions, as well as the pathways through which recovery and healing occur. These mechanisms of healing, which took me a while to detect and understand, really have to do with identifying, dismantling and rebuilding disempowering, fear-based and negatively-oriented conscious and subconscious core belief systems.

After introductions, Mia quickly opened up and described her problems to me.

M: When I'm driving, I wonder what would happen if I let go of the wheel. The only thing that prevents me from letting go is not that I would harm myself but that I might harm other people.

Mia explained that she had a long history of severe depression. She was raised in a poor family with a very controlling, alcoholic father who verbally and physically abused his wife and children on a daily basis. She tried to kill herself three times—at 14, 16 and 21 years old by taking overdoses of medication. A year prior to our appointment her depression had worsened again. She was also experiencing intense anxiety episodes in which she had difficulty breathing. I asked Mia if she was sleeping well at night and feeling well-rested in the morning.

M: No, not rested. I haven't felt rested for many months. I feel as though every cell of my body hurts when I wake up in the morning and it's not from physical fatigue. It feels like my muscles are anchoring me to the floor. I'm so tired that my whole body hurts. But even though I'm tired, I have no choice. I have to wake up to go to school, to study and go to work. I have withdrawn socially and I just want to sleep. I feel so exhausted all the time.

Mia added that her physician discovered she had papillomavirus (HPV) precancerous cervical lesions, for which she had been treated medically several times, yet with a poor prognosis. She also mentioned that she had tried and failed over many months to lose weight. She described her diet issues, and the fact that she consumed too much coffee and smoked many cigarettes. Mia did not use recreational drugs, but she took on the habit of drinking a glass or two of wine at night, or a beer, to stop her sadness and pain. In addition to having a job, she was in college and when she got home each day, she was responsible for all the chores. She admitted that she was in a destructive (verbally, emotionally and physically abusive) relationship with her husband who had addiction issues and serious health challenges. They were constantly in serious conflict, and she had gotten to the point where she was secretly wishing for his death. Mia was in turmoil about staying with him but was also afraid to leave.

Furthermore, Mia described to me her strong fear of death, and how her ideas about life and death were limited to what she had read in the Bible. She concluded that she had done everything her doctors recommended yet nothing had helped. She felt extremely overwhelmed and tired.

Considering the severity of Mia's case and her critical state of mind, I decided to begin by using two techniques. The first was hypnotic regression, which requires the clients to return to the onset of their symptoms to investigate the subconscious sources of their issues. The other technique was subconscious mind optimization, which involves dismantling the disempowering and negatively-oriented beliefs within the subconscious and conscious thinking and replacing them with positive ones. This would help the clients return to a positive and optimistic state of mind.

In hypnotic regression some clients regress to a younger age or to childhood where their symptoms or issues originated, while others regress beyond or before their current lifetime. It is truly remarkable how the exploration of the subconscious mind can take a person to seemingly foreign territories such as the survival of consciousness after death (the afterlife), and reincarnation (the existence of the same soul—same consciousness—in multiple lives). Without a doubt these are controversial topics. Many of the debates about their "truth" reflect not only various philosophical and religious beliefs, but also the suppositions that medicine embraced, that consciousness—the mind—is the product of the brain's activity, and if the human being dies, the person's consciousness ceases to exist. However, recent research on near-death experiences is starting to point out that consciousness may exist and function without the help of the brain.

To access the subconscious mind the client needs to be deeply relaxed as if in meditation or hypnosis. It will appear as though he or she is asleep in the dream state, in REM sleep (*Rapid Eye Movement*, when the eyes are fluttering under the eyelids), but is actually in a state of focused concentration. The person is not asleep.

To begin our hypnotherapy work I instructed Mia to sit comfortably, close her eyes, relax as deeply as she could, let her thoughts go and follow my guidance. I encouraged her to try to stay as still as possible in order to facilitate the deep state of relaxation in which the subconscious is accessible. I explained to her that this is a normal state of mind that we all experience every day and night.

I then directed Mia verbally to help her relax all of her muscles starting from the top of her head and moving all the way down to the tips of her toes while gently focusing her attention inward. Through this process of guided meditation, Mia gradually moved into the dream-like state (the alpha brain wave state), then into the deep relaxation state (the theta brain wave state) and into the REM state. Through this process of guided meditation both the conscious and the subconscious levels of awareness are active, and the conscious mind is in a quieter state than usual—in an observer state. When her whole body was relaxed, I suggested that she imagined herself completely enveloped and bathed in a warm, golden light. I asked her to detach from the sensations of her physical body and to imagine that she was climbing a staircase of light, the steps of which led upwards to a big, bright, golden Light, warming her like the sun. (I will later explain what this "Light" is.) I then suggested her to enter the Light as she let go, allowing her higher levels of consciousness to show her the events or situations that represented the source of her current symptoms. I never tell my clients where to go. I let their higher consciousness direct them to the real source of their present challenges.

MIA'S PRIMITIVE LIFE

Once Mia entered the Light at the top of the stairs, I asked her to look with her mind's eye at her feet, to see if she was wearing any footwear, how she was dressed, and to describe in detail what she saw, felt, heard or realized.

M: I see furs on my body. It's winter and it's cold. Everything is frozen and I'm by myself. There is no one around me.

Dr. G: What else do you see in your surroundings?

M: I see a cave. It's cold and dark inside. It's as though no one has ever been in here before… I live here. It's familiar. I'm walking and it seems I know where I'm going. I've been living in here for a while but I haven't always lived here. And it's completely dark. I don't see anything around me. I can't even see what I'm stepping on, and it's cold.

Dr. G: Does anybody live there with you?

M: No, no.

Dr. G: How did you get there?

M: I walked here.

Dr. G: If you look at yourself, what can you tell me? Are you an adult or a child?

M: I'm a man. I'm a man...

Mia did not regress to her childhood. This regression to the source of her symptoms became what is called in therapy a "past life regression." Past life regression therapy is based on the concept that a soul can live multiple lives that can influence each other, and the past lives' traumas, fears, and vulnerabilities can manifest in the current life as symptoms, diseases, fears, phobias, and so on.

I have not explored the concept of past lives before beginning to study the subconscious mind. However, after researching the work of prominent hypnotherapists such as psychiatrist Brian Weiss, MD, psychologist Michael Newton, PhD and Dr. Bruce Goldberg my skepticism regarding this concept eroded. When my first client accessed her past lives, I was well prepared on how to conduct the regression process, and aware of the remarkable benefits of past life exploration.

Hypnotherapists are inevitably taken by their clients into what they describe as their past lives, which seem to reveal the sources of their current issues or symptoms. Regardless of how implausible their experiences may seem to be, the scientific method is to observe and study clients' experiences, and to take all data into consideration.

Some of the clients are comfortable with the concept of reincarnation because it's part of their philosophical, cultural, spiritual, or religious belief system. Other clients—those who believe that we live just one life—often interpret these experiences as remarkable metaphors of the mind that teach them powerful lessons about their current challenges. Nevertheless, I have found that my clients' opinions regarding this topic do not interfere with their recovery process when participating in past life regression therapy.

Dr. G: How are you dressed?

M: With many furs. They are very fine.

Dr. G: Where did you get the furs?

M: I got them myself. I hunted, I fought. (Mia answered with pride.)

Dr. G: Where did you come from? Where are the rest of the people?

M: I don't know. I'm by myself and I think this is how it supposed to be. They either died or exiled me.

I observed that the way Mia answered me was masculine. Her maternal language (which is my maternal language as well) is a Latin-based language which has masculine and feminine connotations to words that does not exist in English language. She used the masculine word for being by "himself." I also noticed that she seemed detached from her current personality as Mia, and her mental connection was becoming increasingly stronger with the man she described as herself in that life.

Dr. G: How do you feel there?

M: I feel calm but I'm afraid. I have to be careful of every step I take. There are many creatures around. It's a constant battle for survival. I could die at any moment.

I asked Mia what this man looked like, and with a proud voice she told me that she was a strong, handsome man with black, shoulder-length hair and white-yellowish skin. I asked if she could find something to show the man's reflection, and she gave me an interesting answer:

M: I will look. Let me go outside. Oh, it's so cold!

I was surprised by Mia's response. It seemed that she was experiencing the past life's sensations in the present moment rather than merely recalling them as memories.

M: There's ice everywhere. It's so cold! Everything around me is white, covered in snow, lots and lots of snow. There's nobody around. I don't know if there are any other creatures like me. Brr... brr... (Mia made these sounds as she shivered. She breathed in and out deeply, trembling from the cold.) Look! I think I can look here... But I don't see myself clearly. I'm a strong man, you can tell by my arms. I'm tall and well-built. I can do everything by myself. I can't see my facial features but I have a big mark on my right cheek. I feel it when I put my hand on it. And it seems that there are more marks, not just one, and they are large and deeply furrowed in my cheek... They are scars from a fight with an animal.

Dr. G: Do you only wear furs or do you wear pants or clothes that are handmade?

M: I don't even know what exactly that looks like... *pants*? No. Furs! I skinned the animals and I put the furs on my back.

Mia seemed fully connected with the primitive man. I guided her to the next event related to her current issues.

M: I'm barefoot, I'm cold and hungry. I know that if I'm hungry I have to eat. I need to find food.

Dr. G: What kind of animals do you hunt?

M: Whatever I find: rabbits, foxes and fish. But I don't like the fish. I have to search. I must be clever in order to eat because the animals are smart.

Dr. G: How do you eat the food? Raw or do you prepare it somehow?

M: I eat it raw as well as prepared.

Dr. G: How do you prepare it?

M: I leave it outside in the sun but I have to guard it so other animals won't eat it.

From here, I instructed Mia to relax deeper and go to the next important event that was related to the depression and weight issues of her current life.

M: I don't know where I am. I'm still barefoot. I don't know what's going on but it's as if I'm lurking. I'm watching something and something is watching me. I feel tension and I don't know exactly what's going to happen or what has happened. I'm probably hunting... Now there's a fight, as if a large animal... I want to say it's a bear but it is not a bear. It's a beast that wants to eat me, and I want to eat it. Oh, my feet are frozen and I can't move! But I continue to fight and I'm scared... Now the beast, the animal is on the ground. But I'm on the ground too, and I can't move... Now it seems that something is pulling me away from the beast. It's taking me somewhere in the dark. Oh, I'm frozen... but I don't feel anything else. It's cold and it's dark.

Mia's breathing became even deeper and faster. Her rapid and deep breathing, the shivers, all of these physical reactions did not appear to be the result of her imagination. What she was experiencing seemed so real to her that her body responded accordingly.

I wondered if the difficulties and the struggles of this caveman in obtaining food and his fear of not having food manifested in Mia's current lifetime as the habit of excessive eating. Or was she putting on weight or holding on to the excess weight because it helped to protect the caveman's body with layers of fat in the frozen environment? These could have been some of the subconscious roots of Mia's habit of overeating. I guided her forward in time.

M: Same situation but on different days. Strangely, I'm still alive. I'm still here. During the fight the beast bit me. It attacked me somehow and I killed it, but now I'm very weak. Something came and grabbed me from behind. It dragged me somewhere. I don't know who or what it was because I don't feel anything anymore.

Dr. G: Go forward to the moments before your death and relieve the last moments of that life.

M: It seems that I'm in a shelter and someone is taking care of me. I don't know what it is but it's as though it's licking my wound where the beast bit me. My legs are covered. I can feel its warm breath but I'm not afraid that it wants to eat me...

Dr. G: What is happening now?

M: It's... it's not... hmm... nothing. It's dark but I'm not there anymore.

Dr. G: How are you feeling there, in the dark?

M: I feel... I don't know how to describe. I don't feel anything. It's as if my place is not here.

Assuming that Mia exited the caveman life, I directed her to go toward the Light.

Dr. G: Do you see the Light?

MIA' S LIFE AS LIZ

M: Yes. I see a blue, beautiful light at the edge of a forest. It's night and there's a tent. There's a circus. It's a circus!

Dr. G: Look first at yourself. Describe what you look like.

M: I'm a young woman with chestnut-brown, long, wavy hair. I'm wearing some gypsy clothes and I'm barefoot. I have many layers of colorful jewelry with a lot of charms in the form of coins. I have some around my neck and ankles, and I have earrings too.

Mia had spontaneously moved to viewing another life. Many people are able to view multiple lifetimes within one session.

Dr. G: What are you doing there?

M: I'm going home, to my carriage without horses.

Dr. G: Do you have a family?

M: No, no. My parents are no longer here. I was told that they died and I'm an orphan.

Dr. G: Who are the others in that community?

M: They aren't near me now. They are the circus people. Yes.

Dr. G: And what do you do there? Do you have any role in that circus?

M: I'm not good at such things. I clean, take care of them, cook… I'm not of the same ethnicity. I'm white and the others are Gypsies with dark skin and dark hair.

Dr. G: Are there houses around the place where your carriages are?

M: Yes, yes, beyond the forest. You must pass the forest to get there. It's a city. It's somewhere in France. Le… Dijon? It starts with D, something like that. Yes. But I don't speak French.

Dr. G: What year is it?

M: I don't know. I have to look, maybe ask. 1800s? Something like that.

Dr. G: What language do you speak?

M: I don't know but I don't speak the language spoken by the people in the city. I speak the language spoken here, in the community. They say that they speak Gypsy.

Dr. G: How did you get to live in this community?

M: They found me. They adopted me when I was 6 or 7 years old. My parents were killed and they took me in.

Dr. G: Do you remember your parents?

M: Yes, a little bit. My mother was very beautiful and my father was a handsome man. My mother would hold me in her arms and sing to me. She was thin, beautiful and tall. Her hair was chestnut-brown, wavy and long. She had green eyes. She was as beautiful as an angel. And there was someone else with us. She would call my mother "Madame" (French for "Madam"). She was like a second mother to me.

Dr. G: What name did your mother called you by?

M: Liz… Liz.

Dr. G: What was the house that you lived in with your parents like?

M: It was really big, with a lot of people around us. I used to run around the house a lot.

Dr. G: What do you remember about your father?

M: I think my father had an important position. He always had meetings, but he was gentle with me. He used to take me in his arms and play with me… But I had no siblings.

Dr. G: Do you remember when the people from the circus community took you in?

M: Yes, I think so. My parents told me that we were going to an aunt's house. My father's sister or my mother's sister had a baby, and we went to them by the carriage. At some point in the forest something happened, and the horses started running. I heard my father getting agitated and started to scream. My mother took me in her arms and then the carriage rolled over. After that, I saw a lot of people around us, but nobody said anything. Only my mother was crying, and then she stopped moving. Afterwards, I was taken from there.

Dr. G: Who took you?

Here, Mia used a term that only children would use to describe an adult male. Interestingly, she was speaking from the perspective of a child, not of the adult who remembered her childhood. I asked her to tell me more about that man.

M: I was really intrigued by his shirt. He had a mark on his chest, and I've never seen my father wearing his shirt unbuttoned like this man.

Mia reveled that this person was not from the Gypsy community.

M: He took me somewhere, also to a big house but it was ugly. There were a lot of children and women dressed in black and white. And they were beating us. They kept beating us!

Dr. G: What age were you when you got there?

M: About 3 or 4 years old.

Dr. G: Until what age did you stay there?

M: I didn't stay there too long. At about 6 or 7 years old, when I realized that my mother wasn't coming to look for me, I ran away to look for her.

Dr. G: Didn't you know that your mother died?

M: No. I saw that she cried and then she just stopped moving. I didn't know that she died.

Dr. G: What about your father?

M: My father… I saw blood coming out of his nose and mouth, so I came to realize that… Actually I didn't realize at that time but when I told other children from that big house, they said he was dead.

Dr. G: Where did you go when you ran away?

M: I ran and I ended up here, in this place with many people. They were speaking another language and I cried, and I told them in my language that I wanted to stay here. And someone took me in and fed me. He was the leader.

Dr. G: And all these years you stayed with them?

M: Yes. We traveled all over the world. I consider them my family. Yes, yes, yes. And Pierre takes care of me. He is like my father. He is the leader of the small community.

Mia described Pierre as being a handsome 50-year-old man whose wife died a long time ago. He didn't like to talk about his wife and he never remarried.

Dr. G: Does Pierre have children?

M: No, but he has many nephews. He wants to marry me to one of his nephews.

Dr. G: Do you like that nephew?

M: Yes. Everybody tells me that he is not of my race and I won't make a good home with him. But he likes me too. (Mia whispered with a playful and happy voice.) I want to get married and have kids. I promised Pierre that I was going to do whatever I could to make him proud of me.

Dr. G: How do the people in your community make a living?

M: Well, we have defined roles. The majority performs in the circus shows. I collect the money, and all of us decide what to eat. Otherwise, we wash at the river, eat around the fire, have fun and tell stories. It's a very beautiful and peaceful life. And we have women here, in the community, who *works* as fortune tellers. But they told me that they don't actually *predicts* the future, that they *tricks* those white women, who *is* more stupid, like that. But people should not know about this. It's a secret. (Mia said whispering.) And there are women who seek the fortune tellers out. So this is how we live: we travel, we buy things, people bring food to us… that's it. It depends on how long we stay in each place.

Mia's expression in this regression proved how deep her mental connection with Liz was, who was most likely illiterate.

Mia, as Liz, also described how her best friend Rossi provoked a big scandal in the community by having a child before marriage.

M: She finally got married to the father of her child two weeks ago. She doesn't love him that much anymore but he loves her. Pierre is a little upset that I'm friends with her. He says that she should have a more organized life, take care of her family and not think about other men. Pierre is afraid that if I marry with his nephew I'll do the same thing. Yes.

Using "Yes" to conclude her statements was another interesting aspect of Mia's expression as Liz. Mia's ability to retrieve so many vivid details about Liz's life was remarkable. I could actually visualize

Liz's life in my mind. I continued by asking if the children in their community were receiving any schooling.

M: No. We don't have time for school. School? (She seemed amused by my question.) Pierre says that the most important schooling for us is to learn to survive and to learn the things he teaches us: to read and write our names, but not more than that. School is not for us, 'cause we don't have time.

Mia also said that Pierre was calling her Muro, short for Muroshavu.

M: It's nice here, I like it. I'm very happy here.

When I guided Mia in regression, I asked her to go to the sources of her issues, especially to the sources of her depression and weight challenges. So far, it seemed that she was happy in this life as Liz. Regarding her weight, I asked if she, as Liz, had a well-proportioned body.

M: Yes. My body is very beautiful. Everyone envies me, and it's the way that they like a woman to look. I'm a beautiful woman. I'm not scrawny like those who have nothing to eat. I have all of the necessary shapes and I'm very appealing. Aha, yessss.

Mia, as Liz, seemed very proud of her physique. I wondered if Mia's current physique was "born out" of Liz's lifetime. Perhaps Liz's beliefs regarding physical appearance somehow affected Mia's subconscious mind and body. Being curvaceous was a sign of beauty in those times, and Mia's subconscious could have been holding on to that belief.

Dr. G: Are you seeing Pierre's nephew?

M: Yes, but nobody is supposed to know 'cause it's against the rules. We should get married first before we can see each other. Otherwise, they exile us from the community. But we go into the forest and we kiss, we kiss… He doesn't care that I'm white. He said that he loves me the way I am and that he wants to have kids with me. Yes.

I instructed Mia to go forward to see the next important events of that life. After a few moments, Mia began to speak with a different tone, with a more mature and serious voice.

M: I'm about 40 years old. I'm a mother. I'm still here with the community but not in the same place. I'm not that happy anymore, and I'm by myself.

Mia described having three sons, the oldest being 20 years old and getting ready to get married. The other two boys were 16 and 14 years old.

M: The children's father is my husband, Marc, but he died about ten years ago, when the little one was about 4 or 5 years old. He got caught on fire... My boys are handsome and strong. The little one is white, like me, and he is a clown. The middle one resembles his dad. He is black and beautiful, with beautiful blue-grey eyes, just like mine, and does acrobatics. But I don't let him climb 'cause I'm afraid of him falling. We always argue on this subject and I say: "What? You want to leave me just like your dad?" The eldest one helps to set up the circus tent, to move it from here to there. He can pass either as a Gypsy or as a white man. I raised them well. Too bad that Marc isn't with me anymore.

Mia, as Liz, revealed that her boys knew only to count on their fingers and to write their names. She also shared that Pierre was not the leader anymore because he was old and had to stay in bed. But he was the wise man who everyone sought advice from. Marc then became the leader, but after his death someone else took over.

M: He is awful and mean. He does only bad things and puts pressure upon the community. It's hard but where else can I go? My boys want to leave but our tradition says for us to stay together.

Dr. G: Did you remarry after Marc died?

M: No. With whom? And with three kids? I couldn't because my children would have judged me.

Mia shared that the traditions of the group would have allowed her to remarry but she thought it would have been disrespectful to Pierre. Everyone was family there. She would have had to marry one of her husband's cousins and she couldn't. She also revealed that they were now in a different country, on the outskirts of a city.

M: These people speak another language. They were very happy when they saw us. We travelled for a few months to get here. The city is bigger and has one of those complicated names. I can't memorize it. There are a lot of people, all white, and dressed, not like us, but also with happy colors. They look like they're all from the same mother— blonds with curly hair, green or blue eyes and pink cheeks. You rarely see one with brown eyes. They are very well made. The women are very well put together, like me. They eat well.

Mia's description made me think of Germany. When I asked her what country she thought they were in, she gave me an interesting answer.

M: I don't know, 'cause... no, I don't know. Maybe I'll ask Pierre tomorrow. We just move along with the community. Us, women, don't know much about things. We must take care of food.

There are just moments when you couldn't help but smile. And again, Mia took me by surprise by saying, "Maybe I'll ask Pierre tomorrow." Shouldn't she remember what already happened in that life? She spoke as though she was actually *living* the events from the past, not as though she was *remembering* events from the past, nor as a detached observer of something happening in the present moment. This made me think of quantum physics, which reveals that time is nonlinear; the present, past and future are occurring simultaneously.

Mia also shared that she and her sons didn't own many things. Her life was very simple and peaceful, and she really enjoyed it. This story is a beautiful reminder of how people could feel happy and content by living a simplistic life; that happiness does not come from material wealth.

M: We travel a lot, we see many places. Pierre says that I'm lucky 'cause if I had stayed with my parents, I wouldn't have seen so many places, and maybe I wouldn't have had a life as happy as this.

It is exciting to work with people like Mia who have the ability to connect so deeply with their other lives. In my opinion, what Mia described didn't seem to be figments of her imagination. One would have to be a very creative person and a gifted actor to put together such an elaborate charade. And why would anyone who is desperately seeking therapeutic help do that? I believe that the last thing on the mind of a depressed person with very little will to live, who also complains of being perpetually exhausted, would be to bother orchestrating an act like this.

After guiding Mia to the next important event of that life, she replied with a tired voice.

M: What can I say? I'm old 'cause I look at my hands and the skin is wrinkled. I'm around 60 years old or past 60. I'm skinny and I'm in bed. The children come to help me, and now they are debating whether I should go with them or stay here. And no, I don't want to go. The oldest one and middle one embarrassed me and got married to white girls.

Again, Mia made me smile. As Liz, she identified so deeply with her gypsy community that she forgot she was the same race as those "white girls." She continued to explain that her boys lived in the city, and "they got together with the strangers," except for her younger son who stayed with her because "he hadn't managed to find anyone." She also shared that Pierre died of old age and had an easy death. Liz had organized a beautiful funeral with the help of the community. The community, still being led by the same ineffective leader who had succeeded Marc, was completely disorganized.

M: We are no longer like how we used to be back in the day. These young ones do whatever they want. Everyone is trying to get more money. I'm lucky with the boys, who, despite the way they are…

'cause they embarrassed me… still *comes* to visit, and *brings* me this and that so that I can survive.

Mia also shared that her older sons got employed at a factory in the city.

M: They *writes* newspapers. I don't know how many francs they give them there. We came back to France but in another place, and my boys are working elsewhere. By the time they get to me it takes maybe a week. Their women wanted to be further, to not have anything to do with us. They are good women but they are not our kind, and that's that, 'cause now I'm one of their own, the Gypsies. After all, if they get along there, what can I do? I couldn't keep them near me my entire life. If they didn't like any of our Gypsies… Eh, in the end, they're grownups and have their own families.

Mia also described that she had difficulty walking.

M: I can't do chores by myself. I'm lucky with Rosi who comes and helps me. I use a cane to move around because I had paralysis. I spend most of my time in bed. I lost weight and I'm like one of those scrawny women. I don't think I'm gonna live much longer.

I noticed that Mia was having difficulty breathing like a person with pulmonary insufficiency. It was time to guide her to see the last moments of this life.

M: My back hurts really bad… It's like it's breaking and my heart is beating really fast… It hurts.

Being deeply connected with Liz, Mia felt the pain in Liz's body.

M: I'm in bed but I'm not with my Gypsies. My children are with me. My middle son's woman is knocked up again, awaiting another child. I'm really old, dearie… It's like I'm suffocating… And I'm hot, really bad. It feels like I'm on fire.

Dr. G: What do your boys tell you?

M: That everything is going to be fine and they love me. They are all crying… and crying…

After a brief pause Mia surprised me by saying:

M: I think I see Marc.

CHAPTER TWO

Beyond Life is Life?

"Wisdom never lies."
Homer

The most exciting part of past life regression therapy begins when the regression client accesses the moment of death, when the soul emerges from the physical body. The soul's journey after physical death has been the subject of very little research to date.

Dr. G: So Marc, your husband, is waiting for you?

M: Yes. He is so handsome…

Dr. G: How do you feel when you see Marc again?

M: Relieved of pain and worry. I feel young and beautiful again… I'm going to go with Marc, 'cause it's hard for me here by myself.

It seemed that Liz had passed away but her consciousness survived. People in regression typically perceive the moment of their death as a liberation from suffering, and as a moment of joy. They realize that they continue to live beyond their human bodies in a different form (as an energetic field, a consciousness, a soul). This idea may be very "far out," but it's a pattern that I've observed consistently while working with a large number of clients. Many other doctors and therapists who practice past life regression therapy have identified and recorded this pattern as well.

When physical death occurs and souls leave their bodies, they are usually greeted by their Spiritual Guides, who accompany and guide them to the nonphysical dimension where souls go after death. The Guides are highly evolved souls who mentor and direct other souls toward spiritual evolution. Sometimes, souls who just passed away are greeted by loved ones who have previously died and who may also be their Guides. Mia, as Liz, seemed to have found her husband after death. Could Marc be her Spiritual Guide?

LOVE BEYOND LIFE

Dr. G: What does Marc look like?

M: He is handsome and young. I didn't marry him for nothing… It's as if he has a body but we can't touch each other. But I know it's him. We are so happy! He says he's taking me to a beautiful place and tells me not to worry about anything. He says that now everything has ended and it's going to be fine. We're going to remain together, like how it's supposed to be. He is going to make me happy. But he doesn't speak. I understand him telepathically. And it's really warm.

Dr. G: Ask Marc what lessons you learned in this life as Liz. What was your purpose?

M: He says I was here to take care of Pierre who was by himself. I made Pierre's life happy and Marc's life happy too, and I brought three beautiful souls into this world. I was an example for the community and I learned to be a strong woman. I struggled by myself, and I learned to not be alone along with my loved ones. Marc says even when he wasn't physically next to me he was always beside me and waited for me.

This made me realize that most likely Marc was Mia's Spiritual Guide. The Guides are always with the people or souls they advise and protect.

M: Oh, it's so hot! But I'm happy, and all of my worries have ended; all of them.

Looking at Mia, I noticed that her forehead was covered with beads of sweat despite the fact that the office we were in was cool. No matter how vivid one's imagination is, it is impossible to cause one to sweat in a cool room. Mia's experience was clearly physical. It didn't seem to be a figment of her imagination.

Dr. G: Where are you and Marc going?

M: Somewhere like, hmm… toward the sun because it's really hot. It's beautiful but it's hot!

The Light that Mia described as bright as the sun is a common phenomenon for those who witness the moment of their death during past life regression. Most clients report that they are attracted to this bright Light that may also look like a tunnel of Light. At the same time, they feel lighter and free of any physical or emotional pains or burdens.

(Since it is a unique type of light, I capitalize the word *Light* when I make reference to it.)

Dr. G: How do you travel toward the Light?

M: It's as if he took me by the hand, but at the same time it's as if he is carrying me in his arms. It seems as if he is floating or flying.

Dr. G: What do your bodies look like?

M: They aren't bodies. They are like an image, but no, nothing like a body.

Dr. G: Do you mean, "nothing like a physical body?"

M: Yes. It's like energy. Only now we can touch each other.

Dr. G: If you look into Marc's eyes, what do you notice?

M: Oh… wow! (Mia seemed astonished.) They are black.

Dr. G: Do they seem black like human eyes?

M: No. They're black, black, black, as if you can look beyond them. But at the same time they are warm and they don't scare me.

Dr. G: Ask Marc: "Where are you taking me and what are we going to do there?"

M: He said that we're going for a stroll, and then we're going to give life again.

Dr. G: Before you give life again (reincarnate), tell Marc that you would like to see your permanent home where you stay after physical death.

M: He says that's where we're going. But it's really hot here because we're getting closer and closer to the sun. I asked him, "Why is it so hot?" and he said, "It's just an illusion." We have to pass beyond the Light, and then we'll get to where we need to go.

Dr. G: If you look around, what do you see?

M: The Light reflects somehow into blackness and radiates such unique and beautiful colors. I don't know if the human mind can conceive of them. It's beautiful here but there's nothing around. It's like the night sky.

THE GATE OF LIGHT

M: Marc says that we have to pass through the gate of Light. And I'm really, really hot. The Light is very powerful and almost blinds me. We spend quite a bit of time in it. I've never seen a gate this long… It looks more like a tunnel. If I look back, everything closes and becomes black again behind us. But ahead of us it's white light. It's very interesting… Look, we've arrived!

THE GREETING HALL

M: We've arrived in a place that looks like… I don't know how to describe it. It's like a hall, a huge area, but I don't see any walls. Around this hall there seem to be huge staircases, and it's as though some of the souls are positioned above the others…

Dr. G: Are there others in that hall with you?

M: Oh, there are many here.

Dr. G: Do they look like you?

M: No. They're like some… I don't know how to explain what they're like. It's as if each one of them is a concentration of air, like a transparent balloon, only not a balloon because if you blow at them they turn into a smoke. They are of different sizes. The bigger ones are the size of ostrich eggs, and some are smaller, like quail eggs. Marc is not like I knew him. He is also steam-like, just like them. But he says that I'm like him, too. He just asked me: "Don't you see yourself?"

Dr. G: Ask Marc: "What happens in this area?" What are you two doing in this place?

M: He said that we are waiting to give life.

Dr. G: How do you feel there?

M: I feel peaceful and liberated. And it's as if I'm not afraid of anyone. I feel surrounded by friends and people that I'm not afraid of. I have faith.

Dr. G: Do you have faith in Marc as well?

M: Yes. I have faith in Marc.

Dr. G: Tell Marc that you would like to see your group of souls. Are you a part of the same group of souls that Marc is part of?

M: He said: "Yes, by association. Here, everyone can take part in whatever group they want. If someone wants to associate with someone else, they are welcomed. No one rejects anyone. Somehow, we all know each other, and everyone is happy even when someone is just visiting. No one tells you to leave. We respect each other deeply. No one does or says anything mean." Marc said that I can take part of any group I choose.

Dr. G: Ask Marc if soul mates exist. If yes, is he your soul mate?

M: Yes, soul mates exist but he is not my soul mate. He is just someone who wanted to help me discover myself, discover my strengths and abilities. But he is not my soul mate.

WHAT IS THE PURPOSE OF INCARNATION?

M: Marc says that every time we go somewhere to incarnate, whether we are aware of it or not, we carry with us certain experiences and information that we transmit further, to others. Thus, we contribute in the process of evolution. At the same time, because we gather here, we succeed in having happy lives over there, where we are incarnated.

Dr. G: What are you referring to when you say *here*?

M: Marc says *here* is this place where we all come from and where we return to after every physical life. Here is our Home. It's where we reunite with others who are here, and where we are all one big happy family.

It seemed that Mia and Marc used the word *Home* to refer to the nonphysical plane of existence from where we all originate; the heaven or paradise where so many people hope to go after physical death. (I have chosen to capitalize the word *Home* in this book when referring to this ultimate nonphysical reality).

Dr. G: What is the purpose of life on Earth? Why do we incarnate on this planet?

M: To grow energetically and to help each other.

Dr. G: Why is it important to grow energetically?

M: So we can create more universes.

Dr. G: What are we, in fact?

M: We are energy that nourishes itself with energy.

Dr. G: How can we increase our energy?

M: By collecting love and positive feelings, while incarnated in our physical bodies, and by living that limited lifetime. The more we succeed in every life to gather as many positive feelings as possible and to offer positive feelings to others, the more the positive energy of the universe increases. Marc also says that one of our key roles on Earth is to open pathways to new lives and new experiences. Every woman has the right to give birth, and every person has the right to bring children into the world.

I was beginning to realize that Mia, who initially told me she had no knowledge of this nature, was somehow accessing the universal wisdom that transcends our personal belief systems, and reaches beyond our scientific understanding and limitations.

HOW DO WE CHOOSE OUR PHYSICAL LIVES?

Dr. G: Please ask Marc whether you have the freedom to choose your next life or it is chosen for you?

M: He says that in principle nothing is dictated here. Here, no one tells you what you should do. *You* choose whether you want to reincarnate or not, and in which life you want to reincarnate. You can organize your life anyway you desire. If you wish to discover other aspects of yourself, you can choose challenges and to try to do only good. But nothing is forced on you. If you don't want to choose another life you can remain here longer. You don't have to go back immediately. You can even choose to stay at Home permanently.

Marc seemed to suggest that it is up to each soul to choose to live just one life or to reincarnate multiple times.

Dr. G: Do you have the option to choose who you will come with in the next life?

M: Yes, you have the option to choose. Nothing is imposed upon you. You can program your life in such a way that you can come in with whomever you want. You can also choose a life that will be challenging, in which you come into contact with souls you probably haven't met previously, or souls that are very small, young or inexperienced.

Dr. G: Did you and Marc plan the life you have just reviewed?

M: Basically Marc decided to help me grow spiritually and energetically because he considered it his duty, though it's not really a duty. It's a matter of friendship to help each other. He tells me that in most cases, when he chooses to do this, he decreases in energy and can end up regressing vibrationally.

Dr. G: So if the purpose is to grow in energy, why do souls like Marc have the kindness to help others, but at the same time risk decreasing their energy? What is the point?

M: Everything is linked to happiness and love. If you give, you will receive back. He decreased energetically at first, but when I came back I returned with more energy and he recovered the energy he gave me. When you return Home, you recuperate the energy that you gave to others.

WHAT KIND OF ENERGY ARE WE?

Dr. G: Marc said that we are energy. There are all kinds of energy: electricity, electro-magnetic energy, caloric energy, etc. What kind of energy are we?

M: The physicist who can identify our energy has not been born yet. You could say that it's a combination of all energies. We are electricity, yes. Look! He's asking if it ever happened that you felt an electric shock when you touched someone.

Dr. G: Yes, it has happened to me.

M: Or has it happened that you felt the magnetic attraction when you fell in love? It feels like you always want to be with the person you are in love with.

Dr. G: Yes. This, too, has happened to me.

M: That's what we are: a complex, intelligent energy with special characteristics and properties—the energy of life.

Dr. G: Mia, if you look at Marc, at his energy, how big is he compared to the others?

M: He is pretty big. Now, I can see that compared to him I'm a small dot. There are only a few others like him here.

Dr. G: Does his energy have a color?

M: Yes, but the colors are changing into beautiful, vivid colors. Marc's energy is now red, yellow and blue. I don't know why they are changing… Marc says the colors aren't changing based on any specific reason. We are all energy, and we have all the energetic colors. It's just a natural fluctuation in energy.

Dr. G: So Spiritual Guides' energy fields don't have specific colors according to their evolution level?

M: No. Marc says that all Spiritual Guides are evolved, and all of them have all the colors. Categorization of the Guides is based on other criteria.

WHO IS MARC?

Realizing that Mia was accurately transmitting the information that Marc, the Spiritual Master (SM) was sharing, I decided to address him directly.

Dr. G: Marc, you were Mia's husband in the life we have just explored. Are you one of her Spiritual Guides?

SM: Yes, I am. (When the answer came, there was no change of voice tonality, no change of Mia's face expression, no change at all.)

Dr. G: Are you her main Spiritual Guide or one of her Guides since it seems that people can have more than one Guide?

SM: I am her Spiritual Master. I am her Master Guide.

This reminded me of psychiatrist Brian Weiss's book "Many Lives, Many Masters," in which his patient, Catherine, was able to transmit messages from the Masters. I wondered if Mia could be another Catherine.

The Spiritual Guides are highly evolved souls who have extensive experience in incarnation, having lived many physical lives.

The Masters are the most evolved of all Guides. They are the mentors and the Guides of the other Spiritual Guides.

SPIRITUAL MASTER'S PERSPECTIVE REGARDING MIA'S PREVIOUS LIVES

Dr. G: Marc, from your perspective why was it important for Mia to review the caveman's life?

SM: Well, you asked for Mia to see where her current issues originated.

Dr. G: So it was another life that her soul lived?

SM: Yes.

Dr. G: It was a life linked to her weight problems, right?

SM: Exactly. It happened long before your era in what is today European territory. There is not much to say about it. It was a primitive life.

Dr. G: Why was that caveman by himself?

SM: He was banished from his tribe for stealing food. He was at the beginning of spiritual evolution, and he did things that others weren't happy with.

Dr. G: Did they know how to make fire?

SM: No.

Dr. G: How did they communicate?

SM: They didn't have a language because their cerebral cortex and speech center weren't developed enough. They communicated through sounds.

Dr. G: When did Mia's soul live the life in the gypsy community?

SM: She was born in 1832 and died in 1902.

Dr. G: Who were Liz's parents and what happened to them?

SM: Her parents were part of the aristocratic class. While on their way to visit a relative, they were attacked and robbed. Both sides had weapons and during the confrontation her parents were killed. Her father was a lawyer, but he wasn't an important enough figure to be found in historical records.

Dr. G: How old was Liz—Muro—when you two married? And why did they call her Muro? Did that name mean anything?

SM: She was 17. In that old Gypsy language Muro meant "Gypsy child."

Dr. G: What happened to you in that life? It seemed that you died young.

SM: I died while I was trying to start a fire for cooking. I poured too much kerosene onto the wood and I was caught on fire. I had to exit that life so that Mia could learn certain lessons.

Dr. G: But you left behind three young children.

SM: These are decisions we make at higher levels. In her previous lives, Mia had the tendency to cling to people. As Muro, she needed to learn to fend for herself and develop a stronger, more independent personality. Therefore, as her Guide, I made the choice to incarnate with her to teach her what love really means, and to help her become stronger. She had other previous lives with relatively happy romantic relationships with other souls, but never with a soul on the same level of evolution or higher. So as Muro, she felt that humanly strong love that you feel when there is perfect compatibility in your relationship. And when she became most attached to me, I had to leave so that she would learn her lessons.

Dr. G: Why was it important for Mia to review her life as Muro?

SM: It was important for her to know me consciously because at the subconscious level I'm always with her. I had to introduce myself, for her to know who I am. It was also important for her to remember how it feels to be happy and peaceful. She also had to rediscover Home and to begin revealing to you the science that you want to present to the world.

Left almost speechless, I thanked him for his answers. I realized that Marc had no trouble whatsoever transmitting information through Mia's mind. Mia herself had no way of knowing about me wanting to reveal anything to the world. I began writing about the human mind approximately one year prior to meeting her, but hadn't shared this with any of my clients. Situations like this remind me how little we know about what is really going on.

WHERE DO SOULS COME FROM AND WHAT IS THEIR DURATION OF LIFE?

Dr. G: Mia, please ask Marc where do souls come from.

M: He says that they are born from the universe, from the Source of Life. As they evolve, they gather energy and most importantly grow vibrationally.

Dr. G: Does every soul have a certain place at Home where they can stay between incarnations?

M: Marc says that there isn't a particular place for each individual soul. The home of all souls is here, at Home. If you wish, you can go somewhere and stay alone, but this doesn't happen. At least it hasn't happened so far. Basically, all souls wish to stay together and share the accumulated experiences of life.

Dr. G: About how long in human years can a soul live?

M: So long that the human mind simply cannot comprehend. Only if you were here, at Home, could you understand our lifespan. For a human mind you could say it is eternity.

Dr. G: Can you increase your energy at Home?

M: No. Souls can only increase their energy when they incarnate.

It seems that when souls leave the Home's comfort zone and incarnate into our world of duality where positive and negative energies coexist, they get the chance to evolve into higher levels of energy and develop a more advanced consciousness.

WHY IS THERE SUFFERING ON EARTH?

Dr. G: Please ask Marc why some people have lives full of pain and suffering.

M: A person feels alone or suffers on Earth because they consider, subconsciously, that in a previous life they did something wrong. Therefore, that soul chooses to incarnate to balance out what it did in a previous life. Suffering could lead to accumulating life experience, which cannot be gained only through happiness. Souls who choose to incarnate have very good intentions, and ambitions to reach higher levels of energy. The problem is that some of them forget to make others happy in order to become happy themselves. They are driven to acquire life experience believing that only in this way can they acquire energy. But the energy comes from the happiness and emotions experienced by the people you affect in life.

Dr. G: Is there another way to attain spiritual growth other than through illness, pain or suffering? And if there is, why would souls still choose to go through such hardship?

M: Everything that happens to the human body is brought on by the accumulated life experiences of the soul, and that gives birth to other experiences in life. In fact, souls do not choose to experience pain, but pain is one of the tributes paid for returning to Earth in order to live a new life. If you don't want to experience pain, you can remain at Home because no one forces you to go back and reincarnate.

I was pleasantly surprised by Mia's amazing ability to perceive and transmit the information that Marc revealed to her. Not many people manage to get so deeply connected to their higher selves and to perceive with such ease and clarity. Some people receive the information in visuals, which they try to explain, while some convey what they hear. Others receive it directly in the form of thoughts, which they somehow interpret through the filters of their current conscious knowledge and beliefs. The most valuable information comes from those who do not have any prior conscious knowledge in this area, and do not even remember what has been discussed. When this is the case, ideas are relayed in their purest form, unaltered by the person's limiting beliefs.

THE PURPOSE OF LIFE

Dr. G: Mia, please ask Marc what is the purpose of your life.
M: Marc says I have chosen to come back because I've decided to help many people. He says that my role is to make others happy because this way I grow in both experience and energy. Every time I make someone happy or content, I gather energy that will elevate me to a higher level of vibration. My increased energy will enable me to create a life that will give me greater life experiences compared to the ones I have now. He says all I need to do right now is gather as much energy as possible by trying to do as much as I can for others, not only for myself. I can help others by offering them unconditional love and positive energy, regardless of what they do or say. I can show them that I care for them, and help them understand that doing this (offering unconditional love and positive energy) is actually the only meaningful thing in life.
Dr. G: It is important to make yourself content and happy too, right?
M: Marc says it's a law of reciprocity. When you give love and happiness, most of the time, it will be returned to you two or three folds, and thus, you will increase your energy and vibration. By helping others you actually help yourself. So if you help yourself, you help others, and if you help others, you help yourself. You can help yourself by thinking well of others, and at the same time you help them too. The happiness you inspire in others will bring your own happiness. Happiness represents positive energy, which elevates you vibrationally.
Dr. G: So it is wise to love even when the love doesn't seem to be reciprocal?
M: Love and happiness have never hurt anyone. If the love you offer is not given back immediately, that doesn't mean that the soul hasn't been touched by your love. The soul who receives your love can transmit it further to other souls, and from that you will receive energy as well. So no matter how much love and happiness you give, it will always be rewarded and given back. All that matters is to love others because this way you love yourself, and as a result you evolve into higher energetic levels. Marc also says that no matter what others do to me, I have to try

to help them and be a good person. When he says "a good person," he refers to offering as much positive energy as I possibly can. And when he says "to help others," he is also referring to making them understand that to live is not enough, but to feel is everything. I should tell them and teach them about what I perceive and what I experience.

PERCEPTION AND EXPERIENCE VERSUS KNOWLEDGE AND INFORMATION. SPIRITUAL EVOLUTION

I asked Mia whether they were suggesting that her purpose is to help others become aware that they have these same perceptual abilities, so they can begin perceiving in their own turn.

M: Well said *perceiving* and feeling. When people say that they believe without feeling, they don't truly believe. But when they open up their perception, they will understand that basically the positive energy doesn't only save their souls, but also their temporary, physical lives. This is how the healing of their bodily diseases actually takes place— through the acquisition of positive energy. Therefore, those who help others understand who they really are will be immensely rewarded beyond the comprehension of this material life.

Dr. G: So we all have this ability to rediscover who we are and to reconnect with Home's plane of existence, right?

M: All people have this ability, but it depends how much they want to see beyond the material world. It's as easy as closing their eyes and asking their Spiritual Guides to lead them toward the Light and positive energy. And they will find within themselves the strength they need even if they won't understand where that strength comes from. All people have the ability to project themselves beyond the physical world.

Dr. G: How important is it for people to discover their abilities and use them?

M: It's very important for their souls and their energy, so that these temporary, physical lives are not journeys made for nothing. The moment when you come to realize there is much more than your physical existence on a small piece of land is the critical turning point of your life as a human being. From that moment on, you begin to work on attaining positive energy because by awakening, you reduce the negative energy you've accumulated and start increasing your level of positivity. This way, you elevate as energy onto higher levels of vibration. By giving unconditional love to others, and thus seeding positive energy in them, they will grow their own level of positivity too. As a result, your soul's positive energy will increase as well because *you* have taught and helped them. You could say it's a chain reaction, like the inner workings of a watch because every single cog is necessary for the entire system to move, and if a single component stops, the whole mechanism stops as well.

The science of physics has helped us realize that our bodies and all physical objects are basically composed of vibrational energy, and that we are all connected in the infinite ocean of energy that exists around and within us. We, as souls, as conscious energy fields, are integral parts of this all-encompassing system, which is described in literature by many different terms: *the unified field of consciousness, the quantum field, the ethereal field, the energy matrix, the divine matrix, the mind of God,* and so on. These are just words trying to describe the same paradigm. In this book, I will use the term *ethereal field* because it is the term Mia's Spiritual Master used. However, if it doesn't resonate with you choose one that you prefer. Don't let the words limit the greater context of message intended for us.

M: Marc says there is no use trying to convince people who don't believe what I'm saying because I can't increase my energy if others don't increase theirs and vice versa. To feel is the most important thing because sometimes what you see or hear is not convincing enough to resonate with what you feel. That's why you have to access and experience the inner universe personally, in order to convince yourself.

Personal experience helps us achieve a different level of understanding, whereas other people's experiences allow us to only imagine what they describe. The exploration of the inner universe is not achieved through using the analytical mind but rather by reducing it to silence.

M: Marc tells me that people seek the truth but they want to find it in a form that they can process through the filter of their limited, conscious minds; in a way that makes sense to them as human beings, not as souls. But through this route minimal information reaches the subconscious. *The soul* needs to access this information in order to return Home.

Dr. G: What does the size of the soul reflect?

M: The size of the soul, which is an expression of its spiritual evolution, reflects how much love that soul has accumulated. The process of becoming a bigger, more powerful spiritual being does not occur in a single lifetime of love. The soul's evolution requires many lifetimes of sharing and gathering positive energy.

DO WE CREATE OUR OWN REALITY?

Dr. G: Is it true that we create our own life and reality with our thoughts and beliefs?

M: Marc says that when you are born, you come into the new life with the experience you've accumulated in previous lives. Therefore, in each new life you bring with you more power, more strength and more energy. Without realizing it, the moment you start a new life your mind is already created, but it's not the mind that you know—your conscious mind. It's the mind of your soul—your subconscious mind—the one that controls your experiences. Your subconscious allows you to create your new life based on the beliefs and experiences you have amassed in other lifetimes.

Dr. G: So you actually create your reality with your subconscious mind?

M: Yes because the subconscious mind determines and oversees the conscious mind.

This explains why the exploration and understanding of the subconscious mind and universe becomes extremely valuable in understanding our human existence, and in bringing our lives to harmony and balance.

THE END OF MIA'S JOURNEY HOME

I asked Mia to send Marc my gratitude for the extraordinary knowledge he had shared with us, and to describe how she currently perceived Marc and everything around her. She shared that Marc's energy looked like translucent and beautifully colored precious stones that constantly changed colors. The other souls present were radiating different colors of light as well.

M: What I'm noticing now is that this hall is huge. I don't see walls that define it. Maybe it doesn't have walls. I say it's a hall because we arrived here through that tunnel of Light... It's a very peaceful atmosphere. There are discussions regarding experiences from various lives and possible alternatives like, "what could have happened if..." Marc is now having a discussion with a friend.

Dr. G: A friend?

M: I guess so because we are all friends here, as we are all part of a bigger source of energy... There are souls who choose to leave, to reincarnate. Everything unfolds in an organized matter and in a calm atmosphere but without anyone controlling anything. And honestly, I don't feel like leaving!

After a brief pause Mia continued in a whisper.

M: I'm talking to Marc. He tells me that there is so much to experience together. Basically, this experience I'm living right now, here, at Home, will help me in my physical life. He tells me that right now my place is not here, that I have things to resolve, but he promises me that I will return and he will wait for me. He tells me to allow myself to be guided by my intuition because those intuitive feelings are given for a purpose. I've lived many experiences that have heightened my intuitive senses. He tells me that he will be here for me whenever I need him. He says it's time for me to go back to where I came from... He is sending me back.

MIA'S REVELATIONS

While Mia slowly returned to her conscious state of awareness, my thoughts carried me back to one of my very first clients and I wondered if Mia would have a fast recovery as that client had. She was a young European lady who had suffered two devastating miscarriages in less than a year. She went into severe depression, which negatively affected every aspect of her personal and professional life.

During three hypnotherapy sessions, I guided her to the sources of her depression and miscarriages. She reviewed meaningful previous lives that pertained to her current circumstances. Curiously, they were presented to her backwards, as lives that started in the old age and unfolded into childhood.

As a result of accessing her higher consciousness, reviewing those previous lives and the lessons they presented, learning the benefits of positive thinking and beginning to carefully monitor her thinking processes, she began to feel increasingly better. The depression lifted and in a few weeks she announced that she was pregnant again. She did not seek other treatment and did not take any medication. This pregnancy presented no problems, and today she has two beautiful children. She had never even considered the concept of reincarnation until she actually saw herself, during our sessions, living those lives.

A few years later, she told me that the experiences she had during our sessions, of reconnecting with her greater self, proved to be a vital turning point in her life. Not only did her health and emotional state improved, but her life circumstances also changed for the better. This occurred through assimilating new wisdom that changed her way of thinking and ultimately helped her spiritual evolution.

Since this client I have been privileged to work with many other people, constantly being reminded of the incredible benefits of subconscious mind exploration.

With each client, I noticed that hypnotherapy was yielding amazing therapeutic results. However, it still wasn't clear to me how the recovery process worked, or how the healing actually occurred. How could I account for these results and what factors contributed to these successful cases? How was it possible to help people overcome lifelong depression and anxiety in such a short time, and to quickly help them find peace and harmony? How was it possible for a person to go from infertility to pregnancy, from physical suffering to a body that is free of pain, from insomnia to sleeping peacefully through the night? I had yet to discover the answers to these questions, and it was with Mia's help, this seemingly ordinary young woman who displayed incredible abilities.

Mia began to move slowly and still in a state of wonder she told me she was very surprised by her experience. I was astounded by how completely unaware she was of her amazing gifts.

M: It's so beautiful where souls go after death! I couldn't say that the hall had walls or a ceiling or a floor, but I could just sense it. It was like a mist. I could see shadows but nothing solid. It looked like an amphitheater. I had the sensation that I was sitting on a step, but there weren't spots where everybody had to sit, and nobody was coming to talk to us. (Mia got up and began walking around the office to stretch.) The energy of the souls seemed like small flames of fire, but they weren't fire. In a sense they looked like air bubbles, but they weren't defined. Or like gas bubbles that changed form and color, and if you blow on them, or if there was a wind blowing, they would disperse like smoke, and then gather back into their original form. Actually, air or wind or anything like that doesn't exist over there. It's almost like when you turn the gas on really high, and you can see the heat above the flames. That's how it looks. And you can understand what they're saying, but they don't speak with their voices. You hear them somehow but, actually, you just know because you understand them telepathically. You can see the particles according to how they change color. Marc's color changed from a pink sapphire into amethyst, then into the color of topaz, then into a beautiful blue and then into a mauve. All the other souls looked pretty much alike but were various sizes. Originally, I saw Marc as a man, but after we passed the Light I saw him as energy. Neither of us was in human form anymore.

We continued the session talking about the lives Mia accessed and how they mirrored her current life in order to integrate the information. As a result of her caveman life, Mia's soul—her subconscious mind—was probably still holding on to the fear that if she didn't find something to eat, she would die. She was also probably holding on to the belief that being curvaceous was desirable, and that she was more attractive with more weight. It is well documented that our behavior related to food is an automatic response to our conscious and especially subconscious belief systems. When we change the unbeneficial beliefs, the behavioral responses to our diet also change.

The lives Mia reviewed didn't seem directly linked to her depression, but young Liz's life in the gypsy community was a reminder for Mia of how it feels to be happy and to live your life with hope. Depressed people lose their hope. Depression is a result of operating from negatively-oriented, fear-based and disempowering beliefs.

To help Mia's recovery, I gave her an audio recording, which I specifically designed to encourage positive thinking, a healthy diet and healthy weight loss. I suggested that she listen to it daily for several weeks so that both her conscious and subconscious could incorporate this new, empowering information.

M: What a peaceful life I had in the gypsy clan! I felt extremely connected with Marc. He had a very gentle and soft look. At first, he seemed to be an ordinary man, but if you focused a few moments on his features you noticed that he was handsome. I was married to him, right? I had three children with him, right? I felt very happy, very in love with him, very appreciated and beautiful. And interestingly enough, I had a beautiful, pleasant, quiet death. It was the end of all of my turmoil and suffering over the sharp pain in my back. I didn't understand why I wasn't feeling the pain anymore at the moment of my death.

Mia experienced how death feels. When the soul exits the body the turmoil ceases. It is replaced with serenity and happiness. Experiencing this process through regression helps people overcome their fear of death.

M: So that's how the other world looks like, huh? That universe is so beautiful! It's superb! I tell you, it's very exciting. The moment you pass through that tunnel of Light you become curious because you don't know what to expect. It's strange because you can't say that beyond the Light is dark, yet you can't say that there is light. It's just impossible to explain. It's somewhere beyond the expressiveness of words.

The description of Home probably depends on each person's ability to perceive what exists in that universe, or may even be entirely beyond our intellectual ability to process the information because we don't have any reference points. How do you describe the indescribable? Since Home is a nonphysical universe governed by different laws and structured in a different way it's nearly impossible to describe, understand or explain it without the guidance of the universal mind.

M: While you're there, you're so calm that your mind is empty of thoughts. To be honest, I don't have many questions even though I haven't read any books about these things and what I saw is completely new to me... And I don't really remember the conversations with Marc except for a few details.

Mia didn't even remember that she didn't want to come back at some point. This revealed that the information she accessed did not originate from her mind or memory. It was transmitted to her consciousness by the Spiritual Master.

M: I can't believe that I was in the place we come from to incarnate! I was in the place we go after death! I didn't think I could do this, but now I know I can. I can't wait to go back there!

Some people, like Mia, are able to relax very deeply and to connect with their higher levels of awareness immediately. They are able to stay in those elevated states for a while and to communicate with ease with their Spiritual Guides. Other people go lightly but most fall somewhere in between. There are also people who need some practice quieting their conscious mind. A very analytical and critical mind with limiting beliefs and a strong negative ego can block the entire experience. On the other hand, people who practice meditation are usually able to easily connect with their higher levels of awareness.

TIPS FOR RECOVERY

Addressing Mia's depression, I advised her to monitor her thinking, to detach from her critical mind—her negative ego—and to redirect her thinking toward positivity, optimism and unconditional love. I suggested that she become aware of what she says out loud, for what she says is a reflection of her thoughts and beliefs. I encouraged her to visualize herself living the life she desires, feeling great, being at her ideal weight, and doing what made her joyful. Studies show that when we imagine a certain situation, the brain reacts in the same way and produces the same chemicals as when actually living that situation.

I encouraged Mia to be present in the "here and now," to enjoy her life and keep her goals in mind. She was the only one who could change her thoughts and beliefs, and by doing so, she would change the way she felt. I also encouraged her to eat healthy food and to begin exercising. I gave her the following daily affirmations to help redirect her thinking toward positivity: "I am happy, peaceful and healthy. I feel great about myself and my life. I am positive and optimistic. I love myself and others unconditionally. I think only positive thoughts and hold in my mind only positive images. I feel increasingly better every day. My life is beautiful and worth living. It's very easy for me to lose the excess weight in a healthy way. Every single day I lose weight until I reach my ideal weight, which I easily maintain. I like how I look. I feel calm and at peace with myself, and in harmony with the universe."

If any of the levels of the mind—the subconscious or the conscious—run negative programs of thinking, they can sabotage our progress and desires. When we interrupt the negative patterns of thinking by replacing the unbeneficial information, our responses and the way we feel change. The human brain has an extraordinary capacity to absorb new information, to form new neural connections between our brain cells (where the information is stored) and to discard the old data. If we repeat positive statements about ourselves and our life, the brain forms new neural networks. The old neural connections dissociate, and the brain discards and forgets the old unbeneficial data. This ability of our brain is called neuroplasticity.

Studies show that the way we think determines what we feel and influences our health. Thinking beautiful, relaxing, optimistic and happy thoughts causes the body to release endorphins and serotonin, the so-called "happiness hormones," which determine a state of well-being. At the same time, the number of the immune system cells increases and the human body becomes more resistant to diseases. The state of meditation or self-hypnosis has the same effects. When we think negative thoughts, the brain produces catecholamines, the "fight-or-flight hormones" or "stress hormones," and we feel accordingly. The number of the immune system cells decreases below normal limits, causing a lower resistance to diseases.

In order to help Mia overcome her severe depression and anxiety, I also advised her to return for another session to continue working on optimizing her conscious and subconscious thinking, and redirecting her focus toward positivity. We would also focus on correcting her unhealthy eating habits, by instructing her subconsciously to eat only healthy foods and in healthy quantities. I also intended to help her quit smoking and eliminate the excess coffee and the wine from her diet.

By the end of this first session, Mia realized she could no longer leave her life to chance, and that it was time to get actively involved in her healing process.

THE OPTIMIZATION OF THE SUBCONSCIOUS AND CONSCIOUS BELIEFS

After two weeks, Mia returned for a second session. She was already feeling better. She had followed my advice, and had even begun repeating the affirmations on her drive home from our first session. Although she sometimes felt that she was lying to herself by saying she felt happy when she actually did not, or that she was beautiful when she felt the complete opposite, she didn't give up. She realized that she had nothing to lose and everything to gain by repeating positive affirmations. Gradually, it became easier for her, and after a while she began to repeat them with conviction, and then to actually believe them.

She also listened daily to the audio recording I gave her and tried to be as positive as she could. In a short time, she realized that she no longer felt so bad, and that her suicidal thoughts had disappeared. She even began to lose weight. But she also wanted to make a confession to me.

M: After I left our session, I was thinking how I was telling you about my serious problems and you were telling me to think how beautiful life is. I was telling you that I wanted to die and you were telling me to think about how beautiful and happy I was. I started to cry. But then, I remembered that you told me not to forget to think positively, and to repeat those positive affirmations regardless of whether I believe them or not because it doesn't cost me anything to tell myself positive affirmation. And in a little while I actually began to see the difference. I realized that it wasn't that bad anymore and that I felt better.

It may be difficult to understand how these techniques work and to identify the mechanisms through which the mental and emotional changes occur. By no means is Mia my only client who has experienced this mental conflict and confusion. Actually, most of my clients with depression experience this rebellion of the critical mind. If you suffer from depression, the critical and skeptical part of your mind—the negative ego—is very strong, and could convince you that it's impossible to change anything, and that it's foolish to even think positive and optimistic thoughts. It will try to make you believe that positive thinking is a waste of time and that you are lying to yourself. But after a while, hypnotherapy clients begin to realize that they do have the right to be happy, that they are the ones in charge of their thinking process, and that they can choose to think optimistically. Then, they begin to say the affirmations with conviction. Their mental conflict and confusion eventually dissipates and the depression and the other symptoms ameliorate.

A very critical person who has a deeply entrenched disempowering way of thinking would have difficulty in accepting the concept of positive thinking. The change involves doing something different than what led to depression. As Albert Einstein said: "You cannot solve a problem with the same level of thinking that created it." The fastest way to *truly* come out of depression, which is a result of operating from negative programs of thinking, is through embracing positive thinking.

When Mia shared with me that the only thing she cared about, at the moment, was for those around her to be well, without including herself into the equation, I realized I needed to design for her affirmations that would help her acknowledge her personal value and increase her sense of self-worth.

After the session, Mia left relaxed and empowered. She felt that she was truly on the right path. She understood that she needed to become proactive in monitoring her thinking process, have an attitude of gratitude and appreciation, and find joy in every moment of her life.

CHAPTER THREE

"I Can Say I Have Been to Paradise"

"Only a life lived for others is a life worthwhile."
Albert Einstein

MIA'S HEALTH IMPROVEMENTS

After the session with Mia I returned in the United States for about three months while her psychiatrist continued monitoring her case. When I went back to Europe, Mia came for an appointment and as soon as she entered the office I noticed the change. I could read the tranquility and joy on her face. She looked great and had lost a significant amount of weight. She seemed healthy and full of energy.

M: I feel much better, much more positive and peaceful. My suicidal thoughts are completely gone and I didn't have any anxiety episodes anymore. I became confident that this approach would work for me when I opened my eyes, right there, at the end of our first session and realized that I felt rested. I hadn't felt rested for months. I still had a lot of thoughts of confusion and contradiction, but at least I didn't feel that tired anymore after our first session.

Mia continued with a proud and excited voice.

M: In the last three months I went from 145 to 122 pounds. I lost 23 pounds! Before, when I tried different diets, there were times when everything went black and I felt dizzy as if I was going to pass out. I would need to rest so I could gather enough energy to keep going. But now I don't have those problems. I have absolutely no craving and I don't overeat anymore. My brain or body decides what and how much to eat so I wouldn't be hungry. And I eat everything healthy. I've lost weight easily and without stress this time. More than that, I didn't lose weight suddenly so my skin isn't sagging, and I don't have any stretch marks. Another important detail I want to share with you is that after our first session I stopped taking antidepressants. I got scared because I felt worse and worse when taking them. I also didn't want to become dependent on any medication. I feel much better now so there is no reason for me to take antidepressants anymore. My psychiatrist is very happy to see me doing better.

Dr. G: Did you continue listening to the recording I gave you?

M: I listened to the recording you gave me quite often, but I don't remember much from our first session. I did remember some of the details right after the session, but I forgot almost everything.

Being very pleased with Mia's progress, we decided to continue investigating the root causes of her depression. I was eager to find out what information Mia would access this time, and what mysteries the Spiritual Masters would reveal. Silence filled the room as I invited Mia to get comfortable on the couch, close her eyes and try to remain still in order to redirect her attention toward her inner universe. I guided her in progressive relaxation noticing how with each breath her body and facial features became more relaxed. I suggested Mia to imagine a golden light enveloping her body and protecting her. I told her to visualize the light relaxing all her muscles and filling up all her organs, tissues and glands. I suggested she detach from any physical sensations and background noises, and imagine herself flying, like a bird of light toward the sun. As she focused her attention on the sun, the sun would become the Light. Her eyes began moving under the eyelids, indicating that she was in the state of rapid eye movements (REM) and connected with her subconscious awareness. As I counted from fifteen to one, I suggested that she relax even more deeply and approach that bright, golden Light. At "one," she would enter the Light and go to the real sources of her depression.

MIA'S LIFE AS JOSEPH

M: I'm somewhere in the countryside, in a forest. I'm barefoot and I'm a child. I'm running and I'm happy. I don't see anyone around me. I just see a lot of trees. The light is shining through them.

Dr. G: What is your name?

M: My name is Ios, Iosif. (I'm not sure about the spelling. It might be Iosip; in English Joseph.)

Mia described herself as being a 6 year-old blond boy with black eyes, and having six siblings: two older brothers, two younger brothers and two younger sisters.

Dr. G: What can you tell me about your parents?

M: My mother is at home and my father is at work. He is a blacksmith in the village. My mother takes care of us and the house. She works all day long. She cleans, does laundry, and makes really good food.

Mia, as Joseph, described her oldest brother, age 16, as already working, helping people but without a steady job. She also described her family as living in a village in Yugoslavia, in their beautiful three-room house. Joseph had run away from home to the nearby forest. He wanted to play even though his mother had asked him to watch over his younger twin siblings Michaela and Josh. Joseph felt "sick and tired of taking care of others." He loved being in the forest by himself, where it was quiet.

Dr. G: How long has it been since you ran away from home?

M: Not long. I don't think my mother has realized that I ran away yet. But when I return, she will probably yell at me because I left Ari, Arianna, my younger sister, to take care of the twins. I think I should head back home, but it's so nice here! There's lots of greenery.

Dr. G: Do you notice any connection so far between this life and your life as Mia?

M: I'm surrounded by people. I like to be alone but not totally. I seek refuge in nature and I'm not rich, in the sense that I come from a relatively poor class of people but rich in the soul.

After guiding Mia to the next important event of that life, she spoke with a sad and tight voice.

M: I'm over 30 years old. I'm wearing a suit, and I just found out that my twin siblings, Josh and Michaela have died. They were run over by a train. I'm afraid to tell my wife. She is pregnant. I have to go home.

Dr. G: Where is your home? Is it close to your parents' home?

M: No. It's not close to my parents' home. I need to travel by train to get to my parents. I live in the city now.

I asked what city Mia as Joseph was referring to, and I could not understand clearly if she said "Zingrad" or "Zagreb Grad." "Grad" means "city" in Croatian and Serbian.

Dr. G: What has happened with your other siblings?

M: Arianna married a doctor. She finished college as well. The twins were also supposed to go to college. They were apparently at a party. I don't know exactly what happened to them. I will have to find out. My father has died already and my mother will have to carry the pain by herself.

Dr. G: Did you tell your wife?

M: Not yet. I don't know how she will react. She is very sensitive. This is our first child. She was pregnant before but she had a miscarriage. Her name is Kristina and she is 29 years old. I call her Kristi or Krista. We met at the university.

Dr. G: What kind of university did you attend?

M: The law university. I'm a lawyer, and I managed to open a private practice. Kristina always blamed our marriage for not becoming a lawyer. She remained a jurist. But we have a beautiful marriage.

A jurist in Eastern European countries is like a paralegal in the United States.

Dr. G: Where did you go to university, in what city?

M: Here, in Zagreb, for six years.

Dr. G: How many years of school did you complete before you became a lawyer?

M: Many because I've been in school since I was 7, and I graduated somewhere around 29 years old after taking all my exams. Kristina laughs and says that I spent my whole life in school.

Dr. G: What kind of lawyer are you?

M: I mainly work on child protective cases. Here, most parents don't yet know and don't want to understand that we all have rights, including children.

I asked how long Joseph had been together with Kristina and to describe her.

M: I think it's been over fifteen years since we met at the university. She is tall and well-made, with medium length blond hair and green eyes. She always likes to dress up trendy. She is an only child from the city. Her parents didn't really approve of us because I'm from the country. But that didn't matter much. At first, they thought I was simply a friend with whom she had fun, but when I asked for her hand, they realized it was more than just friendship. They helped us a lot after that.

Dr. G: Did you get home to deliver Kristina the news?

M: Yes. She is next to me now. She is like ice. She doesn't know what to say. I'm afraid of scaring her too much, but I know that everything will happen according to God's will. This child has been a blessing. She is already five-and-a-half months pregnant. We don't know what it will be. I'm hoping for a girl. She wants a boy.

Mia amazed me again by how deeply she connected with Joseph, being able to access his thoughts and feelings. Imagine how much remarkable information she could reveal by exploring a life during the time of a long forgotten civilization.

M: We are preparing to go to my mother's, to take care of the formalities and everything necessary for the funeral. I don't really want to take Kristi with me. I'm afraid she won't be able to handle the trip and the situation in general, but she is being stubborn about coming with me.

Mia explained that Joseph's family name was *Krisko*, and that his deceased siblings were in their twenties.

M: They have always been inseparable wherever they went. And neither of them managed to get married. They were somehow dedicated to a religious cause. We are Catholics. My mother is so old now. She has white hair and is wearing a headscarf. She is crying… My older brothers, Ruben and Karol, are here along with their wives and children. Kristina is looking with so much love at the children. We want a child so badly! I'm so afraid of her losing this one, too. What a life my poor mother has!

Dr. G: Has the funeral taken place yet?

M: Yes. We couldn't even recognize them. There were a lot of people at the funeral and so much pain. It was a nightmare. And I thought how difficult it must be for my mother to bury her children; just as hard as it was for me when Kristi suffered the miscarriage. I feel so empty right now. It's like I can't even cry. I'm wondering if I'm selfish because I can't feel the same way the others feel. For some reason I never felt close to this family, not even to my brothers. I felt like I didn't belong to anyone. I always felt alone. I cared and I care for them but it's like I can't feel. I don't feel for them as I feel for Kristi or how I felt when she told me she suffered the miscarriage. It was like a piece of me fell apart.

Dr. G: You don't feel alone anymore, now, that you are with Kristi?

M: No, I don't. Kristi gets me. It's as though we communicate on the same wavelength. She supports me in any decision I make. She is a good girl. I was lucky.

I asked Mia what modes of transportation existed there besides trains, and she said cars and buses, and that they also wanted to buy a car.

Dr. G: What kind of car would you like to buy?

M: Skoda is in fashion now. A new model is on the market and Kristi wants one. The problem is that right now we don't have enough money and I don't want to ask her parents. We may have to wait a while.

Skoda is a very well-known car brand in Eastern Europe that began production in the first years of the 1900s. This life seemed to be a very recent life. Mia continued with the description of Joseph's wife's pregnancy, and the following events of that life.

M: It was a rather complicated pregnancy for Kristi. Even though she is a strong woman, she had to spend whole days in bed. The doctors say it's possibly twins considering that her belly is so big, but we don't know for sure. I hope that no matter what it is, it will be healthy. That's what we both want. I'm so impatient! It's three o'clock in the morning and we are waiting to see if everything is okay. I'm at the hospital with my in-laws. We are all concerned.

After several seconds of pause, Mia continued with a happy, enthusiastic voice:

M: It's a boy! The doctor just told us! He says there is a problem with the baby. Kristi is fine but the baby has to stay in the incubator for a few days. I think the umbilical cord was wrapped around his neck. He will have to stay under medical supervision. But the doctors are assuring us that he is well, and that such cases are very common, not to get scared. And Kristi is well too. She is resting now. I can barely wait for all of us to go home! We've prepared the nursery already. The doctor is telling us that we should go home but I don't want to leave Kristi by herself.

Dr. G: What name did you give your baby?

M: What Kristi wanted: Yura. I'm looking at Yura, my son. He is so small and strong! I would like to hold him… The waiting is killing me.

Dr. G: What are you waiting for?

M: For Kristi to wake up, for the doctor to come and tell us what's wrong with Yura. Kristi tells me to go home, get cleaned up, change and come back later. She says that everything is fine. My mother-in-law came so she will stay with Kristi. I'm going home to take care of business. I can't believe that the baby we so wanted is finally here! He is so beautiful! I would love to take him home with me… I don't understand why it takes so long for Kristi to be able to come home with Yura.

Dr. G: How long has it been since she gave birth?

M: Two weeks. Kristi is not well. She is not allowed to breastfeed him. I don't know what's happening exactly. It's as if the doctors are avoiding me. Yura is still in the incubator and Kristi is on intravenous therapy. Something's not right. It seems that Kristi has developed an infection and she can't nurse him. They keep giving her antibiotics.

After a few moments of silence, Mia began breathing deeply and crying. I asked what was going on, and she answered with a heartbreaking voice, tears flowing down her cheeks.

M: I can't believe this! Kristi just died.

Dr. G: And Yura?

M: Yura is still in the incubator, but Kristi… why?

Dr. G: Why did she die?

M: Because of a complication, an infection from giving birth. I'm not sure what happened. I guess a toxin developed during childbirth… I'm wondering if Yura is going to be okay… I have the feeling that I'm cursed. I can't live without Kristi! If Kristi died, then I… it doesn't make sense for me to continue living.

It seemed that Joseph's life was most likely one of the major root causes of Mia's depression.

Dr. G: What is going to happen to Yura if you die?

M: I can't take care of everything now. I don't want Yura if Kristi is not with me. It's because of him that Kristi died!

After Mia spent more than a minute in silent introspection, I asked her to continue telling me what was happening.

M: I feel like I'm going somewhere. I don't want to know about anything or anyone. I don't want to think about Yura. I want to find Kristi and bring her back. I see Yura further and further away, and I'm beginning to see more and more darkness.

The pain caused by his wife's death was overwhelming Joseph. I realized that his awareness was detaching from his body. Just like in our first session, Mia was strongly connected with the previous life. She was describing what was going on in that life as if living it in the present, and not as if she was accessing memories of past events.

THE JOURNEY TOWARD THE LIGHT

M: I feel like I'm floating and flying, but I can't see myself. I can't see or perceive anything. I'm in complete darkness.

Dr. G: What are you doing right now? Are you waiting for something to happen?

M: I don't know what I'm waiting for. The strange thing is that I can't feel a thing. I don't feel the fear of the unknown, I don't feel happiness and I don't feel pain. I don't feel anything. It's hard to explain. I have the sensation that I'm in an abyss. I don't see my body, nor can I feel it. I don't feel any kind of emotion. I wish that I could scream, or cry, or laugh, but I don't feel any of these. It's as though I don't exist, like I never existed.

Dr. G: And yet you have consciousness. There is something that you are thinking with.

M: That's true… I feel alone as if I'm floating in darkness.

Dr. G: Are you going toward something?

M: I would like to think so but nothing exists. It's as though there is only darkness, and it seems that I'm floating in endless circles.

Dr. G: So you're not staying still. You are moving at a certain speed, right?

M: A very slow speed. It's as if I'm looking for something, or maybe I'm expecting something to happen; only nothing is happening.

Had the pain of Joseph's loss caused him to become insensitive, unable to feel anything? Or did his inability to feel any emotion have to do with the darkness he was in? Between the Earth's plane of existence and the Light there is an inter-dimensional plane, called *the astral plane* or *ethereal plane*, through which souls travel when going to the Light and Home, or when leaving Home to return to their physical bodies. There also exist *lower dimensions of existence*, located on lower vibrational levels than Earth.

Was the darkness Joseph was experiencing a lower dimension of existence? And if so, is it an environment where souls are devoid of feelings? Is that why in the darkness Joseph was unable to access an emotional state? When his wife died, Joseph suffered tremendously. Therefore, his soul's vibration wasn't very high, which could explain why he would find himself in such a vibrational environment.

I told Mia to call her Guide, the Spiritual Master, to help her find the Light. After a few seconds, she interrupted my train of thoughts.

M: I see two lights. One on the lower right side, very powerful, and the other one in the upper right, but that one seems very far away. I don't know where to go, which one to go toward.

Dr. G: How big is the one on the lower right?

M: It's very large and very bright, having a golden color of maximum intensity. It's blinding me.

Dr. G: And the other one?

M: It's a frail daylight. It has the tendency to increase in size and then, like a flame, to flicker and turn off. Now it disappeared. The light from the bottom is bigger, but I don't know what to do, whether to go toward it or not... It's almost touching me. I don't know how to describe myself but I feel it's touching me. And I'm scared of going into the Light.

Interestingly, in this state, Mia as Joseph was fearful of going into the Light. Souls who are overwhelmed by sadness and other negative feelings have low vibrational frequencies and often report this hesitation. This reminded me of what Plato once said: "The real tragedy of life is when men are afraid of the light."

Dr. G: What do you feel when the Light touches you?

M: Warmth.

Dr. G: Is it a nice feeling or not?

M: I don't know what or how to feel. I am without feelings, as if all that's happening to me is not actually affecting me. Without my will, the Light absorbs me like a vacuum. I'm trying to look beyond the Light but I can't see anything else because it's blinding me.

After a pause Mia whispered:

M: I'm in the Light.

Dr. G: How do you feel in the Light?

M: Bright? Very bright. I'm like a light that is part of the Light. I feel weightless and full. I don't know where I'm heading.

Dr. G: You feel full?

M: I feel like a ball, like… not necessarily a ball, but like something that's round and full, tangible somehow, but not necessarily. And I feel that the more I go into this Light, that much more I'm finding and rediscovering myself and I'm becoming whole again. In the darkness I only felt that I was floating. But now, in the Light, I feel as if I have some weight. I'm floating, but at the same time I'm something tangible.

Dr. G: You said that you are part of the Light. Do you have a distinct identity in the Light?

M: I think so because I feel one with the Light if I look around, but personally, I feel different.

Dr. G: Can you see your shape?

M: I can't say that there is a particular shape. But I feel that those arms and legs that I should have, or I have had up until now, are somewhat round, like a ball. I feel full.

Dr. G: Are there others like you in the Light?

M: I can't distinguish anything in the Light. It's such a blinding light that I have the tendency to believe that I'm one with it. If I didn't feel so full, I would just say I was the Light.

Dr. G: Do you feel better in the Light compared to how you felt in the darkness?

M: Feeling-wise I feel alive. I feel as though I would like to be with many people. I'm thinking of Kristi and wondering, "which Kristi?" I perceive her as that dear person of my life but it's as though I'm detached or detached. (Mia used the masculine form first and then the feminine). I'm alone but I don't feel lonely. It's an extremely pleasant feeling. It's a feeling of rediscovering or finding myself, becoming whole again. I feel like crying with joy…

Mia did begin to cry. Being in the Light is such an intense and pleasant experience that most of the clients begin to cry with joy. The Light is very beneficial for souls. It helps them release their negative feelings and to become energetically pure again. It recharges them with love and positive energy.

M: It's such a complex feeling, so complete and extremely pleasant that I can't explain it in words… I'm wondering if I'm by myself or if anyone else is here. I can't see and I don't feel anyone, but I wish there was someone else here to ask them whether they feel the same.

Dr. G: Is the Light still so blinding or can you see around you now?

M: I'm beginning to distinguish myself in all this Light. It's as though I'm a globe of glass, of crystal, but it's not a tangible glass. I'm colorless in this huge Light that now seems to be going away.

Dr. G: How big is your globe?

M: It's pretty big. Hmm… I'm like an enormous crystal balloon, an immense, colorless globe. It appears to be glass but it's not glass because the only thing that I can think of is the imaginary idea of being able to touch it. Inside of it is not air, but I can't see what it is. And it's as though I'm rediscovering myself, and I feel full.

Dr. G: So that globe is not solid; it's nonphysical.

M: Correct, it's not solid. I would say it defies the laws of physics. It's probably energy. I don't know exactly. It's more of an imaginary idea that something tangible exists. It exists, but it's not something material that you can describe. Pure and simple it just exists.

Dr. G: And where are you in that big orb?

M: I'm everywhere in it.

Dr. G: If you could see yourself from outside, how would you describe yourself?

M: The Light flows through my globe forming the colors of the rainbow. And these colors fluctuate.

Dr. G: Are you still a part of the Light or have you gone beyond it?

M: I will probably come out soon.

Dr. G: Can you see the edges of the Light?

M: No. It's like being in the middle of an infinite ocean, and no matter where you look, you can't see any edge. There isn't even the idea of the ocean meeting the sky; of that line on the horizon. Such a thing doesn't exist here. The darkness I was in was exactly the same, in the sense that it was infinite, limitless, endless.

This vivid journey into the Light and beyond is representative of what is reported to me by my clients who have good perceptual abilities, like Mia.

HOME

After several moments of silence Mia tells me:

M: I would like to know if there are others like me here. The Light seems to be turning into a mist of various colors, and it seems like I'm floating over different realms.

Dr. G: Do they seem to be physical realms?

M: Yes, they do. And I'm hearing a lot of pleasant crystalline voices and laughter. It's as though there are lots of children. It's such a wonderful feeling! Now I feel that there are others like me around here, but I can't see where they are. In fact, to be honest, I don't even know what exactly to look for because I don't know where I am. I'm floating, and I'm like a ball, a balloon. What fabulous colors around me!

Dr. G: What are those colors?

M: The others and I are those colors, and I feel that someone wants to talk to me. I wish I could see who but I can't. I only feel. I feel that they are next to me. There are more of them and they are like me. They are telling me to stop and to look around me so that I can see them. They're telling me to not allow myself to be carried by energy. Everything is so beautiful! It's so difficult to explain. It's such a wonderful feeling!

I have not found any literature with a description as clear and coherent as Mia's about how it feels to be in the nonphysical form, at Home, in this universe we, as human beings, know so little about.

THE REUNITING WITH THE SPIRITUAL MASTERS

M: I stopped to look around like they told me to, and everything turned black. Then they told me I could have any color I wanted, any combination of colors that exists. (Suddenly, Mia changed her phrasing.) He is telling me that everything that's happening is exactly how I want it to happen, and that here, we are all one family.

Dr. G: What else is *he* telling you?

M: To not be afraid and to change the scenery. Now I feel like I'm in between some cliffs with a superb sunset... but I will still change the decor. When I asked him if he was Marc, my Spiritual Guide, he smiled.

Dr. G: What does he look like?

M: He is also like a glass ball that is changing colors. We're somewhere on some spectacular meadows with a divine sky of an almost unreal color. I can feel the scent of the fresh grass and the breeze of the sea. It's very pleasant. And I have so many questions to ask him...

Dr. G: Ask him who he actually is.

M: He tells me that I will find out all in good time, for me not to rush; that as long as I'm rushing I will not understand anything. He is asking me if I like it here. He says that if I don't like something, I can change it to exactly how I want it to be. And if I don't like it again, I can change it up to the perfection that I envision. Here, everything is done according to everyone's desires. He says that I'm creating my own universe both here and in the physical realm. He is telling me that we create both lives and the countless lives, and that the physical life I just came from is nothing but an illusion.

According to my clients' reports, at Home, souls are able to instantly create. Their thoughts and wishes are mirrored back to them, taking the shapes, colors, sounds, and fragrances they desire. There, everything can be perceived as physical, although it's all nonphysical.

M: He welcomes me back. He is glad to see me again.

Dr. G: Who is he?

M: He says that my mind can conceive of him as Marc, although he has no name. He tells me that as long as I accept him, he can be with me anywhere. The strange thing is that I'm not scared. I wanted someone to come and talk to me. He says that if I will look around carefully, I will see the things I have ignored or I'm ignoring. Most of the time, I'm used to seeing with worldly eyes, but the truth always lies beyond the material things. I asked him to help me see the truth, and to take me into his universe, the universe created by him. I'd like to see it.

Dr. G: Is he accessible to you anytime?

M: He said yes, as long as I accept him. Every time I call him, he will be there. (Mia began laughing.) I asked him if this somehow makes him my Guardian Angel. He is telling me that Angel or Spiritual Master or Guide, or however I want to call him, he is the same one.

Dr. G: Does each person have a Spiritual Guide or is he the same for all of us?

M: He tells me that it depends. A person can have several Spiritual Guides, and that he, Marc, can be the Guide for many others as well as for me. He also tells me that although I don't know it, I already am one.

Dr. G: You don't know but you're already what?

M: That I'm a Spiritual Guide too.

It didn't surprise me to find out that Mia was a Spiritual Guide. She had proven to have extraordinary abilities while connecting with her higher states of awareness, which reflect a certain spiritual maturity.

Dr. G: What does Marc look like now?

M: He is asking me how I would like to see him. Hmm... Wow! It's difficult to choose how to speak with him because he can change his form into a flame, a waterfall, a lily, a cloud or even into a beautiful child.

HOW DO SOULS COMMUNICATE?

Dr. G: How do you communicate with Marc?
M: It's more telepathic. It seems that we can also understand each other visually, and he can gesture as long as he takes a form. But we communicate mostly through telepathy. There are certain waves that I perceive. We don't use a specific language but I understand him, and he understands me. I'm asking him things while thinking and we communicate through our thoughts. And he is telling me that thoughts are energy too.

WHAT IS THE RELASHIONSHIP BETWEEN THE SOUL AND THE SUBCONSCIOUS MIND?

Dr. G: Can the soul, over the course of a human being's life, extend from the physical body to travel, and return into the body at will anytime it wishes to?
M: Yes, whenever it wishes to. A human being can travel into our realms, and into all the other places where it wishes to travel only with the mind, meaning the soul.
Dr. G: Which part of the mind is the soul?
M: The subconscious mind is the mind of the soul. The subconscious actually determines the conscious mind.

While asking Mia questions, I noticed that it was as though I was talking directly to her Spiritual Master. As she had said, she was communicating telepathically with him, receiving the information as energy waves that her mind and brain were transforming into language. These answers did not originate from Mia's mind; they were only articulated by her. Mia's Spiritual Master perceived my questions telepathically through her mind as well. Thus, Mia had the ability and capacity, which I believe all of us have, to transmit information from the nonphysical dimension into our physical universe. This is a way of accessing the universal mind. Knowing that the information was originating from the Spiritual Master and not from Mia, I decided to address myself to him directly.

WHAT IS THE DIFFERENCE BETWEEN THE SOUL AND THE SPIRIT?

Dr. G: Marc, you said that the mind of the soul is the subconscious mind. In literature the spirit is described as being what we call the higher self—the superconscious mind. How would you explain it more

clearly? Which is the soul and which is the spirit in Mia's regressions?
SM: The soul and the spirit are one and the same energy. The difference is given by the dimension, the plane of existence in which it finds itself. The soul is that which dwells in every human being. So in the human body is the soul, and after it extends from the body, passes beyond the Light and arrives Home it becomes the spirit. When Mia stands next to me she is the spirit, and when she exits the Light to return into her physical body she becomes the soul.

Mia had actually described this transformation from soul to spirit. When she died and exited her body in the gypsy life she was in the soul state. She could identify Marc as well, who was waiting to guide her Home. As she left her body, she noticed that their bodies were not physical anymore, but rather ethereal or energetic. After they entered the Light and went beyond it, they had a different form. They were in the spirit state, becoming those balloons, globes or orbs, as Mia described them.

Dr. G: Where are the memories of a soul's lives stored? What holds them, the soul or the spirit?
SM: The spirit. Only here, at Home, can you access these memories of everything that the spirit has ever lived. The soul doesn't hold the information from other lives. To access these memories the soul has to come Home. When the spirit returns to its physical body and becomes the soul, it doesn't hold the memories of previous lives or what is happening at Home. The spirit is the sum of intelligent energy—the energy of love—that the soul accumulates in every incarnation. The memories of the spirit—the Akashic memories—can be accessed only at Home, by the spirit.

The term "Akashic memories" or "Akashic records" comes from the Sanskrit word "Akasha," which means "ether." These records represent a live encyclopedia of the universe's existence or history, including human life. As the Spiritual Master said, these Akashic records are available to be accessed at Home. At this point, I became curious whether Mia was familiar with the term "Akashic records or memories."

Dr. G: Does the soul remember what happened at Home after returning to its physical body?
SM: When the soul returns to its physical body it remembers just partially what has happened at Home, and only when the spirit decides it.

From what Marc said, it seems that the relationship among the spirit level of consciousness (the superconscious mind), the soul (the subconscious mind), and the conscious mind is extremely complex, and affects our lives at all levels.

WHAT HAPPENS DURING SLEEP?

Sleep is an extremely complex process, one that is not yet fully understood, and without which the human organism could not function.

You would think that the human brain's activity is reduced during sleep, but in fact during REM sleep the brain increases its activity and blood flow except in the part of the brain that is responsible for logic.

What really happens during REM sleep? Researchers say that the brain sorts the information gathered during the day and stores the useful data. But what are dreams really, and how do they form? Why do some people feel so rested after a night of sleep while others feel tired when they wake up though all of them slept the entire night? What actually happens during sleep? Is there a part of us that travels? Many of us have dreams in which we fly or we are aware that our consciousness is outside of our body engaged in different life scenarios. Are dreams really imaginary? Some of them seem very real, very intense, and the feelings we experience during them are not imaginary at all.

SM: During sleep you extend from your bodies and come Home. Your souls are coming Home. Each one of you has the ability to come here and talk to us, the Spiritual Guides, or whomever you want. While you sleep, you are simply opened to the world from Home, but also to other dimensions of existence including the lower dimensions. You can become channels of information, and you can choose to communicate, as souls, with whomever you wish or to go wherever you wish.

Dr. G: What do we do when we come Home?

SM: At Home you recharge with energy and positivity. You come here to rest, to consult with us, and receive our suggestions.

Based on what the Spiritual Masters said, we may be traveling during REM sleep (when our eyes are moving under our eyelids) and then resting and recharging with positive energy at Home during deep sleep, a phase that is essential for human life.

SM: There are signs we give you through dreams. You have the power to remember what happened when you came Home, but you remember only partially. Most of the time, you barely take with you as little as one percent of the information. Sometimes, you have vivid dreams that you remember. Those are in fact astral travels in the state between sleep and wakefulness.

I have personally had such dreams during which I was aware that I was dreaming. Researchers who study dreams call them "lucid dreams" because you become lucid or consciously aware during them. You can take conscious control of the dream and directed it however you wish. The lucid dreams I had were extraordinarily pleasant and beautiful, with amazing feelings of pure love and happiness much more intense than the ones we feel in our human lives.

Dr. G: Am I right that the feeling of absolute happiness that we experience sometimes during dreams is what one experiences in nonphysical form, at Home, as a spirit?

SM: Yes, that's right. That's what you feel when you are at Home. And sometimes you access and experience your past lives during sleep as well.

During dreams we shift to the subconscious and the superconscious states of awareness. These are the same states of consciousness that we reach in hypnosis, only hypnosis is the state of REM sleep but without being asleep. The difference between lucid dreams and the therapies that use hypnosis is that during therapy *the therapist* guides you to reach those higher states of awareness, whereas during sleep you become lucid spontaneously. In other words, in both situations you get the chance to become consciously aware during the journeys of your soul. However, in therapy we access certain past lives for the purpose of recovering from symptoms and illnesses. In my opinion hypnosis, astral travels, lucid dreams and meditation basically occur in the same states of mind, with the same process of reconnecting with the higher states of awareness. The soul extends from the body and begins traveling in one direction or another with its destination and purpose being more or less influenced by our conscious desires.

Dr. G: What happens when we have nightmares? The feelings of fear and anxiety we experience during them become physical. They seem very real, they don't seem imaginary at all. Usually, people wake up in the morning more tired than when they went to sleep.

SM: When you have nightmares, you are chased through the universe by low vibrational energies—negative energies. You are drawn into the low vibrational dimensions and you exhaust your energy. And because you're not coming Home to recharge, you feel tired.

This means that there is a tight connection between our soul's level of energy and the level of energy and vitality of our physical body.

Dr. G: When the soul travels, let's say at night, does it leave a part of its energy in the body?

SM: Yes, it leaves a part of its energy behind to ensure the normal functioning of the human body.

The idea of the soul's extension from the physical body may trigger feelings of fear in some people, but there is no reason to feel this way because we go through this process all the time. Our souls have been extending from our physical bodies throughout our entire life, but we were just unaware of this process. We have all had the sensation when we became lucid during certain dreams that we were outside of our physical body engaged in different scenarios, while actually our physical body was still in bed. We just didn't know what that meant. The body we have when we travel during dreams is called the "ethereal," "astral" or "dream" body. It is our soul extending a big part of its energy and awareness to travel toward Home.

Dr. G: What is the purpose for our conscious mind to be shut off, to "go to sleep," while the subconscious—the soul—travels?

SM: Have you ever considered that the conscious mind, the one that "goes to sleep," is doing so because the soul has things to resolve at Home? That it may not yet be the time for that person to become aware of what really exists? And that what is discussed at the subconscious level is superior to the physical plane and the human mind? That maybe the human mind is not yet equipped to understand the complexity of what is happening beyond the physical world?

ARE PEOPLE GENIUSES?

Dr. G: How do we come up with all the exceptional ideas?

SM: Have you ever woken up in the morning with a great idea, and when you put it into practice it yielded great results? What do you think is the reason why the idea, which came over night, could yield results?

Dr. G: I would say maybe the idea has been suggested to you; your consciousness may have captured it from the intelligence of the universe.

SM: Definitely. An idea is nothing but an energy that you capture when you let your soul or spirit free, when your soul wanders through terrestrial realms or universal spaces. It is possible that your soul comes into contact with other souls, and makes an exchange of information, of energy. And then, when your soul returns into your body, the idea would just surface into your conscious mind. That's how those so called "genius" ideas are born. This is how you bring information and knowledge that already exists into your life.

What the Spiritual Master described made me think of Leonardo Da Vinci, the Renaissance genius who had extraordinary, visionary ideas. There are scientists who are said to have been inspired in their dreams and visions with brilliant ideas that helped them solve the scientific theories they were working on. Albert Einstein described to have been enlightened in a dream in which he was traveling at the speed of light with an idea that influenced his theory of relativity. Niels Bohr managed to remember details from a dream that helped him develop the model of the atomic structure. Nicola Tesla's brilliant ideas about alternative current, wireless communication, and other inventions that uplifted the human condition came from dreams, images and visions he had about light. He actually said: "My brain is only a receiver. In the universe there is a core from which we obtain knowledge, strength, inspiration."

Painter Salvador Dali described his paintings as reproductions of images from his dreams. Sometimes musicians reproduce music that they hear in their dreams. Some of the grandest ideas come not from observing physical reality, but by focusing on one's inner world. People we call geniuses had exceptional minds, but maybe they have also been exceptional vehicles through which the knowledge of the universe flowed freely, when they quieted their conscious minds and connected to their higher levels of consciousness. They may have mastered the connection with the universal mind and downloaded information from it.

We spend about six years of our lives dreaming. In light of what the Spiritual Master said, we may spend, as souls, at least six years of our lives traveling or recharging with energy, relaxing at Home and gathering and exchanging information. Obviously, without sleep we would not be able to survive. Although we are physical beings living on planet Earth, we may spend our time in both planes of existence, Earth and Home, or even in more than these two without even realizing it consciously.

HEAVEN OR PARADISE, THE HOME OF SOULS

Dr. G: What does the universe that souls live in look like? Is it indeed a universe governed by different laws?

SM: The laws of physics are applicable only in the physical realm. Here, at Home, everything is different. When I say different I mean that the human mind can't yet perceive it. And why it is not yet perceptible is because many people, instead of increasing their positive energy, increase the negative energy they already have created or accumulated. There is the desire for power in the physical plane, for wanting to assert themselves as people, not as souls. It happens that some of those souls have something positive to contribute to humanity. Others, most often, forget the purpose for which they affirmed themselves, and choose a path that is to their disadvantage in terms of their energetic, vibrational growth. Humanity would probably need a few more thousands of years to even be able to perceive, let alone to understand what is here, at Home. In the physical world everything has a beginning and an end. Here, nothing has a beginning or an end. Everything is endless. Here, there is infinite continuity of absolutely everything.

Dr. G: Do you experience at Home the strong feelings and emotions that we experience on Earth, or are they different?

SM: They are different. We have only positive feelings here. The emotions we experience as human beings have a beginning and an end. In the human mentality, to have continuity of absolutely everything, forever, may seem boring but there is nothing like that here. You would have to come here, consciously, to experience it and then you would know.

People who relive the moment of their death from previous lives and go into the Light during regression therapy experience the wonderful feelings of relief, peace, clarity of mind, happiness and joy. That is how souls feel at Home as well, when they go beyond the Light. Mia explained that the feelings of being in the Light and at Home are absolutely amazing, and very difficult to describe in words.

DOES GOD EXIST?

SM: Yes. God is the Source of Life from which the spirits, the souls are born.

Dr. G: Marc, can you access God?

SM: Yes. God is here, at Home. (I will use the masculine when referring to God because that's what most people do, but God is not defined by gender.)

Dr. G: What would be the most accurate description of God?

SM: God is an intelligence and an infinite energy with unimaginable characteristics from the perspective of the physical plane, and of the limited, conscious, human mind. You can perceive as human beings who God is only when you come Home consciously. We are all part of God. Our spirits are detached from this energy that we refer to as "Chi Energy." Whatever you call this supreme consciousness: God, Universe, Chi Energy, Source of Life Energy, Great Spirit, Creator, Brahman, Allah, Tao, it is one and the same.

WHO IS MARC REALLY?

Dr. G: Do you, the Masters, as highly evolved Spiritual Guides, have different attributes and responsibilities at Home? And if so, what are yours?

SM: Beside the fact that I'm sharing my experience with the other Guides, my role is what in the physical world would be considered a judge. I'm the judge of the truth, and I'm the one who makes justice. I represent the righteousness and the truth. Souls who decide to incarnate choose their physical lives with me, and it is also with me that the souls of all human beings decide when it's the time for them to return Home.

Dr. G: But the number of people who are constantly born and who die is very high. How can you, just one Master, take care of so many?

SM: Because I have the ability, just as the other evolved souls do, to divide my energy in many parts, and to be in multiple places simultaneously. It is that property of the soul that I'm sure you have heard of, called omnipresence.

Dr. G: Do the other Masters have the same responsibilities as you?

SM: As Guides, we're always in contact with those who are calling us, who believe in us and need our help. We're always together with the incarnated souls and we share our wisdom with them. The other Masters also have other attributes and responsibilities. They greet and welcome the returning souls from their physical lives, evaluate their progress, reintroduce them to Home, help them plan and prepare for their next incarnation, and so on. We have many attributes.

Dr. G: How do you see us, human beings, and know all these things about us?

SM: Because we're always beside you and amongst you.

The Spiritual Guides and Masters are at Home, but at the same time present with the incarnated souls that they guide. We are never alone, we never were. Although we don't see the Guides with our physical eyes, they are amongst us as part of this energetic network, the quantum, unified field or ethereal field that interconnects us all. The communication at the soul level is telepathic. Therefore, the Guides have the ability to read our thoughts and energy fields, and to understand our concerns and challenges. They read our minds as we read an open book.

Dr. G: Do you see what we look like in our physical bodies, as human beings?

SM: Yes, of course. We see you as a physical body, as an energetic field, and as a spirit. As a spirit, it's not much to see, that's what you can't understand. For you, to consider that something exists, a visual image must always be created in your mind. As a spirit you're felt. That's it.

Dr. G: Marc, I know that this was your name from the life that you've lived with Mia. I'm sure you have lived many other lives and you had many names. What is the name you're known by at Home?

SM: It is Iam. You can call me Iam. (Phonetically pronounced /ja: m/.)

Dr. G: In what way do the Spiritual Guides and Masters influence our lives?

SM: The Guides are the ones who mentor, advise and provide opportunities for every human being. But it depends if people want to be helped by their Guides and if they ask for their help. What the Guides can do is observe and intervene when their help is needed. However, if aid is not requested, then a soul must elevate its vibration by itself.

Dr. G: That is what Jesus was probably referring to by saying, "Ask and it shall be given to you."

SM: Exactly. If help is requested, then the Guide can intervene either with a suggestion, with a certain teaching, through influencing various situations, or by using their positive energy and light to help people heal.

SOUL MATES

Dr. G: What are soul mates?

SM: Soul mates are souls that are on the same level of evolution.

Dr. G: We understand that the concept of soul mates refers more to the husband-wife, boyfriend-girlfriend—romantic type of relationships.

SM: No. At Home it's different. The souls, the spirits are androgynous. Here, the idea of sexuality does not exist. In the physical life, when two soul mates come together in boyfriend-girlfriend, husband-wife type of relationships, their energy is much stronger. But the energy can be also strong when two soul mates come together in platonic love type of relationship—in friendships. The energy is also strong when two incarnated souls on very close levels of evolution and vibration are in relationship with each other.

Dr. G: How many soul mates does a soul usually have?

SM: A soul usually has an infinite number of soul mates. In the case of highly evolved souls, the number of their soul mates becomes limited. In some of its incarnations, a soul can meet with one or more of its soul mates, or in other lives with none of them. If none of the soul mates are incarnated, it doesn't mean that person can't be happy with a soul from a near higher or lower level of vibration. Love can exist at any level.

The more evolved consciousness you are, the easier it is for you to adapt in the relationships with souls that have different vibrations than yours. Love and being in love is everything that connects all these energetic levels of souls.

SPIRITUAL MASTER'S PERSPECTIVE ON MIA'S LIFE AS JOSEPH

Dr. G: When did Mia live as Joseph Krisko?

SM: *Kriskov*. He died in 1980, and in a few years his soul reincarnated in this present life as Mia.

Dr. G: To me, Joseph's life seemed to be a root cause of Mia's depression.

SM: It's true. As you have learned, it was a life in which Joseph went through much suffering. Also, Mia had the fear of losing a parent, of what would happen to her in such a situation because there is affection and connection between family members. And as Joseph, Mia has seen what happens when a parent dies.

Dr. G: Joseph's wife died as well.

SM: Yes. Initially his father died and afterward two siblings. Then his wife died and lastly his mother. In addition to this, don't forget that through the obligation Mia currently feels toward her husband, she was afraid of what would happen if she were to leave him. Now, she is not afraid anymore because Joseph's wife died, and he survived in one way or another. And Mia learned from that.

Dr. G: Approximately how long did Joseph live after his wife's death?

SM: He lived fifteen years but he never remarried.

Dr. G: During Mia's review of Joseph's life, when his wife died, his awareness detached from his body and began traveling. Then Mia called you to talk to us. Did Joseph faint or what really happened?

SM: Joseph initially had fainted because his soul wanted to go with his wife. But he returned to his body because he realized that their child needed him, needed the support of a parent. Then Mia also detached from that life because she had learned her lesson. She remained at Home so that we could be talking now, and Joseph returned into his body.

I was lacking certain information to fully understand what the Spiritual Master was referring to. Weren't Mia and Joseph the same energy, the same soul who lived that past life? Only if the past and the present were occurring simultaneously would the Master's statement make sense. I still needed much more information to understand in depth his explanation.

Dr. G: What was that darkness where Joseph said he was empty of feelings?

SM: It was a lower dimension of existence. Joseph went there because he was extremely upset about his wife's death, and as a result his soul had a low vibration.

Dr. G: So actually our conversation is happening somehow outside of Joseph's life? You said Joseph returned into his body when we began our discussion.

SM: Yes because Home is beyond the physical planes. It's beyond time and space.

MIA'S RETURN INTO THE LIFE AS JOSEPH

At this time, Mia came back to the forefront of the conversation.

M: Marc says that we will talk more. He tells me to come back here, Home again because we have much to talk about. He made a mist around him. I can't even see him anymore, he left. I see fog and it's as though I'm returning the way I came, through the same Light where it's very, very hot. But I'm heading faster and again going through the darkness. It's as if it's a movie on rewind.

It is fascinating how similar the experiences of people in this elevated state of awareness can be. Mia perceived her return like a movie on rewind. Other clients had said almost precisely the same thing after their Guides told them to return to their bodies. For example, one said: "It's fast, everything flows away quickly, and I'm going backwards on the same path I came. It's like I'm in a movie on rewind."

M: I'm back in the hospital. Kristi is not here anymore.

Dr. G: What is going on with your baby?

M: Yura is fine. He will be coming home with me. I feel like I'm in a violet light.

Dr. G: How do you feel in that light, are you fine?

M: No.

I told Mia, as Joseph, to step out of the violet light, and as she did she felt better. Then I guided her to see the end of Joseph's life.

M: My in-laws are with me. I'm in the hospital.

Dr. G: How old are you?

M: No more than 50 years old. It seems that I have a heart complication. Yura is big, he is already a teenager. He has the same green eyes as Krista.

Dr. G: What were the lessons you had to learn in this life?

M: To love others as I loved Krista. And I didn't know how to love the others, only her.

Dr. G: Did you love Yura the same way?

M: No... I'm ready to leave. Nothing is holding me here anymore.

I asked Mia to send love and forgiveness to all the people she knew in that life, including Joseph. Then, I guided her to fully return into her body and open her eyes.

MIA'S REVELATIONS

After Mia fully returned to her conscious awareness, she couldn't remember the details of the conversation with the Masters. However, she remembered Joseph's life and her journey into the Light and beyond it. She was not familiar at all with the concept of Akashic memories or records.

MIA'S EXPERIENCE IN THE LIGHT

M: When I arrived in the Light, I simply felt that I became round and full. My experience in the Light was so intense that even now I feel like crying, but with tears of joy. It's such a complex sentiment that I can't find words to explain it. It's not about becoming invincible or powerful. It's pure and simply a sense of rediscovering yourself. It's a feeling of contentment, but contentment at a different level, not at a worldly level. You become extremely happy; so happy, that you feel as though you could explode. I burst into tears there. I don't know if many people have experienced crying of happiness. That's how I felt. Afterwards, the Light began to fade, or perhaps it didn't necessarily fade but I perceived it that way because I began to move. I can't say whether I was moving up or down, to the right or to the left, but I had the sensation of floating. When I came out of the Light I saw a big balloon that was transparent like glass. I could see through it, beneath it. It looked like a crystal globe. It was Marc. After I passed beyond the Light, I saw myself as being very big; huge, actually. But, compared to him, I felt like a grain of sand. I felt embarrassed but that's how small I saw myself compared to him.

THE WAY SOULS TRAVEL AT HOME IN THE RIVER OF LIFE

M: When I exited the Light and reached Home, it was as though I was in a big bubble of "air." I essentially was that big bubble of "air." I was carried somewhere as if on the breath of the wind, though there was no wind; or as if I was carried by water, though there was no water. It was like the flow of a river, or like when the wind blows and carries leaves or dandelion seeds.

THE ABILITY TO CREATE AT HOME

M: I saw extraordinary colors like those of a sunset, so sublime that I don't know if you have ever seen this kind of thing in your life. It is beyond the power of imagination. And at some point when Marc approached me, he told me that I could create whatever I wanted. And I created a beautiful meadow with cliffs. I sensed a faint wind that brought not only the smell of green grass but also the sea breeze. It was superb! The sky looked so blue, something very difficult to explain. It looked gorgeous, stunning. I can barely wait to go back there!

Mia had difficulty finding her words. By the way she described this universe she created the impression of a magnificent realm, as one would likely imagine paradise or heaven.

Dr. G: What did Marc look like?

M: I asked to see him, and he changed his shape first into a flame, then a river, a waterfall, a flower, and finally a gorgeous child. He can project any image. He can transform into all of these. For us, as human beings, the idea of seeing with our visual sense is very important. That's why I told him that I wanted to *see* him.

TELEPATHIC COMMUNICATION

M: At some point, I was talking to Marc and the flow of thoughts, information or energy that was coming from him was so big that I couldn't convey everything. He said: "You see me the way that you wish to see me. Do you think that if we want to communicate we have to talk? We don't have eyes to see each other, we don't have mouths to speak with, but we understand each other anyway. Do you really need to see me in a particular way to feel and know that I'm here?"

HOW DO SOULS FEEL AT HOME?

M: I don't think that you can live or experience such feelings as a human being; or perhaps *I* just haven't experienced them. I can't explain what this feeling is because until now I haven't experienced anything like that. It's so complex that is not just a feeling of peace or calm, but it's also to be completely free of worry. It's an incredibly pleasant feeling! There are no words to describe it. I can say I have been to Paradise.

WHAT DID MIA LEARN FROM REVIEWING JOSEPH'S LIFE?

M: I can honestly say that I didn't like this life. I felt like a stranger in my own body. I basically lived only for my wife, and this was a lesson for me. It felt like a slap in the face that she died at a young age of 30 years old. I didn't feel any love toward my family or toward myself. It was as though I actually had not lived. It was a life lesson to love all those around me just as deeply as I loved Krista. The first life I saw when I lived in the gypsy tribe was different. I gave and received love, and I lived amongst people. This is my purpose in my current life—to make other people happy—because this is the only way I can be happy. As Joseph, I tried to make myself happy through my wife and not to make her happy so that I could also be happy. I shouldn't have tried to make myself happy through her existence. If I think about it, even in this life I still have that tendency. No matter how sociable I am, how easily I interact and talk to people, I have moments when I want to be by myself and I don't want to talk to anyone. And those moments are starting to scare me because it's not good to be this way. The house I now live in depresses me, and it's as if it's not letting me leave. It's a very strange energy. I know that my husband is a carrier of negative energy and drains me of positive energy… Probably the idea that I have to understand is that if I make others happy, I too will be happy. As Marc said, it's important to make yourself happy thinking of others, not thinking of yourself with that ego of negative energy.

I was very glad to see that Mia understood the teachings about love and positivity that were important for her to embrace in order to overcome her depression. By reviewing those previous lives, she realized what mistakes she had made, and what changes would be beneficial for regaining her health. By reviewing Joseph's life, a major root cause of her depression, Mia's conscious mind learned the lessons she had missed in her previous life about how to shift toward health and happiness. In addition to this, by identifying and replacing the fear-based beliefs she was holding on to at the subconscious level, her soul had the opportunity to grow as well.

I was confident that what Mia experienced in this session would help her tremendously in viewing her life from a larger perspective and regaining peace of mind and emotional balance.

Joseph didn't find the Light in his life as Mia did in her current life. They are the same soul, the same energy, but with two different destinies, two different paths in life. Joseph allowed himself to be overwhelmed by the tragedies of his life and lived his life in sadness. Mia, although she lost herself for a while on the same path, found a way to rediscover herself and understand the true meaning of life.

"I Can Say I Have Been to Paradise"

CHAPTER FOUR

We and the Energies of the Universe

> "The whole secret of existence is to have no fear."
> Buddha

MIA'S HEALTH IMPROVEMENTS

Almost five months after beginning our work together Mia returned for a fourth session radiating happiness. In my opinion, she had reached her ideal weight and seemed very happy with her new physique and life. She was no longer depressed or anxious and no longer had thoughts of suicide. The new Mia was confident and relaxed. She felt rested, calm and emotionally balanced.

M: I've made a 180 degree shift. My mental and emotional states are so different than when I came to our first session. I was so depressed and pessimistic! I had been thinking of suicide and I actually wished for my husband's death. More and more bad things kept happening to me and I practically had both feet in the grave. At the end of the first session, when you told me to think in a positive and optimistic matter, I felt that I wanted to strangle you (Mia smiled to show she was kidding) because that didn't seem possible. I mean, I felt like I had reached rock bottom. I can't explain how you've changed my state of being! How did the change occur? I still don't understand. I don't understand how the affirmations worked, the positive thinking and the positive self-talk. And how did I regain the confidence in myself? I followed your suggestions. I repeated the same positive phrases every day and listened to the audio recording you gave me. I made a sort of prayer out of those affirmations. You told me to repeat that I'm healthy, beautiful, smart and young, that I look good, I'm at my ideal weight and I have all the possibilities of succeeding in life. Before the session I saw myself depressed, tired and fat. And now, every morning when I look in the mirror, with every passing day I'm that much more beautiful. And the way I see myself is the way people around me see me. It's not just a matter of attitude. It's the fact that my eyes always sparkle now. They say that the eyes are the window to the soul. I feel as though I'm smiling with my eyes and I'm constantly feeling joyful and happy.

Mia also shared good news about the relationship with her husband.

M: Our relationship has become very calm and friendly. We don't yell at each other anymore. He is stubbornly trying to win me back but I've told him that I just want to be friends. Now I really appreciate the atmosphere in the house, of respect and understanding. I told him we're going to leave things the way they are to see in what direction life will take each of us. The idea of staying together until old age or having children together doesn't exist for me. I just want everybody to go on their own direction in a kind way and to help each other.

I was relieved to hear that Mia wasn't being harmed by her relationship with her husband anymore. Attaining emotional balance affects our relationships in a beneficial way. It also seemed that Mia was no longer afraid of leaving her husband, as the Spiritual Master pointed out during the previous session.

Mia made herself comfortable on the couch, ready to continue her journey of self-discovery. I guided her through progressive relaxation as usual, and invited her to continue exploring the sources of any issues she was still experiencing in this lifetime. I wondered what scenarios of life she would uncover this time, and what life lessons would be revealed.

MIA'S LIFE AS HELEN

M: I'm wearing a pair of very elegant green shoes. I'm at a party and there are a lot of people around. I'm wearing a very beautiful green dress, but at the same time it's very heavy. The music is pleasant. It's a nice atmosphere and everybody is laughing.
Dr. G: What kind of dress is it? What style of fashion?
M: I would say of aristocracy because it's made of velvet and has gold embroidery, puffed sleeves and a train.
Dr. G: Look at your hands. What details do you notice?
M: I'm wearing green gloves but my hands are white. By the way they

look I could say that I'm about 17, maybe 19 years old.

Dr. G: What is your hair like?

M: It's long, wavy, red… reddish. I have a golden crown with very beautiful gems.

Dr. G: What is happening around you? Where are you now?

M: I'm in a large hall. People are singing and dancing in the middle of the hall and there are others sitting on chairs all around. I'm waiting for someone to invite me to dance. It's a very pleasant atmosphere, with laughter and classical music. There are musicians who play the violin and the piano, only it's not a piano but something similar—an organ. They are playing the horn, the trumpet and the harp. It's a very relaxing, beautiful, danceable music. It's not very loud because I can hear what people are saying. And you can hear the clinking of glasses. Everyone is drinking.

Dr. G: Who did you go to the party with?

M: With my mother and my father. My father is very well put together, partially bald and usually wears a hat. He is very well respected. His name is Frederic Duval (Mia pronounced the name with a French pronunciation). He has a very interesting ring that he calls his seal. It has a large red stone. He is about 50 to 60 years old. My mother is called Countess and she has long red hair. Her name is Stephanie but my father calls her Tiffany. She wears a dress the color of oranges. It matches very well with her hair. She also wears very expensive jewelry, at least that's what my father says.

Dr. G: What is your name? What do your parents call you?

M: My mother calls me Helen. (It might be Hélène, the French version.) My name is Helen Christiana Duval.

Dr. G: And what is your date of birth?

M: 1792, March 13.

Dr. G: What is your father's occupation?

M: He works at the palace. He has an important function because my mother always says to be careful how I behave. And the governesses who educate me are always telling me that I must be a young lady with class.

Dr. G: What does your mother do?

M: My mother takes care of our education, and she is always there for my father. She supports him in every way, but she doesn't really spend time with us. She is always composing music, always writing something.

Then Mia, as Helen, shared that she had two brothers. The older brother, Stephan, was three or four years older than Helen. The younger brother, Victor, was about 11 or 12 years old at the time.

Dr. G: In which country do you live?

M: In London, in England, but we travel extensively. During the summer we usually go to Paris. My parents have a home, a palace near Paris, and we usually go there when my father needs to go to France. We stay at the estate.

Mia's life as Helen didn't seem to be very difficult, living in a wealthy, high society family in nineteenth century Europe. I was curious to see if Helen was able to find her happiness or if she found reasons for sadness and suffering. I asked her how she got along with her family and she sighed.

M: I can't really tell them what I want. I don't want to get married. They want to marry me to a Baron whom I don't like. He's much older than me. I haven't even met him yet, but it seems that I'm supposed to meet him tonight. My father says it's very important to smile, be nice and dance with him. But there's such a big age difference between us! And my mother says that if I'm not going to marry this Baron, it will be very difficult for me to find a match.

Dr. G: What's happening now?

M: I'm looking around and I'm admiring the gowns, the jewelry and hairstyles the ladies are wearing. I feel so ugly compared to them! But everyone is smiling at me and treats me nicely. My brother has a girlfriend and he is already dancing. I'm a little afraid because I don't really know how to dance. There are so many rules and I always get them confused! And what if the Baron comes here now? I don't want to embarrass my father. So many people are looking at how I'm dancing! I would so like to leave this place! Yet my mother and father have insisted that I come here. I don't want to get married yet! I think there's still plenty of time for that. In fact, I don't really ever want to get married. My mother says that I have to, and that I also must have children. She says that I'm already getting old... I want to go outside. The more I think about this party, the more I realize that everything is an act.

After several moments of silence, I asked Mia what was happening.

M: Nothing interesting. I've decided to go out to the balcony and get some fresh air. It's nighttime and it's so nice! The jasmine smells so good! The guests are still arriving. Another family is coming out of a carriage: a lady with two small children, a very elegant gentleman, and a well-built knight. I wonder who he is. When is this Baron going to arrive so everything can be finished, so I can go home? I wish I could meet someone interesting! These types of parties bore me so much! It's such a waste of time.

It seemed that Helen found it difficult to live in the moment and enjoy her life. I asked her to go to the moment the Baron arrived at the party, if he ever arrived.

M: My mother and father are talking to another family. They are delighted, and my father gestures me to come over to them. He introduces me, and that young knight introduces himself by kissing my hand and inviting me to dance. My father said to go ahead and dance with him.

Dr. G: How did that knight introduce himself?

M: Pierre. Pierre Calden. He is tall, with green eyes and dark hair. His little mustache amuses me. He is not older than 24. He is maybe about Stephan's age. I apologize discretely that I don't really know how to dance. But I'm confused. I don't understand why my father said I could dance with him, with Pierre, when I came here to meet the Baron... But Pierre is very nice. He is so gentle and knows how to dance so well. I'm afraid that I'm going to make mistakes while dancing. I feel nervous. Pierre tells me that I look good when I blush, and I shouldn't be afraid of anything. There are so many rules for dancing! But he is helping me and telling me what I need to do. I'm so embarrassed! I feel like running away. I keep looking at my father. He is still continuing to talk but he is also watching us. I don't understand what kind of arrangement is this. Why do I have to dance with Pierre when the Baron is probably the one talking to my father? Would Pierre know something more than I know? If I ask him, would I be considered impertinent? My governesses always tell me that a woman from high society never asks a man. She always waits for the answers to the questions she may have.

Mia again connected very deeply with the life she was exploring, allowing me to see that society through her eyes, and to get a glimpse of the beliefs, rules and views prevalent during that period of history. She conveyed Helen's thoughts with such clarity! I decided not to interrupt Mia's narrative sequence with any questions.

M: The dance is over. I'm looking at my father because Pierre invited me to go to the balcony to get some fresh air, but I don't want to do anything without my father's permission. I don't know if the Baron is still coming or the Baron is the one talking to my father. I don't know what to do. I need to ask my father first, so I'm going to interrupt his conversation because I'm put in such an imposition. My father introduces me to the Baron. His name is Jacques Calden, and Pierre is his nephew from Norway. I'm returning to Pierre to ask him more about himself now that my father has given me permission. Maybe he has more answers. Maybe it's an arrangement that I'm not aware of.

Pierre has harsh features even though he is young. I'd like to see him smiling. Is his expression a mask imposed by society? He tells me that he came here expressly to meet me. He is looking for a fiancée and his intentions are some of the most serious. If my parents agree, he would be happy to court me. Hmm… I'm thinking that it's better than the old Baron at least! I asked about his uncle. I thought the idea was for me to be married to a Baron. He tells me that he's a Baron as well, and the agreement was for him all along.

I'm very confused! How can I possibly tell him that I'm not actually interested in getting married, having children and taking care of an estate? And if I had children, I wouldn't want to hire a governess just because that's what society expects me to do. I want to spend more time with them. I don't want to be like my mother, always withdrawn into her writing. I don't even have many memories of my mother.

I can't seem to pay attention to what Pierre is telling me because my thoughts are running away with me. On the other hand, as a life partner, he wouldn't be such a bad arrangement considering that he is young. I think that I could love him. He is pleasant to look at, and probably in intimacy he could even smile. I'm wondering if he is sad. Does he need to get married because that's what his family is telling him to do, or does he really want to get married? I can't imagine why others have to choose for us. Maybe he doesn't even like me. Perhaps his proposal is strictly business, considering that my father is…

How many times have I asked my mother what a marriage arrangement is based on? She said that it wasn't the time yet for me to learn about such a thing, all in good time. I don't know what this arrangement involves, and it makes me question whether or not I really want to get married. My mother has girlfriends, Countesses and Baronesses who come to tea parties, and I'm hearing all kinds of stories. What if Pierre is one of those Barons who lay down the law of the house through aggression? Looking at his harsh features I could guess that he is a harsh man, but I shouldn't judge him on first sight, based on his looks. Perhaps beyond this mask he is a good soul. My mother always tells me that I think too much and I should limit my questions. And then, why is Pierre asking me if he should court me when it doesn't even depend on me? Maybe my father has already agreed, and even if I say no, it doesn't matter anyway. I would ask Pierre if he has someone waiting for him back home, someone who already exists in his heart, but that is a totally inappropriate question.

The enormity of Helen's waves of thoughts was astonishing.
M: For some reason I feel uncomfortable in Pierre's presence. I want to go back to the ballroom but not necessarily to dance. I told him that I'm

cold and I want to go inside... He just gave me his military jacket. He put it on my shoulders, so now I'm wondering what other excuse I could use to go back inside and look into my father's eyes to figure out what's happening. And I'm asking myself how long do I have to stay here? When can we go home?

After guiding Mia to the next important part of Helen's life she described the following scene:

M: I'm wearing a black dress with black lace. I'm looking in the mirror and I feel as if a hundred years have washed over me. I feel burdened. I'm about 35 years old. I have an 8 year-old boy. His name is Chris. We thought that from Christiana, Chris would be a nice name. And then I thought that my mother also named her first child after her, who was a boy as well.

Dr. G: To whom did you get married?

M: Pierre, Pierre Calden. Currently, my name is Helen Calden. I'm back home again because my father has died. I'm trying to take care of my mother. I might take her home with me.

Dr. G: Where do you live?

M: In Norway at one of Pierre's estates. The family has gotten smaller. Stephen is not with us anymore. He died in the war between France and England because we have estates in England as well as in France. There were big problems and we lost the estates in France. Stephan always thought that for those like us it's worth the fight.

Could Mia, as Helen, have been referring to the Napoleonic wars that took place after the French Revolution of 1789 and lasted until around 1815?

M: Then my husband also died. He got terribly ill and nobody knew what was wrong with him. He was about my age, about 35 years old. This happened about five or six years ago. I was thinking about remarrying because my financial situation is not the best, but I think it's difficult considering that my Chris is still young. He is too young to understand why another father came to take his father's place. And I don't think it would be appealing to a possible suitor. I'm already past my first youth, with a child and a shaky financial situation. Maybe I should consider selling the properties because I can no longer afford to keep them with all the employees. I don't see any other way and I'm thinking about returning home to my mother. Victor has practically taken over the family business. I don't even know how to tell my mother about my financial situation. She always considered that it was the best. I never really dealt with money. I don't know how to manage or run things. My education didn't include this aspect.

Dr. G: How was the wedding with Pierre?

M: It was a beautiful wedding with many guests. I was happy with him during the courtship. We wrote each other a lot, and we saw each other maybe three or four times. We became very close and I discovered that he was a very good man with many feelings. But he could never love me too deeply. He told me that his love remained with a peasant girl, and they couldn't be together because of society. She was one of the servants, a simple person, not one of the educated employees of his estate. His parents would have never been able to accept her because she didn't have noble blood.

Dr. G: How long after you got married was your son born?

M: I think somewhere around three or four years. I got pregnant again but I wasn't able to sustain the pregnancy until the end. I don't know what happened, probably the climate and the worries. Pierre had always been extremely understanding, and even if he got sad he did everything to make me feel good. I think he did his best in our marriage although I never felt him completely present. But I was never completely there either. Our marriage was more of convenience, imposed by our families. But it was a pleasant time, nothing out of the ordinary, no feelings that troubled our existence.

I asked Mia to go to the next significant event of that life.

M: It's night. I'm trying to write a letter to my mother by candle light. I want to tell her how much I missed her in my life, and that everything I didn't receive from her I try to give to Chris.

Dr. G: How old is Chris now?

M: Chris is going to get married. He is extremely in love. She is a young lady from a good family and very well-educated. She apparently loves him as well. He is 27, 28 years old. I know that he may have waited too long, but I always told him that for such an important decision he should be ready and sure. And as long as I was here, he didn't have to worry about social pressure. I told him to do only what he wanted to do and he shouldn't feel pressured by anyone. I probably would have wished... I'm living this life through him, as I would have liked to live my own life, but I had no choice. I'm not complaining. I had an easy life, maybe too easy compared to others, but I feel that I didn't live it fully. I feel that the essence of happiness escaped me, and everything was like a game, like a shadow.

It is amazing how through the regression process, people from other times of history can teach us powerful life lessons in such a direct way. Helen never dreamed that she could impart her life experience with an audience two hundred years further in time, and her own life would become a lesson for her future self in another life.

M: If my purpose on Earth was to make Chris happy, I hope that I succeeded. He has been the engine that gave meaning to my life. I would have liked him to have gotten married sooner. Perhaps by this age he could have had his own children. I could have been a grandmother. But it's never too late. I'm convinced that it's better for him to take as much time as he needs to be happy than to do something in haste and later to regret it or to be unhappy. I told him that from my point of view, to choose whomever he wanted no matter if she was an educated girl or not. We will somehow cover up these inconveniences and nobody will ever know. A person can be beautiful even without education or a title. I'm happy for him, and I'm writing this letter for nothing. I'm writing it as a thought to my mother because she is no longer with us. Shortly after my father died, she died too. It seems that she loved my father, although she never told me about their marriage. She never told me if it was or wasn't arranged, but it seemed that they found the desire to grow old together. Or maybe it was all for convenience as in my case? Will I ever get the answers to my questions?

Next, I guided Mia to review the last moments of that life.

THE TIME OF DEATH

M: I'm outside and it's daylight. I feel like my breathing is being cut off, and I feel a terrible pain in my chest.

Mia felt the pain from Helen's body, not from her present life's body.

M: I wonder why nobody comes to help me. I see a lot of flowers… I'm looking at the sky and I'm wondering if this is the end… then I'm ready.

I asked Mia, as Helen, what was going on with her family at that moment. She said that her son was married to the same woman he had courted. They had 11 or 12 year old twins—a girl and a boy—and they were happy. They lived in Norway as well, about two hours away from where Helen lived.

Dr. G: What is Chris's occupation?

M: He is a councilman, an advisor for the state. He is an important man. I'm so proud of him!

Mia said that she, as Helen, sent Chris to very well-known universities in London to prepare for this profession.

Dr. G: How old are you?

M: 69, 70 years old.

Dr. G: What mode of transportation do you use when you visit each other?

M: Still with the carriage. Chris explained and showed me in the newspaper that people invented a car that uses steam. But I don't travel in it and I don't believe in it too much. What if the car breaks down and I get stuck in the middle of wilderness? The worst case scenario, with the horse and the carriage the horse gets to rest and then we continue from where we left off. He told me that a trip from my place to his, that takes around two hours with the carriage, would take about half an hour with the steam car. But I still don't believe it. For me, it's easier with the carriage.

Dr. G: Are there other means of transportation such as a train?

M: I think that's the car with steam that Chris was talking about. It's made of iron, and it's big and long.

The steam locomotive was invented in 1802 and the first railway in Norway was inaugurated in 1854. Mia already mentioned that Helen was in her late 60s and was born in 1792. The years seemed to match.

M: I see the sun becoming larger. At first, it was like a shadow, but now it lights up the sky and its rays are so warm. I see the sun more and more... I feel like someone is putting their hand in my chest, and they are squeezing. They are squeezing and releasing, squeezing and releasing. Now I feel a state of liberation, and I see an immense light that seems to get inside of me and free me. I feel like I want to reach the sky. I feel weightless and without pain.

Mia has relived the moment of her death as Helen.

Dr. G: If you look back at this life, what do you think you had to discover or learn?

M: I probably had too many restless thoughts. Maybe I wanted a much closer relationship with my mother, or maybe I just wanted a different life. I was happy, but happy just on the surface. For me, happiness was only an empty word or concept. I didn't *feel* the happiness as a sentiment. My goal in this life was definitely Chris. The link with my current life is to be happy, to discover the true value of happiness and not to be pressured by society's expectations. Probably the teaching is that I should learn to live through myself, not through another being. I should enjoy life at a different level—the level of feelings—not just complying with those around me.

Trying to find happiness through others (as Joseph tried through his wife and as Helen through her son) seemed to have been a pattern in the last two lives Mia reviewed. Reliving these lives helped her discover and apply in her life the transcendental wisdom: "Love is all that matters," "It is very important to enjoy life at the level of feeling," "Learn to feel happy through yourself, not through others," and "Love others because this way you love yourself" since "The happiness you give to others will bring your own happiness."

THE JOURNEY TOWARD HOME

M: Now I'm trying somehow to reach the clouds because I feel like I'm floating.

Dr. G: Can you still see the Earth?

M: Yes, I can still see the Earth and I also see clouds. If I look ahead, I can see that pleasant sun and a clear sky with white clouds. Downward, there're white and gray clouds, and sometimes I see a mist. It seems pleasant and warm. It's like a soft sheet of cotton that covers me.

Dr. G: What do you look like right now and how do you feel?

M: I don't see myself. I feel light, and like I'm floating without any effort.

If this is what really happens, if this is how people really feel when they die, then death doesn't seem to be such a horrible experience after all.

Dr. G: How do you know where to go?

M: Something is attracting me easily and smoothly as though it's opposite of what I'm thinking, yet everything I'm thinking… It's hard to explain. It's a desire that makes me float, and at the same time a magnet that draws me to it. But I'm not resisting. Pure and simply it's not me who knows where to go or how to get there. It's beyond what I think.

Dr. G: What do you see around you now?

M: Infinite blue and clouds. And it seems that there is a boundary that I can't go beyond, but it just looks blue with clouds as if it was part of the background. I can't seem to go beyond that limit. And that sun that I was heading toward earlier it's now somewhere below me. I can see it.

Dr. G: What is the color of the sky?

M: It's a light, bright blue; a vivid color that I can feel. I keep trying to pass this boundary. I keep trying to go forward and backward, to see if there is an entrance in this backdrop or whatever it is. Downward, there is a splendid image; the sun with clouds and a sky of an amazing blue color. It's interesting. I always thought that the sun had rays like very thin thorns radiating out, but it has a beautiful aura with thousands of colors…

Dr. G: Do you feel someone's presence?

M: No. So far I feel like I'm by myself. I feel like there must be something beyond that boundary. And I'm trying to find an entrance because otherwise I don't understand what I'm doing here.

Dr. G: In what direction are you going?

M: Sideways. I'm curious if it's really the way I see it. It's as hard as a wall... I see now like a waterfall of colors! I'm going with the waterfall.

This was the first time one of my regression clients had encountered such a "boundary" or "wall." I decided to ask the Spiritual Masters to help us understand what was happening.

THE RIVER OF LIFE

Dr. G: What color is the waterfall?

M: Various tones of light blue, but not as water. It's more like the sky because there is nothing liquid that can get anything wet. It's more like air in the form of a waterfall, like an optical illusion.

Dr. G: In what direction is that waterfall flowing?

M: It seems to go sideways. I can't necessarily tell you that it's going up or down, left or right.

Dr. G: How fast is it flowing?

M: It's flowing normally, and it slowly pours into something bigger.

Dr. G: What is your interaction like with this waterfall? Are you flowing alongside the waterfall or are you part of it?

M: It's as though I'm a part of the waterfall, but it's not exactly a waterfall. I could say that it's a flux, a stream of energy. And it's not just me. There are many energies here, and they are all going in the same direction. I feel them even though I don't see anything specific.

After passing beyond the Light, many of my clients had seen themselves flowing in this *River of Life*, which is a stream of energy formed by millions of energies (spirits, essences or consciousnesses— whatever you choose to call them). The River of Life takes them to different *locations* or *places.*

M: Now I see a clear night sky with many stars situated on various levels; many suns, many planets and many moons. It seems like I'm floating, and I'm amazed by what is happening around me. Below me is an Earth from fairytales surrounded by a layer of colors that aren't defined. They blend and complete each other as though one color transforms into another. And it's night but it's very illuminated by light. Now I see a very, very large tree where there is a lot of energy.

Mia was astonished by what she was witnessing, and so was I. Home is a nonphysical, infinite universe, but it can be perceived as physical. I could only guess that the very large tree she was seeing was a formation of energy that resembled a tree.

M: I feel like there are millions like me. There are also larger energies embodied in something that could be described as snowflakes. And you can get in contact with others. I can hear them singing as though they're all praying in unison in a unique and beautiful melody.

Dr. G: What do you look like now?

M: I look like a jellyfish that's somehow floating in this atmosphere; like an energy that changes its color in orange, blue, yellow, pink, red, violet, yellow, white, a fluorescent blue, a fluorescent mauve… The colors are probably changing according to the energy of the others that are around me.

Dr. G: Do you want to call the Spiritual Masters to come and talk to us?

M: I'm going to ask Marc to come because I've spoken with him before.

THE REUNITING WITH THE SPIRITUAL MASTERS

In about ten seconds Mia spoke again.

M: He says they were wondering when I would come back.

Dr. G: Thank them for coming to talk to us.

M: He thanks me as well for returning to speak to him, and he is very happy for you. He says that he is impressed that in such a short period of time you have managed to access so much information.

I was taken by surprise that Iam (Marc), the Spiritual Master, was talking about me. He addressed me directly.

SM: You have an extraordinary capacity for understanding the information we are giving you. And it's very impressive that you are not afraid of what we can show the world, of what is beyond physical death and the material world's appearances. There is much, much more than people see. You are on the right path. Every human being has the desire to see beyond what it sees with the physical eyes. And we are trying to show to everyone, but not many have the capacity to perceive. It's a mystery that wants to be revealed. It's not a secret. And the faith that there is much more than what meets the physical eyes has always been the one that took souls beyond the limits of the physical universe. Beyond these appearances there is that which you will too discover soon. We are impressed by how you receive the information and how you use it. The access to this science has been opened to you, and many amongst us are even wondering whether we are not giving you too much information at once.

Dr. G: I don't think it's too much information. The secret is in understanding the information correctly. I still have many questions. And the more answers I receive, that many more questions arise in my mind.

SM: Your perception is one of the most accurate. You are guided by very positive and loving forces, which are very grateful for the effort you are putting forth in this life.

You may wonder why these loving forces—my Spiritual Guides—would be grateful for my efforts. The Guides are the ones who oversee and help the spiritual growth of humanity. They increase in energy concurrently with the souls they guide, according to how much positive energy those souls accumulate in their physical lives. The Spiritual Guides and Masters make remarkable efforts to guide and help souls evolve, and those efforts are rewarded. Ultimately, the energetic, spiritual growth determines the expansion of the positive energy of the universe.

All the Spiritual Guides and Masters are connected to each other and to Source Energy, The Source of Life. In religious terms you could call them Divinity's forces. There is a continuous exchange of information amongst all of them. They are part of the streams of positive, intelligent energy of the unified field of consciousness, the ethereal or quantum field in which we all exist as energies, as consciousnesses. This electromagnetic field incorporates energies of all vibrations from the highest to the lowest. In other words, it incorporates the entire spectrum of energies from the most positively-oriented to the most negatively-oriented.

SPIRITUAL MASTER'S PERSPECTIVE REGARDING MIA'S LIFE AS HELEN

I asked Iam about Mia's life as Helen, whether her father was really a Count. He confirmed that he was a French Count, and his name was Frederic Duval.

SM: They lived in France, but they traveled and also stayed at the palace in England. Some of the experiences Mia accessed were from England. What she had seen was correct.

Iam also shared that Helen was born in France, and that she married Pierre Calden. He was French but of Belgian descent and had estates in Norway.

SM: They haven't been very happy in their marriage, and even in the present Mia doesn't really like Norway.

The Spiritual Master also revealed that Helen's mother was quite educated. Even though she had potential, she never published her work as a composer due to the sexual discrimination that existed at the time. Iam also mentioned that Helen's son's full name was Christian Rudolf Calden, and he has been indeed a Norwegian councilman.

Dr. G: Why was it important for Mia to see this life as Helen?

SM: It was important because at one point, Mia was asking herself why she is having the life that she's having. Her current life is one of the most beautiful and easy lives she has ever had. By showing her previous lifetimes in which she struggled, not so much as others but still struggled, for her to realize and understand that her life is worth living with joy.

I also asked about the hard-as-a-wall boundary of the blue sky that Mia as Helen felt she could not go through.

SM: That boundary she felt was there because people in her family were mourning for her. They didn't want to let her leave. When Helen needed to come Home to the Light, the wave of energy she felt as a wall had the purpose of sending her back into her body. When she felt that wall she wasn't completely out of the Earth's plane of existence of that specific life.

Dr. G: Do you mean that her family's thoughts, feelings of grief and wishes to bring her back actually created an energy wave that she experienced as a wall?

SM: Correct. Her family was trying to bring her back because they I didn't want to let her go.

Dr. G: So when we mourn our departed loved ones we can create energy blockages in their path out of our desire to bring them back, or simply because of our sorrow?

SM: Yes, absolutely.

In that moment, I realized how powerful our thoughts and feelings are, and what a strong impact they may have on ourselves and other people. All of our thoughts, feelings and emotions are energy. We are factories of energy. Maybe the entire process of mourning our loved ones who have died is not quite beneficial. We could hinder their return Home. Perhaps the cultures and civilizations that celebrate the death of their loved ones have properly understood the energetic connotations of this process.

Dr. G: Many people take this concept of the power of thoughts as something abstract or something that has no real basis.

SM: Because they don't understand how the energy functions.

THE VIOLET LIGHT

Dr. G: At the end of the previous session, when I guided Mia back into Joseph's life to see how it ended, she saw herself in a violet light in which she didn't feel good. What was that light?
SM: When Joseph fainted, he was attracted in the lower dimensions of existence because of his suffering. When you've been into a lower dimension, it would hurt when you are enveloped by this violet light energy. You wouldn't feel well in the violet light because it is a positive, high-vibration energy that is too strong for lower vibrations. That's why when you told Joseph to come out of the violet light, he felt relieved.

WHAT IS THE ENERGY WE ARE MADE OF?

Dr. G: You said that we are all energy nourished by energy.
SM: It's difficult for me to explain these things concretely because there isn't any specific theory or science to help you understand how this energy vibrates. The energetic vibration of the soul is of a dimension that is inexplicable to the human mind. It's of a measurement that has not been and will not be discovered by humanity, nor explained by science. It's partially electromagnetic energy, partially electrical impulse, but it has many more particularities and properties. Basically, you can see it either as an electrical impulse or a mist. It has consciousness, memory, information, ability to create and so on. It has the quality to love and holds absolutely everything that is positive, what you would call positivity.
Dr. G: Are there other qualities that we don't know about?
SM: Oh yes, there are, but you wouldn't be able to understand them because as human beings you are constrained by the limits of the human mind. Those qualities of the soul's energy have to be felt to be perceived. There is a lot that you don't know about, but everything will be revealed at the appropriate time.

TELLURIC AND ETHEREAL PLANES

SM: I want to clarify something. Between Earth and Home's planes of existence, which are parallel, there is the ethereal plane, which is also called the cosmic or astral plane. Through this plane, you, as souls, travel as you extend from the human bodies and go toward Home, and when you return into your bodies. Moreover, the Earth's existential plane has two dimensional planes that coexist in the same place: the telluric plane and the ethereal plane. Both planes of existence belong to your Terra. In the telluric (physical) plane you are in a reality that you can see with your physical eyes and that you can touch. In the ethereal (energetic) plane, you are in a reality that you can see when you open your mind's eye to receive knowledge of this science. In the ethereal plane you exist as energies, as souls, and it's where you evolve vibrationally and energetically.

Dr. G: So both planes of existence coexist in the same place. In other words, the energies are always present with us. It's just that we can't see them with our physical eyes; only with our soul's eye—our third eye. But is the ethereal plane limited to the Earth's plane of existence?

SM: No, it's not. Each planet has this energetic field or plane—the ethereal field—and it spreads endlessly across the universe. It continues up to the Light. It is the delineation between your dimension and ours. The ethereal plane is that which happens at the soul level. And once you pass beyond this ethereal plane, you, as souls, are in the Light and then Home.

This ethereal plane, this quantum or unified field as physics calls it, which Albert Einstein dedicated a big part of his life to research, is the ocean of consciousness that is spread everywhere in the universe up to the Light, and in which energies of different vibrations coexist. On the other hand, the universe from Home has a different energetic environment: a pure positive, higher vibrational environment.

Dr. G: Quantum physics suggests that we are all made of the same "fabric," and we are all interconnected.

SM: Right, we are all Chi Energy, The Energy of Life. And as Spiritual Guides we are always with you in the ethereal field, and all the energies are in the ethereal field as well.

I think this is something that we do not realize. We are never alone, and we have never been alone. The universe is conscious. Our teams of Guides are always with us from the moment we exit Home and enter the physical reality, until we die as physical beings and return Home. And it has always been like that, since life began on planet Earth.

THE ENERGIES OF THE UNIVERSE

Dr. G: Please talk to me about the different kinds of energies that exist in the universe.

SM: As your physics describes, there exists positive and negative energy. Here, at Home, we are all positive energy. When one of us chooses to incarnate, from spirit to become soul, the positive energy of the spirit leaves Home and enters a different dimension—the Earth's dimension—situated on a lower level of vibration than Home, by passing through the ethereal or astral plane. The soul enters the Earth's telluric (physical) plane by entering the two cells (the gametes) in the mother's physical body. Compared to Home where there is only positive energy, the Earth's field consists of both positive and negative energy streams. But regardless of the level of vibration, energy is still energy. And the energy fluctuates in every person depending on the emotions of their soul, of what that soul feels, lives or experiences in every moment.

Dr. G: Do you mean that there is energy flowing through our bodies?

SM: Yes. You are vessels through which the energy flows. If people experience feelings of love and compassion and think positively, then their souls vibrate on high levels and attract positive energy—Chi Energy. If people feel anger or hatred, or have thoughts that can harm those around them, they vibrate on low energy levels. As a result, they attract negative energy, which disturbs the proper functioning of the human organism. The persistence of negative energy in the human body leads to the development of illnesses. People who attract negative energy feel stressed, depressed and sick. Basically, the negative energy feeds on our souls' positive energy when we are incarnated.

Dr. G: So there is a force of attraction between the souls' positive energy and the negative energy?

SM: Yes. There is attraction between the positive energies as well as between the positive and negative energy. The attraction between the positive and negative energy it's like the phenomenon that is demonstrated in physics as the attraction between the positive pole of a magnet and the negative pole of another magnet. It is the same with the incarnated souls. When we, as souls, attract negative energy we try to transform it into positive energy. How do you sense the influx of negative energy that goes through your body? You all have experienced this situation many times when you felt a cold current passing through your body and you tried to transform it into a warm current. You feel the negative energy as a cold current and the positive energy as a warm current. There is a cycle though which you can transform negative energy into positive energy. It leads to the disappearance of symptoms and the cure of illnesses.

THE POSITIVE ENERGIES OF THE UNIVERSE

SM: There are two types of positive energies born from The Source of Life—Chi Energy: the spirits or souls, and the protective, angelic energies—angels or angelic consciousnesses—whatever you want to call them. Both types are positive energies but with different properties. The spirits or souls are energies that ascend, evolving energetically and spiritually until they reunite with Chi Energy. The protective energies are particles of pure positive energy that have the role of protecting the souls. Unlike souls, they do not incarnate.

SOULS' LEVELS OF EVOLUTION

Souls are on different levels of evolution and vibration. Though there are infinite levels of vibration, we can simply label them into four categories: new, beginner souls, souls situated on intermediate levels of evolution, evolved souls, and highly evolved souls.

When souls are born, their desire is to reunite with The Source. Therefore, they need to elevate themselves energetically, through physical and nonphysical lives, to those ultimate levels where the union occurs.

Beginner souls are very small souls that have more recently detached from Source Energy. They find their physical lives more difficult because they have very little experience with incarnation, and they are vulnerable to low vibration energies. The more a soul gathers experience and positive energy, the more it evolves on higher levels of vibration and the easier and more beautiful their lives are.

The souls situated on intermediate levels are souls who already have experience with incarnation.

Evolved souls are close to or actually on the levels of the Spiritual Guides, and have extensive experience with incarnation. The souls who reach the levels of the Guides choose to share their wisdom and experience with less evolved souls, becoming their teachers, advisers and protectors. We could compare them to amazing, wise and loving parents. There are also other evolved souls who choose to continue their ascension taking on different responsibilities than those of the Spiritual Guides.

When souls reach the levels of the Guides, it is no longer necessary for them to incarnate to increase energetically because they can achieve this goal by guiding other souls. But they still choose to incarnate over and over again in order to help humanity evolve spiritually. At the same time, they progress even more energetically and vibrationally themselves.

Highly evolved souls are very high vibration energies from the highest levels of Spiritual Guides—the Spiritual Masters—all the way up to the levels where the reunion with The Source occurs. The souls who are close to reunite with The Source or on the levels with The Source are very old (but at the same time ageless) and wise, highly experienced and enlightened. They embody the consciousness of love.

SM: Chi Energy is the one that we all aspire to reach...

Dr. G: Are you able to communicate with all the levels above you, with the most evolved souls such as Buddha, Jesus, Krishna and Muhammad (I will refer to them in alphabetical order throughout the book), or even with Chi Energy—The Source of Life, God?

SM: Yes, of course. At any moment we can communicate with any of them. We all are learning from the most evolved souls, and they will always be open to talk to us. But you must understand that here, at Home, there is nothing that reflects the notion of superiority. Everything is related to the experience and the love that has been accumulated. If asked for an opinion, it is offered with a friendly attitude and accepted in the same way. The ones that are smaller energies respect the ones that are more advanced, and learn as much as possible from the sharing of their experiences. But neither the highly evolved souls nor the less evolved ones consider themselves superior or inferior. Moreover, there is nothing wrong in being a new energy or a less evolved soul. You are energy, you are part of love, and you just carry the love further.

TWIN FLAMES

Dr. G: When we incarnate, do we bring all our energy with us or does part of it remain at Home?

SM: It depends on the soul's level of evolution. Usually, souls incarnate completely. However, after reaching a certain level of evolution, souls can choose to divide their energy into multiple parts. A part could remain at Home, and the other part or parts could reincarnate. Every energy, every spirit, decides what it wants to do. They have the option to either reincarnate into a single human being, or to divide their energy into multiple parts to reincarnate as multiple persons in the same time frame. The incarnated parts of the same spirit would be what you call "twin flames." Not every energy can do this, but it doesn't need to be extraordinarily evolved either. If you are evolved, you have the option to choose what you want to do. As a beginner energy, since you are not that big you don't have much to choose from, and you don't have the experience to handle certain situations.

Dr. G: How many parts can a spirit divide itself into?

SM: Anywhere from two to a very large number of twin flames, depending on how evolved that energy is and the purpose for which it incarnates.

The fact that a single energy or spirit can split and incarnate into multiple human beings might answer the question that many of us ask regarding where all the "newcomer" souls come from, since the world population was much lower in the past than it is now.

Dr. G: If I regress twin flames to review past lives, could they see the same lives since they are part of the same spirit?

SM: Yes because all the lives of a spirit can be accessed by all the twin flames—the people whose souls are part of the same spirit.

That explains why multiple people can access the same lives in regression. Also, you may have noticed that Mia's life as Helen overlapped with her life as Liz. Liz was born on 1832 while Helen was still alive. Mia's spirit divided into multiple parts and lived parallel lives during the same timeframe.

Dr. G: When returning Home, do twin flames reunite or do they keep separate identities? Do they become the same mind, the same spirit, the same consciousness, the same energy?

SM: Well, it depends on when they come Home. At night for example, when twin flames come Home they reunite. They also reunite after the physical death. Most of the time, when a twin flame completes its physical life and comes Home, it energetically attracts the other parts as well and all reunite here.

Dr. G: I assume that all the parts of the same spirit incarnated in different human beings have the same issues, such as the same fears and vulnerabilities.

M: Yes because they are the same energy.

Dr. G: So if one of them manages to overcome one of those issues, will the other twin flames also benefit in their current human lives?

SM: If one of the twin flames solves a problem, it doesn't affect the others in their current incarnations. Only after all of them, as human beings, die and then reunite at Home would they have that issue resolved collectively. In their next incarnations, they will not have that issue anymore.

Dr. G: Do all the incarnated twin flames maintain the same vibration?

SM: No, they don't.

Dr. G: And what will happen when they will get Home?

SM: When they come Home it's a different story. They reunite whenever they get here. From however many parts they are, they become one big energy.

Dr. G: What happens if one of the incarnated twin flames begins to regress vibrationally by getting lost in negativity, and after death doesn't manage to get Home and arrives in a low vibration dimension? Will that twin flame have to start the spiritual evolution all over, separately from the other twin flames?

SM: In that situation, the part or parts of that spirit that have arrived at Home will either draw the other twin flame back from the lower dimension or somehow manage to bring and maintain it in a positive dimension. However, they will collectively regress a little on the spiritual ladder.

Dr. G: So you can actually recover the lost parts of your soul, your lost twin flames.

SM: Yes, you can.

It seems a very wise and safe decision for a spirit to divide itself into multiple parts, and incarnate in the same time frame into multiple people and live parallel lives. The soul will be safe, even if, in the worst case scenario, parts of it regress vibrationally. Additionally, by incarnating into multiple, concurrent lives, a soul can evolve faster by gathering more experience and positive energy. I also believe that a soul incarnated into multiple persons could fulfill very complex plans to help humanity's spiritual evolution.

In the case of twin flames, the idea that hurting others means hurting yourself is literally true. This is an interesting concept to consider.

Meanwhile, Mia was still at Home and the conversation with the Spiritual Masters continued.

CHAPTER FIVE

The Spiritual Guides and Masters

"Know yourself and you will know the Universe and the Gods."
Inscription in the Temple of Delphi

The Spiritual Guides and Masters are basically us in nonphysical form, except that they are the most evolved of us in terms of experience, knowledge, wisdom, power, size, abilities and skills. As part of the positive energy streams (Chi Energy streams) in the Earth's unified field of consciousness (the ethereal field), they are the teachers who oversee the evolution of souls both at Home and on Earth. The Guides and Masters have the option of either reincarnating or coming to the Earth's ethereal plane to guide other souls. Although as human beings we are unaware of their presence since we cannot see them with our physical eyes, we are very well aware of them at the soul (subconscious) level and at the spirit (higher self) level.

Mia was still at Home. Again, I addressed the Spiritual Master.
Dr. G: Why do you still choose to reincarnate if you have already reached these advanced levels of evolution?
SM: We choose to reincarnate to help humanity and to contribute to the expansion of the positive energy of the universe. Also, it's impossible to not want to reincarnate and live as human being because human feelings are so unique. As painful as they sometimes are, they are just as unique and beautiful. Here, at Home, it's wonderful because we are always so happy! We can't even try to be sad because the concept of sadness doesn't exist here. Only those of us who keep reincarnating understand what sadness means.

The Spiritual Guides and Masters have directed the evolution of human kind throughout the history of all civilizations. In fact, at any point in time, many humans are advanced souls who have already reached these high levels of evolution.

Dr. G: Is Leonardo da Vinci a Spiritual Guide?

SM: Yes, he is one of us.

Dr. G: What about Plato?

SM: Plato is also on the highest level of the Guides.

Dr. G: What about Mahatma Gandhi or Einstein?

SM: They too. We are many. And we are Spiritual Guides for souls from the moment they come into existence until they become so evolved and advanced that they reunite with Chi Energy.

We have planned our lives together with our Guides prior to incarnating, and we, as much as they, have undertaken specific responsibilities in the life scenarios we have designed. But it depends on each of us whether we want to accept their guidance or not. We usually accept or block them without being consciously aware of what we are doing. If our thoughts and feelings are negative (angry, hateful, blaming or sorrowful), we would be functioning at a lower vibration, and we would attract and accumulate low vibration energy that blocks our Guides. If we have positive feelings (love, compassion, generosity, gratitude) our soul's vibration would be high, which would allow streams of positive energy to flow through our bodies. As a result, our Guides could easily access and help us. Energetically, we either attract or reject them, depending on the type of thoughts and feelings we have.

Dr. G: Various books propose the idea that people can have multiple Spiritual Guides. Is this true?

SM: Yes and no. It's based on the level of energy, not on the number of Guides because you could have one highly evolved Guide who could represent as much energy, power, knowledge and wisdom as many other Guides together. One person can have one Spiritual Guide or several, or an infinite number of Guides. Usually, one has an infinite number of Guides. When you decide to reincarnate, you decide who and how many are going to guide and take care of you. However, we, the Guides, are all for one and one for all, as you say. Also, Chi Energy can be everyone's Guide as well.

Compared to those of us currently incarnated, the Spiritual Guides have a significantly more complex perspective and understanding of what really exists.

SM: We are here with you anyway, and we see a lot more than you can see as human beings.

SPIRITUAL GUIDES' LEVELS OF EVOLUTION

SM: The Spiritual Guides themselves are on different levels of evolution. Here as well, there is a hierarchy.

Dr. G: Who is your guide, Iam?

SM: It's Chi Energy.

So it seems that The Source is the Guide of the Spiritual Masters.

Dr. G: Are there other levels of vibration above the levels of the Masters, until you merge with Chi Energy?

SM: Yes, there are. And if you choose, you can also reincarnate from those very high levels. There are highly evolved souls that are liaisons between us and the highest evolved souls such as Buddha, Jesus, Krishna, Muhammad and so on. These highest evolved souls supervise and oversee what is going on at Home. And when the Guides decide to reincarnate, they can either choose to be guided by other Guides, or they can be their own Spiritual Guide. A part or multiple parts of their soul can reincarnate into one or multiple people, and another part can become their Guide.

Dr. G: So souls reincarnate only if they choose to, no one imposes the decision on them.

SM: Exactly. Souls that have not yet reached the levels where they can function as Guides, as well as the Guides and other advanced souls decide themselves if they want to reincarnate or not. And they all need Spiritual Guides to guide them so they can achieve their goals on Earth. When the Guides choose to guide other souls and not to reincarnate into physical bodies, they enter the earthly dimension in the ethereal field. They retain their guiding skills without having a physical body. As Guides it's up to them whether they want to be host souls of physical bodies or Guides for others. Yet, when the Guides or other advanced souls reincarnate, it can become problematic for them because they have very high vibrations, and their human lives can cause them to regress vibrationally. Therefore, they have to be very careful when they reincarnate. It is the law of karma. When they come to Earth, there is the risk of accumulating low vibration energies no matter how spiritually advanced they may be. Basically, as Guides, they open themselves up to the other dimensions, including the lower ones, just like any other human being. It's wonderful that they manage to overcome these energetic blockages with your help, for example, or someone else's who uses techniques like yours, but that doesn't mean that they, as incarnated Guides or advanced souls are not experiencing those blockages.

Dr. G: You mentioned *karma*. What is karma actually? Is it the cycle of cause and effect? If you did something wrong, evil or harmful, will you then experience what you have done?

SM: Karma is basically an energy. For example, when a person thinks something bad about someone else, it's normal for that person to attract negative energy, experience that energy, and have negative things happen to him or her. It's exactly the concept of the power of thoughts. When you think and speak positively, and visualize yourself as being a bright light, then you create for yourselves a positive electromagnetic field. As a result, you elevate yourselves to a certain higher level of vibration, such that the low vibration energy cannot reach you anymore. So this is karma. You do good, you receive good, you do bad, you receive bad.

In other words, the concept of karma basically describes what physics teaches us: the energy we put out is the energy we get back.

SOPHIA'S EXPERIENCE AS A SPIRITUAL GUIDE

Before continuing with Mia's session, we will review a client's fascinating experience as a Spiritual Guide. It beautifully illustrates the way the Guides (and also us as souls) see in both of Earth's planes of existence—physical and ethereal—and the challenges they are exposed to while guiding other souls.

Sophia, a 35 year old lady from Beverly Hills, California was an Art Institute graduate working as a jeweler. She had no prior experience with regression therapy, nor had she read about or been exposed to this topic. Although she had many friends, Sophia felt alone and as though nobody really understood her. This prevented her from deeply connecting with other people. She wanted to explore her spirituality and to understand what is beyond the physical experience in hopes of becoming more comfortable in her life. She desired to discover her purpose of being on Earth, and was eager to increase her self-awareness and accelerate her spiritual growth.

After I guided her in regression, Sophia saw, as an observer, the life of a 4 or 5 year-old girl who was living in a very poor area with several other children under the care of a lady. When the little girl returned from a walk she took by herself to admire butterflies, she couldn't find anyone. She waited for several days, but the other children and the lady were nowhere to be found. The little girl finally died. Sophia felt so much compassion for her that she had tears in her eyes as she spoke.

THE JOURNEY TOWARD THE LIGHT

Dr. G: Are you still close to the little girl's body?

S: I'm way up in the Light. I see the lady there. She is waiting for me, giving me her hand. She is very tall and beautiful, and she has long hair.

Dr. G: Do you see the lower part of her body? Do you see her feet?

S: No. And her body doesn't seem to be physical. It's very light. I can see a little bit through her, but I know she is smiling at me.

According to regression clients' reports, the Guides and souls who greet them have bodies that seem transparent and made of light (ethereal bodies). They are able to distinguish the Guides' upper bodies but most can't distinguish their lower body.

S: We are going up into the clouds. She is carrying me by my hand. We're floating. (Sophia's description of the mode in which she travels with her Guide matches Mia's.)

S: She is taking me somewhere higher. It's very sunny and nice, very bright, like golden light. I see the other children here, too. I'm holding her tight because I'm afraid that if I let her hand go, I'm going to fall back. I like being here, it's very pleasant... Now I don't see the lady anymore, but I know she is still here. The children are disappearing. "We should be there soon," she told me.

Dr. G: How is she communicating with you? Is she using words?

S: No. She is not using words... She is letting me go up higher. She is watching me. I'm going even higher now, to another cloud and it feels very good to be here.

IN THE LIGHT

S: I'm now part of the Light. It feels warm and pleasant. It looks like a huge, flat, white cloud.

Dr. G: What's the effect of that huge cloud of Light on your body?

S: I can't see my body. I just feel tickling sensations.

Dr. G: Do you see anyone there?

S: No. It feels very good to be here. I want to stay here. I don't want to go anywhere else yet. (Sophia paused.) Now I feel like I should go higher but I don't want to. I think I have to go back down. I feel like I forgot something. I can't remember but I feel it.

Dr. G: If you could remember, what would that be?

S: The children. They should be with me. I understand them. They are saying that they don't need me, that I can go higher, and I will see them again. It feels so good to be where I am! I'm going higher now.

IN THE RIVER OF LIFE

S: It's very different. I see many little lights, very small golden lights.
Dr. G: How small compare to an egg?
S: Probably bigger. I look like them and I'm floating with them. There are thousands of little lights.
Dr. G: What do you see beyond those lights?
S: It's a little bit darker on the top, but it's light where the lights are… Now I see more lights! They're all over the place. There are so many! I don't have to go anywhere else. I feel like I found it. This is where I'm supposed to be.
Dr. G: Do you know who those lights are? Are they familiar to you?
S: Yes. I feel like I know all of them. They are like magnets. It's very comfortable to be here.
Dr. G: Does each light have its own mind, its own individuality and consciousness?
S: Yes. They feel very friendly, as though they have known me for a long time. Ahead of us it's a very nice, deep, dark sky. I feel like I belong to this place.
Dr. G: Are any of those lights trying to communicate with you?
S: No. They don't need to tell me anything. I feel them. They love me. I feel that I'm not alone and I'm happy. I feel very open. I feel I'm one with them.

Sophia, just like many other regression clients, had described the same route souls take when returning Home that we heard from Mia earlier. They first enter the Light, and, after passing beyond it, they enter Home into the River of Life, where they float together with many other energies, all the way feeling wonderful, free from any earthly pains. They feel a strong sense of belonging and love.

THE WINDOW OF PASSING INTO THE EARTH'S DIMENSION

S: There is a huge whirlpool, and we're supposed to go in. It's very bright. It's made of light.
Dr. G: Does it feel dangerous?
S: No, but it looks very fast. And I know that if I go there, I will go somewhere where I will be important or needed. I'm going toward it. Many other lights are going too.

The whirlpool is the window, the exit through which spiritual energies leave Home to enter the Earth's ethereal field. If they chose to serve as Guides, they remain in the ethereal field. If they chose to incarnate as physical beings, they continue and enter the physical plane in the mother's womb.

S: It's spinning really fast and going downward. I can feel the energy pulling me down and it feels good. It's just very fast. (Sophia began laughing.)

Dr. G: Did all the lights enter the whirlpool?

S: Not all, but many.

IN THE ETHEREAL FIELD OF THE EARTH

S: Now it looks like we're above the world... I can see people. They look so small from here.

Dr. G: Are there many of you?

S: Yes. We are waiting for something... for a while...

Dr. G: What do you see below?

S: I see a big town and lots of people. It looks like it's spring time. I can see some trees but not many.

Dr. G: What do the houses look like? Do they seem to be from recent times or older times?

S: I would say from older times but they look nice.

Dr. G: How do people travel from one place to another?

S: With horses and some funny bicycles. They have wooden parts. They don't look comfortable at all... I don't know what we're waiting for.

Although Sophia was not in a physical body, she could see as a consciousness, a soul, in both planes of the Earth since they share the same space. She was able to see in the energetic (ethereal) plane, where she and the other souls or "lights" were, as well as in the physical plane, observing the town, the houses and people. From the ethereal plane you can clearly see everything that exists in the physical plane, but without being seen by people. Just because we, as humans, cannot see these energies with our physical eyes, it doesn't mean that they don't exist, and that they are not around us.

S: I feel like I should go down there, it feels familiar, but I don't know where to go exactly.

Dr. G: Have you done this before?

S: I think so. I will just know when it comes. It's not time yet. Some of the lights are going down, I see them disappearing slowly. But I'm not going yet. I have to wait.

Dr. G: How do you know that?

S: I just feel it. When it's going to be my time I'll know, and I'll go too.

Dr. G: Let's go to that time.

S: I'm in a house. It seems to be the house of some rich people from the beginning of the twentieth century or maybe the end of the nineteenth. It's a very nice house with hardwood floors and nice old-style furniture. It must be Christmas time. There are a few nicely dressed children playing with many old fashioned toys. They have a beautiful dog. The girls look like little princesses. There is also a boy. He has a dark blue shirt on.

Dr. G: Are you in a human body or are you still a light, an energy?

S: I'm not a human but not a light either. I'm something floating around the children. I'm not one of them. I'm just around them.

Dr. G: How many people are in the house?

S: There is one older lady looking after the three kids. The boy is 3 or 4 years old, another girl 4 or 5, another one maybe 6. He is a nice little boy. I see their mom but I don't see the father. I don't know where he is. The mom doesn't work and they have the nanny too. I'm helping them as well to watch after the kids.

Usually, people in regression see themselves in physical bodies. However, Sophia was seeing herself as an energy with a guiding and protective role—a Spiritual Guide.

Dr. G: Did you change your appearance? What do you look like now?

S: I have a light dress but I cannot see my feet. I can float around them.

What Sophia described was an ethereal body. She was in the soul state, in the Earth's ethereal field. While she was at Home, until she exited the River of Life through the whirlpool, Sophia was a "light," an intelligent energy field, in the spirit state of consciousness. When we exit Home to come to Earth, we enter a lower vibrational environment—the ethereal field—and we develop ethereal bodies.

Dr. G: Do they see you?

S: No but I think the boy knows I'm here. He can feel me and it makes him more comfortable. I think the boy needs me. He is mature for his age. He misses his dad… Now I'm just floating around watching out for the boy. I'm protecting him, but I don't know against what yet. I feel very close to him. I've been here before, some long time ago.

Dr. G: With the same family?

S: With the same boy. I know the boy. It seems like it's repeating, like I've seen it before. I did something wrong, that's why it's repeating. He needed me to help him.

The fact that Sophia's experience was repeating, that she felt she had been there before was a very new idea for me. I was about to find out what this meant.

S: The boy is standing there and I feel like something bad is going to happen. I can't remember... His dad, the boy's real dad, it's about him! But I don't know exactly what it is. His dad isn't here. He didn't come to get the boy. He needed to come back but he didn't.

Dr. G: Is the boy in danger?

S: Yes but I don't see it. I'm forgetting something. I've seen it before. I don't want to be here but I have to be here, and I can't remember.

Dr. G: Let's go forward to the next important event.

S: The boy is gone! There was all this chaos in the house. I lost the boy again! He's gone.

Dr. G: Let's go backward then. Let's see the event from the beginning.

S: His stepfather came. He is not a nice man. He wants the boy to go with him but the boy doesn't want to go. He is hitting the boy with some metal stick. I feel it too. He is hurting the boy's legs! I feel the pain in his legs so strongly! The boy is gone. I lost him! I don't know where he is. I'm missing something.

Dr. G: Where are you now?

S: I'm above the world. I have to wait here. I have to finish. I have to find him and help him. I'm alone. The other lights are gone. I feel the pain so much...

Dr. G: Detach from that pain and go up toward the Light... What do you look like now?

S: I'm an energy, a white ball or bubble. I'm in the universe among the stars. It's very nice. There is no one else here, but I feel like my bubble is broken.

Dr. G: Then imagine a beautiful light surrounding your energy field and repairing it. Connect with the Light.

Through imagination, the attention is directed toward the Light and the souls connect to the Light instantly.

S: I see the Light. It feels good. It's repairing my bubble... I'm being pulled higher... I'm changing colors.

Dr. G: What color are you now?

S: I'm pink and yellow. It's nice. I'm being pulled toward the clouds above me.

IN THE RIVER OF LIFE

Dr. G: What do those clouds look like? Do they look like regular clouds?

S: No. They're spinning, and I'm being pulled toward them. I'm going through them now. It feels like Home. They look like Home. There's much more light here than below. It looks like I'm completing the cloud. We are going to create a lot of light.

Dr. G: Who is "we"?

S: Me and many others around me. They're in the clouds, they form the clouds.

Dr. G: What do they look like?

S: Just like I do. Like a light of white color, but with pink and yellow.

Dr. G: How many are there?

S: I can't count them. There are so many! We create the big cloud and we are spinning. It's a very nice feeling! And it's dark around us.

THE WINDOW OF COMMUNICATION BETWEEN THE TWO DIMENSIONS

S: We're going to make a ball of light. It's getting faster. It's like a game. In a little while we're going to be sent to different parts of the universe. It's spinning faster and faster.

Dr. G: Who is sending you?

S: The center, the center of the cloud that makes us spin. Oh, that's beautiful! We are flying to different parts of the universe. I'm flying away from the center, and the center radiates so much light! It looks like fireworks in yellow, pink and white. I'm going further away now to some part of the universe… Now I feel like a drop of water… I'm in another cloud.

Dr. G: Is it the same type of cloud?

S: No, it's different. It's not as thick and it's not made out of lights. It's a thinner layer of cloud, and I feel cold. I think I'm falling to Earth…

IN THE EARTH'S ETHEREAL FIELD

S: Now I'm in a school, in an old bedroom where children sleep. There are nurses, and there is a little girl with blonde hair tied up in two little ponytails. She has a doll and she is talking to me.

Dr. G: She can see you? What is she saying?

S: She got a new doll and she thinks it's from me. She is very sweet and she is smiling.

Dr. G: What are you saying to her?

S: I'm not talking but she thinks I am. She is saying she is going to see her brother soon. She wants me to stay.

Many children have the ability to sense, see or hear their Guides and to communicate with them. They are able to see into the ethereal field with the eyes of their soul.

S: I'm telling her that I will come back. These children don't have parents. There are so many of them! They have tiny metal beds but at least they're clean and nice. It appears to be a very poor place but very friendly. I want to stay with the girl but I know I have to go… I'm going up toward the sky again, to the clouds, but these clouds are so cold! I'm waiting in the clouds.

Dr. G: What are you waiting for?

S: I have to go and see her brother. I think he is in their house.

Dr. G: Let's go there then. Focus on her brother. Are you moving toward him?

S: Yes, and I've been here before. I don't see the boy but I know he was here… He *is* here! His stepfather is taking him away. The boy is hurt. He doesn't want to go. He thinks he needs to stay there to see his sister, but his stepfather is pulling him away. He has a stick in his hand. The boy is holding back, but the man is pulling him by the hand taking him away from the house. He is hitting the boy with the stick. (It seemed that Sophia was reliving the same situation.) The man wants him to work but the boy wants to stay in the house to see his sister. He doesn't know that his sister was taken away. She is happy but he doesn't know it. The mother isn't around anymore. She died.

Dr. G: And the biological father?

S: He is gone too. He didn't die, and I think he will come back.

Dr. G: Who was taking care of the kids?

S: The older lady. The boy is outside now. The stepfather is taking him away. The older lady isn't doing anything. I need to help the boy, to calm him down, but he can't see me like his sister does. He doesn't talk to me… Maybe he does… He thinks I know his mother. I tell him that he needs to be calm, that everything is going to be alright and his sister is safe. The stepfather is taking him to a different house. It looks like a pub, like an old place. It's not clean. There's a wooden bed. The boy listens, he is calmer. He knows he won't stay there for long. He is right there but I can't touch him. I'm telling him that his father will come and he'll take them both back. He needs to be patient.

Dr. G: Is he happy that you talk to him?

S: He is not happy but he is calmer and he understands. I feel like I can go back now. He is safe for a while… I'm going toward the clouds. I feel really light, as though I'm part of the wind. Now I'm going through the clouds again. It's really nice; cold but nice. I need someone's help to find the father. I can't see the father. I don't feel him…

Dr. G: Take a few moments and mentally focus on him.

S: I feel like I'm floating on a very small boat. It seems to be a lake. There is a big house, even bigger than where the boy lived. The father has some work to do there. He is an important person from the army. He has a hat and is wearing a red and white uniform… Now he is arguing with an overweight man who's sitting behind a table, and who has a big, funny moustache, with gold at the ends. The father wants to go back home. I think he feels he needs to go back. That man is angry with him. It seems to be his superior.

Dr. G: Did he let him go or not?

S: I don't know yet but the father will go either way. Now he is coming out of the building and I'm with him. He is waiting for someone to come so they can go together. The older lady is his mother-in-law but the house is his. She is not very nice to his children. She gave away the girl and she doesn't want the boy either. She wants to have the house to herself. But the father will go home. He knows about the children, he'll take care of them. He's been gone for a long time. The mother thought he died, so she remarried the mean man who took the boy away. He is a friend of the grandma, but it's going to be over now. I can go now. I just want to say goodbye to the girl. We're not going to see each other for a while…Hmm, she is telling me she knew I would come back. She has such a strong belief. She is very strong, stronger than her brother. He is scared and needs more help. I can go Home now… I'm going back to the clouds. It feels like I'm part of the wind. I'm really light, and I can go all the way through all the layers. Now I don't feel cold anymore. I'm just floating in the universe. I'm going back to the Light.

Dr. G: Are there others, like you, going upward as well?

S: Yes, but not too many.

Dr. G: What do you look like now?

S: I look like a bubble, like an egg that doesn't have a solid bottom. I have a hole where my legs should be. The Light is so beautiful and warm!

BACK IN THE LIGHT

S: I'm becoming part of the Light. I'm not the bubble or egg anymore. I don't have form but I have a golden color.

I asked Sophia to call on her Spiritual Guides. After a few moments, she told me they were there.

S: There are three Guides. One of them appears to be an older man. He is all light. He is saying that in my current life I ask but didn't listen, and I spend a lot of time on materialistic things. I've forgotten about them. He is inviting me back. There are two women. They look very compassionate and they make me feel very calm. I can hear them clearly.

THE TEACHING

Dr. G: What was the significance of what you just saw? What are the lessons?

S: They are saying that it's my job, and I have to finish my job and not to leave things undone. It's important because people can't live that way. People need help... The Guide who looks like a man wants me to come back. He challenges me to return. He is there for me but I don't listen enough. Now they're taking me somewhere down through different kinds of light... We're entering a pink, almost purple light that changes color. It's big and looks very flat.

Dr. G: Are you inside that light?

S: Yes. Now everything is just pink. I'm inside of what appears to be a building, a chapel. It's pink light everywhere. In the middle there is a deep well from which the water springs. My Guide wants me to look in and to see my reflection. But I don't see much. He tells me that's the answer to my question. I can see drops of water falling into the well.

Dr. G: Now look in the water and set your mind on something that you want. Can you see it?

S: Yeah... (Sophia seemed very surprised.)

Dr. G: What did you set your mind on?

S: A family.

Dr. G: Now change it. Set your mind on something else that you want.

S: It's my work!

Dr. G: Now do you understand the message your Guide is giving you?

S: I think so. All answers are actually within me. I have the power to create and I am the creator. I have to think of myself this way! He tells me that my work will be creative and I will help people. I shouldn't be afraid if other people think I'm wasting my talent because art comes in many forms. Art is the human soul... He is saying it's time for me to return.

SOPHIA'S INSIGHTS

After the regression, Sophia described her experience, obviously impressed and excited.

S: The part when I jumped into the whirlpool was so amazing! The whirlpool was horizontal, smooth and fast. I could see it coming to us from the bottom, and some of us where taken down into it. It was very comfortable, very warm in there. It was like a door to the physical dimension opening from an upper dimension; a window opening from the upper plane to the lower plane. When I came down from the whirlpool I wasn't a light anymore. (Sophia shifted from the spirit state of consciousness into the soul state, since she entered a different dimension—the ethereal filed.) It was like I disappeared. I couldn't see myself. The other lights disappeared too. The sparkles became transparent energy, like a transparent bubble or orb. (Sophia was describing the ethereal body.) But I felt the same. You could just feel it, but at the same time I could see some of my energy body's parts. It was like in the desert when heat waves come up from the ground, but it felt very normal. It didn't look or feel weird. No one knew I was there, except for the boy who could feel me and the little girl who was able to see and talk to me.

SIMILARITIES IN CLIENTS' EXPERIENCES

People in regression therapy describe their continued existence, without a physical body, after death. They talk about the same feelings of relief, freedom, lightness, peace and detachment once they exit their bodies. They explain the same mode of travel—floating or being carried by their Spiritual Guides toward the Light. They give the same explanations of how their Guides communicate with them—through telepathy—and how both the Guides and them look in their ethereal bodies. They describe the same bright Light or tunnel of Light, and the wonderful feelings of peace and self-discovery they experience in the Light. They explain how it looks and feels to be in the River of Life, and how they perceive the other energies that float there together with them. They even give the same description of the window of communication between the two dimensions. They all describe being an intelligent electromagnetic field in the form of a globe, bubble or cloud at Home, and talk about a wonderful sense of peace and clarity they experience there.

Remarkably, not only do my clients provide consistent information, but their accounts match the data gathered by other doctors, hypnotherapists and other therapists. I would like to mention psychiatrist Brian Weiss, M.D., author of *Many Lives Many Masters*, Dr. Bruce Goldberg, author of *Protected by the Light*, and psychologist Michael Newton, PhD, author of *Journey of Souls*, but actually there are many others who have gathered and published very valuable information.

Many patients who undergo clinical death also report seeing the Light, floating toward it and experiencing the same wonderful feelings in the Light as described by the regression clients. They often report that they have discussions there with wise spiritual beings (their

Spiritual Guides) about their lives and whether or not they should return into their bodies. They report the Guides telling them that it's not yet time for them to remain in the Light, and they should return into their bodies to continue their physical lives.

Human beings possess very rich imaginations, yet if everything described here was pure imagination, then why would there be consistency amongst the cases? If all of these people were imagining or inventing these things, how could they describe the same experiences, the same processes, the same "places," sometimes even using the same words? If all of these experiences were simply figments of each person's imagination, the descriptions would vary, would they not? The fact that all of them report the same details with staggering similarity is amazing and should not be ignored. We know too little about our extraordinary consciousness with its different levels of awareness to rule anything out. We are just beginning to decipher its many mysteries. As Nicola Tesla said, "The day science begins to study the nonphysical phenomena it will make more progress in one decade than in all the previous centuries of its existence."

SPIRITUAL MASTERS' CLARIFICATIONS REGARDING SOPHIA'S EXPERIENCE

I again addressed Mia and the Masters. They revealed that Sophia was quite an evolved soul, and what she reviewed took place when she decided to begin her journey as a Spiritual Guide. It was one of her experiences as a beginner Guide.

Dr. G: She felt the boy's pain. Are the Guides connected emotionally with the people they guide?

SM: She felt the pain partially. We partly feel your pain because we've lived many human lives, and we understand what pain means.

Dr. G: As a Guide, you transform from a spirit form of consciousness to a soul, as you leave Home to enter the Earth's ethereal field to guide other souls, right?

SM: Yes. You become a soul because you're entering a lower vibration environment, the ethereal plane. You are a spirit only at Home.

Dr. G: So that's why Sophia didn't remember all of the details of what needed to be done. As a soul you cannot access all the information unless you go Home.

SM: Correct. You cannot access your entire spirit's consciousness unless you come Home. After these experiences, Sophia decided that she was suffering too much working as a Guide. She realized she was too dedicated to the earthly world and decided to continue reincarnating, to experience life as a human being and not as a Spiritual Guide.

PROTECTIVE ENERGIES

Dr. G: Earlier, you mentioned that there are two types of positive energies that detach from Source Energy: spirits or souls and protective energies. What are these protective energies?

SM: They are what religions have described as angelic energies or angels. They protect the incarnated souls by taking low vibration energy—negative energy—out of their energetic and physical bodies and back into the Light, thus restoring the positive energy flow. They basically cleanse the sites of disease in the human body. Some of the negative energies are destroyed in the Light while others are transformed into positive energies. It depends on their level of vibration.

Dr. G: So diseases are formed by the accumulation and stagnation of low vibration energies in our energetic body, right?

SM: Exactly.

Dr. G: How are the energetic meridians and centers of the energetic body formed?

SM: The energetic body is formed together with the physical body. It nourishes the physical body with energy.

Traditional Chinese Medicine describes the energetic body's centers and meridians. It focuses on balancing the body's energy flow through them, calling the energy that flows through the body Qi, Ch'i or Chi. The Spiritual Master referred to this energy as being the energy of the Source, the energy that we are made of—*Chi Energy*.

Dr. G: What do the protective energies or angels really look like?

SM: Angels are not how religion or famous painters have depicted them: as blond people in white robes and with wings. They are omnipresent particles of Chi Energy with the role of protecting the souls. Every single human being has Spiritual Guides from the level of protective energies as well, and they are known in the Christian religion as Archangel Michael and Archangel Gabriel. The archangels were the first energies detached from the Creator, and they are sort of leaders of the angelic world. Along with the archangels, every human being also has other angelic protectors.

Dr. G: How many angelic, protective energies does every person have?

SM: There isn't a fixed number. A person can have two, three, fifty or even more. Their number varies according to how much help and the type of help you need, your level of vibration, and whether or not you accept the protective energies to help you. And if you accept them, the evolved positive forces that guide you send the angels to you. At that point, the challenge you are facing starts to resolve. The angels are always amongst you.

Dr. G: Do angelic energies live on a different dimensional plane?

SM: When you talk about angels it's like talking about a different universe, but a universe that is still part of Home.

Dr. G: Is there a connection between you and them? Do you work together when you guide the incarnated souls?

SM: There is connection between us and them, you and them, you and us, and you and all the energies because we are all united. We just have different properties each of us.

It seemed that the Spiritual Master suggested a concept promoted in quantum physics, which says that we are all interconnected in this unified field of consciousness, this quantum, ethereal, informational matrix.

Dr. G: So if you wanted to talk about Mia with her protective energies, can you access them?

SM: She can do this by herself, through her angelic Spiritual Guides, Michael and Gabriel.

Dr. G: But if you wanted to speak with the energy called Archangel Michael, can you?

SM: Yes, I can, but I cannot access them *for* her, for what she wants. We, the Spiritual Guides, cannot be mediators between you, the ones who are incarnated and the angelic world. You can do this personally, to ask for wisdom and light. As a result, they will come to you and bring you peace, light, tranquility and wisdom. So only *she* can do this, if, of course, she believes in them.

Was the Spiritual Masters suggesting that Mia did not believe in angels? I recalled that she said she was a religious person.

SM: This is the difference between us and the angelic energies. Our role as Spiritual Guides is to assist you in rediscovering your life's purpose, to help you access and visit your past, present and future lives, and to help you awaken at the conscious level in order to evolve and grow vibrationally. We also have the possibility to reincarnate, while angels don't have the opportunity to live human lives.

Dr. G: These details about the protective energies and the Guides are not well known.

SM: And it may never be known because you, as human beings, are trying to limit all that there is. Everything will probably be much better understood when the planet Earth is elevated to a higher level of vibration. Planet Earth was once on a higher vibrational level than it is now, during the time of the early civilizations of humanity when we could communicate with you without any intervention.

Perhaps that's why we still have so many unanswered questions about our early civilizations, and cannot explain some of the technology that allowed them to build amazing structures that we consider wonders of this world. Maybe they were more deeply connected with the universal mind, and their secrets lay in their ability to access this infinite, universal encyclopedia of knowledge. They may have had a much stronger connection with the universe of Home, with the Guides and Masters, and The Source. Thus, they may have been able to bring in their lives the knowledge that allowed them to advance their technology, and better understand life and the universe.

I had to make an effort to abstain from asking questions about the pyramids of Giza and the ancient civilizations: Sumerian, Egyptian, Greek, Roman, Mayan and even the civilizations prior to them. But I knew that one day I would ask those questions, and suddenly, the Master answered as if he read my mind.

SM: Currently the goal is to again become very closely connected with you, so you can perceive, see and hear us because you have so many questions and you've become chaotic. It's as if you're walking around in the dark. Therefore, we have to shed a little bit of light.

HIGHLY EVOLVED SOULS

SM: Highly evolved souls decide to return to the earthly world frequently, with the intension of elevating the planet Earth to a higher level of vibration, of changing things much faster for the better. They want to give humanity a chance to more easily come into contact with Home, with us and Chi Energy, to offer you our support and love. In a way, these highly evolved energies choose to sacrifice themselves out of their love for humanity because when they return to Earth, they can drastically decrease in energy. They can drop from their high levels of vibration to lower levels. But they consider this their mission, that they must do it to help humanity. These extraordinary evolved souls are capable of offering a great deal of love, and when incarnated, they are exceptional people. Their souls are much bigger than the majority of souls. However, "a measurement" of the soul is not the best description because neither a hierarchy based on soul size, nor the concepts of superiority or inferiority exist at Home. These souls are something that the human mind cannot perceive, nor something that even the humans' souls can see with their mind's eye. They are very powerful, very big and extraordinarily evolved energies. They are pure in everything they do and have no worldly ambitions. Their purpose and desire is to make others happy, knowing that they have everything they need. They have reached the advanced level that no longer requires…

Dr. G: Learning?

SM: They are trying to maintain it so they don't destroy themselves. Returning to Earth, they sacrifice themselves out of their desire to elevate it to a higher spiritual dimension. It's not known how long the planet will maintain itself on that higher level, or if the change will be permanent. Chi Energy will be the one to decide.

NEGATIVE ENERGIES

I asked the Spiritual Master to explain what the negative energies are.

SM: Negative energies are energies that vibrate on low frequency levels. They coexist in the ethereal plane, including the Earth's ethereal plane, with positive energies, and they come from the lower dimensions of existence. Souls incarnated as human beings attract negative energies when they think negatively.

Dr. G: Can you enter Home with negative energy attached to your energetic field?

SM: The energy that you call "the Light," which protects the universe from Home transforms the negative energy into positive energy. The moment you head toward the Light, some of the negative energies that you have with you detach or fall away from your energetic field because they cannot rise on the high vibrational level of the Light. The negative energies that remain attached to your energetic field are demagnetized and transformed into positive energies in the Light.

Dr. G: So then you cannot enter Home with negative energy on you.

SM: No, you can't. Negative energies don't have access to Home. They don't know what is in here, and the only way they can enter is as pure, positive energies. Although there are many souls who want to come Home, not all of them succeed in maintaining themselves in the Light very long because they're attracted by negative energies from Earth's plane of existence.

Dr. G: So this process of connecting with the Light is very healthy, and it basically helped Mia heal. And since she is going Home more often now, she is cleansed of negative energy blockages by the Light.

SM: Correct. At first, she couldn't stay, but now she is no longer interested in many of the worldly matters that could involve her with negative energies.

Dr. G: How are negative energies formed? Are they still the creation of Source Energy?

SM: Yes, they are the creation of Chi Energy who gave birth to them as pure spirits, molecules of pure positive energy. However, they came into contact with low vibration dimensions. So if we, for example, go to a low vibration dimension, it's possible that we may not find the way back Home. When a soul remains in a low vibration environment, its pure energy degrades. It becomes impure. In fact, through this degradation, that soul's pure positive energy is transformed into pure negative energy. To give an analogy, it's like putting blotting paper in ink. The paper gets saturated.

Dr. G: Do negative energies evolve over time and become positive energies?

SM: Definitely. All souls start somewhere lower, and gradually increase their vibration becoming more positive and experienced.

Here is one more reason to have compassion, understanding, tolerance and unconditional love for all people. As humans pass through various stages of development and learning, their souls gradually climb the ladder of spiritual evolution. For the purpose of spiritual growth, many souls experience human lives that don't seem to be pleasant or easy from our human perspective. However, it's important for them to have those experiences in order to become more positive, more loving, more compassionate and stronger.

Dr. G: Were those lower vibration dimensions of existence also created by Chi Energy?

SM: Yes, but relatively speaking.

Dr. G: Was everything in the Universe and in all Universes created by Chi Energy, by God?

SM: Yes. Everything that there is, everything that the human mind can think of, is the creation of Chi Energy or what you call God. However, it is important to know that as long as Planet Earth will exist with life forms, human beings and the possibility of vibrational growth, those lower vibration planes of existence are needed. Through them, souls can evolve and learn lessons of spiritual growth. Many souls need to stay in those lower dimensions, in that *purgatory*, as it's called by humanity, because not all lives are created to transition immediately to the Light.

After physical death, some souls choose to hold on to their feelings of anger, sadness or guilt due to the difficulties they had during life or their death circumstances. They do not find the Light, nor do they want to go into the Light when they do find it. Many of them end up in the lower dimensions of existence.

Dr. G: What was the point of creating the lower dimensions of existence?

SM: It's not Chi Energy as in The Source who created negative energy or the lower dimensions of existence. We, the souls who have detached from Chi Energy created them. When we incarnate as human beings, we open ourselves up to all dimensions. This way, we become vulnerable because we have the possibility to live some emotions that we cannot feel at Home. We get to develop a physical body that we can appreciate, we get to enjoy the fact that we can *see* ourselves, we start to experience pride… all these in addition to having our spiritual powers. Then, it becomes a matter of… without even realizing it, everything becomes so human! And without wanting, we've transformed some of our positive energy into negative energy. This negative energy, having a low vibration, has accumulated and formed those lower vibration dimensions of existence.

Dr. G: So the Chi Energy in us, as souls and human beings created the negative energy and the lower dimensions of existence, not The Source, God, The One from Home?

SM: Correct. We, as incarnated beings have created this negative energy. We could say that it happened without a higher intension, and now, we are trying to fix this issue.

THE LIGHT

Dr. G: Is the Light a kind of a gateway to Home?

SM: You can call it that, but it's a gateway that cleanses the soul because you cannot come Home with negative energies on you. When you return Home at night or after a physical life, the Light is the one that totally cleanses and purifies you.

Dr. G: Is this Light really light?

SM: It's a protective layer of energy of the universe of Home, sort of like a shower that washes the sand off. But in fact, it's not truly light as humans know it. That's just how Mia perceives it.

Dr. G: Other people describe it the same way: as a bright, blinding light.

SM: That's because for them, the Light resembles daylight or the light of a light bulb. It's an energy with special qualities and it can be perceived as taking on any color. It depends very much on the speed of the soul who is returning Home. There are many souls who are attracted very quickly, and, indeed, the colors are formed based on the energy and their speed.

Dr. G: So negative energies have no way of passing through the Light and getting Home with their low vibration. They can only enter Home after the Light transforms them into positive energy.

SM: Correct. And this is from where the idea of Heaven and the gates of Heaven came, along with many other similar ideas described by various religions. However, the word Heaven or Paradise doesn't do justice to what the universe of Home actually is. It's something that the human mind cannot fully perceive or even imagine.

It's difficult to imagine a place even more amazing than Paradise or Heaven... I took this opportunity to ask how Mia was doing.

SM: Mia is bouncing here, near me. She is charged with energy. It helps her to relax. She is very happy here.

I thanked the Spiritual Masters for the answers and clarifications they provided, and I returned to addressing Mia directly, asking her how she felt.

M: I feel very relaxed. It's very nice here. I hear a song, as if the others are chanting a continuous prayer. Marc says I have to go back, and I'm feeling again the energy that seems to pull me back to the River again. Everything is rewinding very fast.

This is the point at which I brought Mia back to her conscious state.

MIA'S REVELATIONS

M: I only remember certain things that Marc said. I feel so good around Marc, so relaxed. Sometimes, when he tells me that I have to go back, I don't feel like leaving. I feel like telling him that I want to stay longer.

Dr. G: Have you ever been to Norway?

M: Yes. I visited Norway, but I didn't like it there. I couldn't wait to leave.

It's likely that Mia's feelings toward Norway may have originated in her previous life as Helen.

Dr. G: What do you remember about what you saw at Home?

M: Flowers, a lot of flowers of all colors. They appeared to be made out of light and have energetic impulses. The one that fascinated me most was like a lily, floating while opening up. It was orange with purple, like orchids or somehow like imperial lilies. I ran, I bounced. Everything is so soft there, like fresh grass. Do you remember at the beginning of the session when you told me to imagine a golden light that relaxes my body? I saw that I have a small hole in my stomach's wall. I wasn't aware of it, and this is the first time I saw something like that. I saw it as if I was looking through a magnifying camera lens.

Mia's ability to see beyond her physical eyes' perception was becoming sharper with each session. I suggested to her to consult a gastroenterologist.

M: At the beginning of the session, when you told me to go upward toward the Light, I saw what appeared to be butterflies. Then they turned into beads of energy that were forming some kind of tunnel. I went up through this tunnel to the sun and the Light. The Light went through all of those beads of energy making them look as though they were made of glass in every possible color. Do you know how when you look into kaleidoscopes you see various colors and geometric shapes? It looked something like that, just that the shapes were round. When the light flowed through the beads, their form wasn't defined anymore. They looked like colors that were blending. It looked so amazing!

What Mia described, according to what the Spiritual Masters later explained to me was a River of Souls, one of the streams of positive energy—Chi Energy—that are everywhere in the Earth's ethereal field up to the Light. Each one of those transparent beads represented a positive, high vibration, intelligent energetic field—a soul. Apparently, these Rivers of Souls are all around us. They are streams of positive energy that also pass through our bodies. These streams are at Home as well, forming The River of Life, which is also a stream of Chi Energy.

Mia continued by stating that she didn't recall the conversation with the Masters, including the one about angels. She added that though she believed in the Bible, she didn't actually believe in angels. This further proves that the information she revealed while accessing the universal mind did not reflect her own beliefs, nor did it originate from her mind. It had, as a source, an impartial wisdom that exists beyond the sciences, religions, philosophies, beliefs, definitions and rules that govern humanity.

However, my personal opinion is that at the base of science, religion and philosophy, there is the driving force to decipher and define the eternal Source of existence and knowledge. As Albert Einstein said, "All religions, arts and sciences are branches of the same tree."

CHAPTER SIX

Reincarnation

"I am confident that there truly is such a thing as living again, that the living spring from the dead, and the souls of the dead are in existence."

Socrates

Two months had passed until I saw Mia again. The progress she had made was remarkable. She felt incomparably better than before beginning hypnotherapy. Her depression, thoughts of suicide and anxiety had totally disappeared. She described herself as peaceful, balanced, happy and confident. She was maintaining her ideal weight effortlessly, and her marriage continued to be very peaceful. Mia even found the strength to give up cigarettes, coffee and alcohol. As she revealed this wonderful news, I could easily read her calmness, joy and contentment.

Mia also shared with me that her husband had both European Union and U.S. citizenship, and they often had to relocate due to his job orders. His next order was in Southern California so were both excited that she could see me at my office in Santa Monica to continue with our sessions.

We continued our appointment as usual with Mia laying down on the couch, eyes closed, as I guided her in progressive relaxation. This time, since Mia had seen a lesion on her stomach wall during our previous session, I added the suggestion to visualize her stomach surrounded and filled with white light. When she reached a deep state of relaxation, I asked her to detach from all physical sensations, to float toward the Light and allow her higher self to show her what was important for her to see and learn at the moment.

MIA'S TRANSITIONAL LIVES

M: I see a large meadow. When I look down I see a lot of grass. But I'm not human, I have hooves. I don't know what I am... I'm tranquil and am grazing.

Mia began laughing. It seemed that what she saw amused her.

M: There is no one around me. It's almost like I'm lost. I'm happy but afraid, and I realize that I'm an animal. I obviously can't see my face, but as I look down and see my feet, they are actually hooves. I don't know what kind of animal I am. I may be a deer or an antelope.

Dr. G: Why are you afraid?

M: I'm afraid because I don't know why I'm here and why I'm by myself. I don't know where I am. All I have to do now is eat, but afterwards when the night comes, where am I supposed to go? There's no forest, only an open meadow. It's nice here, there are beautiful flowers, but I'm by myself.

I guided Mia to review the next important event of that life.

M: It's dusk and I'm in the same meadow. I notice now that there is a lake next to me. Wow! I feel as if a snake-like creature is watching me from over there, waiting for the right time to strike. I'm afraid to run... (After a pause) It's eating me. It bit me!

Dr. G: What do you feel? What's going on now?

M: Hmm... I feel nothing. I don't know where I am. It's dark and cold. Brr... I'm inside some place because I see light outside, and there's blood; a lot of blood. But I can't see myself and I don't feel any pain. I don't feel anything. I smell the scent of blood and I'm not alone. I see a snake-like reptile and I'm afraid. I'm afraid...

After a few moments of silence, I asked Mia if she was still in that life.

M: I don't know. I don't feel anything and I can't see anything. It's quiet. There are no images and there's no color.

Dr. G: Go to the next important event and see what happens.

M: I feel as if I'm floating. There's a lot of water beneath me, like an ocean. I'm floating.

It seemed that Mia's soul emerged from that physical body and was travelling.

Dr. G: Look at yourself. What do you look like?

M: I don't see myself. I'm like wind. I'm floating, liberated and without fear.

Dr. G: What do you think was the lesson you had to learn in that life?
M: To not be alone, to not stay by myself and to trust my instincts. When I feel I'm in danger, to run away.

I must admit that I was very surprised by Mia's experience because I had not previously had any client access a life as an animal. I had heard the theory that prior to incarnating as human beings souls transition through lives as insects, plants and animals. It's an eastern concept and it's also taught in Yoga schools. I had also heard other therapists and doctors mention such cases. But this is, of course, a controversial topic. Some accept the validity of these experiences as genuine past lives, while others insist that they are mere metaphors of the mind. I personally had not thought about this concept much until this session.

I asked Mia to describe what she was seeing. She answered me with a totally different tone of voice, happier, more vibrant and more confident.

M: I see everything as a... as a lily, as flowers that look like they're made of ice with all the possible colors. What a unique spectrum! It's gorgeous and I'm in the middle of that flower. I'm not sure there are any words to describe what I am. I'm maybe a stamen? No, but I'm part of that flower. I'm round like a tomato. (Mia smiled.) Yes, like a tomato.
Dr. G: So you're in the middle of that lily?
M: Yes, but I don't know if it's a lily. It has tall and long petals. It gives off incredible colors as if it's made of crystal or ice. The light shines onto it and reflects amazing colors.

THE REUNITING WITH THE SPIRITUAL MASTERS

Armed, as always, with many questions, I guided Mia toward the Light to call on the Spiritual Masters, to come and speak with us. After a few moments, Mia announced that they were there. Iam addressed me directly.

THE SOULS' BIRTH FROM THE SOURCE OF LIFE. LIVES OF TRANSITION

SM: I'm happy to talk to you again.
Dr. G: I'm happy as well. Regarding what Mia just experienced, do souls incarnate as animals and plants?
SM: Yes. Spirits detach as molecules of energy from The Source of Life—Chi Energy. These small, inexperienced energies arrive initially

to live in the physical plane as water, insects, flowers, trees and all kinds of plants as well as animals.

Dr. G: What do you learn from being a flower besides how it is to live as a flower?

SM: You simply delight in the caresses of divine energy and you evolve. Mia was at the beginning of her life as a spirit. These are lives of transition until the souls become positive and evolved enough to incarnate as humans beings. Love is the only thing that counts for absolutely everyone, everywhere. The majority of animals are very small souls, but they have an extraordinary capacity for love. As they evolve, in future lives they incarnate as humans beings.

Dr. G: Do the souls of animals and plants that are positive energies return Home after their physical death?

SM: Yes, they do.

THE CYCLE OF REINCARNATION

Dr. G: So a soul that is newly emerged from Chi Energy is not evolved and cannot incarnate as a human being from the very beginning?

SM: Oh no, because it could not pass from the ethereal field of the Earth into the mother's energetic and physical body. The energies of the human body are too strong for a newly emerged soul.

Dr. G: At what age does a soul enter the human body?

SM: At the beginning, right at the moment of impact between the two cells, the ovule and spermatozoon. Then, it has a period of about seven weeks to decide whether it wants to remain or not in the embryo. If it decides to stay, then the process of transition from our plane to yours occurs completely. The soul passes from the ethereal field into the physical plane.

Dr. G: There is an idea proposed by various authors that a soul chooses prior to incarnating whether to be a woman or a man. Is that correct?

SM: No. It's not decided at Home because you cannot control such a thing. We know what life the soul will have either as a woman or a man, but no...

Dr. G: Is the energetic body with its energetic centers and meridians described by traditional Chinese medicine different from the soul?

SM: When the soul enters the two joined cells, it radiates its energy resulting in the aura, which is actually the energetic body. You can see the aura of any incarnated soul.

Dr. G: So the soul is like a magnet, and the energetic body is the field of the magnet.

SM: Correct.

Dr. G: If the energetic body is, in fact, the energy of the soul, it means that a physical body without the soul being present in it would not have an aura, an energetic body, right?

SM: Right. The body wouldn't have an aura without the soul being present in it.

Dr. G: Does the soul have a certain location in the body?

SM: The soul, which is a particle of pure, positive energy, doesn't have a specific place where it's located. It can be in a nerve or a nerve center. It can exist in one of the brain's lobes, in a simple neural connection or in the heart. It's about energy not blood flow. It's pure and simply a flux of energy. If you could only realize how small the soul is compared to the human body! It's actually invisible to the human eye, that's how small it is. And yet, it's so powerful that without it the human life could not exist.

Dr. G: So the human life exists only when a body has a soul?

SM: The life that you know.

Dr. G: Otherwise what kind of life would we have? Could the brain think without the soul?

SM: No. That person could not think nor speak, but it could survive as people do in coma. The body of a person in coma is not usually powered by its soul. It's powered by life support machines.

This would mean that the soul of a person in coma is no longer in its body. Some researchers have proposed that we actually think with the soul and not with the brain, and it's true that a person in a coma cannot think, communicate or wake up. Perhaps when or if the soul returns to the body, that causes the person to awaken. Also, Mia connects with her Spiritual Master, who is in the spirit (higher self) state of consciousness. He doesn't have a brain or a physical body, yet he has the ability to think and communicate. These points must make us consider whether we really think with our brain or actually with what powers the brain, our eternal consciousness, our soul?

Dr. G: In other words, as human beings we are the physical manifestation of our souls, the energy detached from the Source of Life. But when we emerge from the Source we are pure positive energy, so how is it that we start our evolution from lower levels of vibration?

SM: When you detach from Chi Energy you are very small. You are a molecule of energy; a microscopic particle. You are Chi Energy at the beginner stage. When you incarnate on Earth, the low vibration energies—negative energies—get to dominate you, and they lower you vibrationally. That's why you start your evolution from a low vibration level.

Dr. G: Is there a succession of how newly detached souls incarnate? Do they incarnate as insects, then plants, then animals, then humans, or can they choose any order?

SM: There is a hierarchy indeed. They are able to first become stones, water and insects, and then to grow energetically as flowers and animals simultaneously.

"Simultaneously?" I wondered. I would understand later what Iam meant by that.

SM: This also happens for the souls who come from the lower dimensions of existence, and manage, as they evolve gradually, to reach Home. When these small energies arrive, they can decide if they wish to remain at Home, or to risk reincarnating to Earth where they might be absorbed by negative energies. This way, they may not be able to return Home. Therefore, they have to ponder what decision would be best.

Dr. G: What happens to a soul who incarnates as a human but regresses vibrationally over several lifetimes, reaching the inferior vibrational limit that separates humans from animals? Does it go back to reincarnating as an animal after it already has incarnated as a human being?

SM: Once you have reached the vibrational level of incarnating as a human being, in order to evolve, you no longer reincarnate as an animal or a plant, even if you have regressed spiritually. After a few lives in which you regress, most often you choose to have a life of suffering. You must somehow repay the energetic debt for mankind and for the plane from Home, and at the same time increase your energy.

Dr. G: Is there Chi Energy in absolutely everything, including matter?

SM: Yes. Chi Energy exists not only in that which has life. It also exists in inanimate matter. Absolutely everything is energy.

The term "reincarnation" that describes the process of souls' evolution, comes from the Latin word "carnis"/ "carnem," which mean "of the flesh"/ "flesh." Therefore, it's understandable if it seems out of place to use the term "reincarnation" for inanimate matter such as water or stones.

Dr. G: Are physical objects such as a table and chairs also Chi Energy?

SM: Yes, but those static things have a different process. They are not creations of Chi Energy as in the Source. They are creations of the Chi Energy and the imagination of the person or persons who created them.

Dr. G: So the purpose of reincarnating is to evolve vibrationally and spiritually by creating and accumulating more positive energy and acquiring experience.

SM: Correct because at Home we can't increase our positive energy. If we could stay where we are, and grow in energy as we are, this work to create positive energy that we are all doing on Earth wouldn't be necessary.

Dr. G: The process of reincarnation through which souls evolve seems to be very well organized.

SM: It is. The souls who decide to live human lives do so to resolve certain problems and overcome certain obstacles. They have their own battles. Every single time they decide to return to Earth to help others, they will live increasingly better lives, without physical pains and problems. For us, absolutely every moment of reincarnation is a success because it advances us along on our spiritual path.

WHY CAN'T WE REMEMBER WHERE WE CAME FROM?

Dr. G: Why can't we remember where we, as souls came from or what we've experienced prior to the current incarnation?

SM: Previous life memories or what you do before incarnation is information or energy that is not stored in your brain for you to access it. The *spirit* holds all of these memories, but the soul does not carry them in its incarnations because it's too much energy to carry. In order to access them, the soul needs to come Home. A human being can access other life memories when it comes Home consciously, as you have guided Mia. At the spirit level of consciousness nothing from another life is forgotten. When you incarnate into a new life, you have all of the experience you have accumulated in your previous lives with you throughout this life, but without you realizing it consciously. Thus, you manage situations that otherwise you wouldn't know how to handle based on your current life experience. To have access to who you are as an eternal being and what other lives you have lived, depends a lot on the wisdom of those around you. It depends on how they raise and educate you because many people are open to this science, while others really don't know what's going on.

THE BEGINNING OF A NEW PHYSICAL LIFE

SM: When souls leave Home to reincarnate, they enter the Earth's plane and their vibrational frequency lowers. Depending upon how powerful and advanced they are, they succeed in withstanding and handling low vibration energies that confront them in their human lives. If they are inexperienced, they attract energies that are not all positive. We and the protective energies look after souls for the first few months of life until they stabilize, after which they begin to assume responsibility for themselves. They begin to follow the path they have chosen for their own spiritual evolution. It was each soul's decision and desire to reincarnate, to attempt to overcome the challenges presented on Earth, the risks they agree to expose themselves to. When souls choose to come to Earth they know what their lives will be. But although the lives are already decided, they can make decisions and change their lives with each step and in every moment. If they know they are not strong enough or can't handle what they have chosen, they can either remain at Home, or change the details of the current life prior to reincarnation or during the course of their life.

THE JOURNEY OF REINCARNATION OF JULIA'S SOUL

Before continuing with Mia's session and the conversation with the Spiritual Masters, we will now review the journey of reincarnation revealed by another client, Julia.

Julia was a well-educated, artistic woman from Los Angeles of South American descent. A successful interior designer, she was eager to find her true life's purpose and use her full potential. Like all of the people presented in this book, she had never investigated her subconscious before coming to work with me.

Growing up as the oldest of four children to a controlling stepfather and a mother who did the best she could to shield her children from the not-so-good moments, Julia's journey started too early with too much responsibility.

J: As far as I can remember, very early on I recall myself searching for something that was missing, but I never understood what or why. A sense of incompleteness has always haunted me, and I only partially felt satisfied. I had been set on a path to focus on achieving my liberation and independence from home to pursue a college education, career and relationship. Despite all the adversity, I can always remember having this unwavering determination or tenacity for everything I set to achieve, and no one could take that from me at that young age. I was unrelenting in my focus or connection with my vision or intention. I thrived on the level of clarity I possessed, as it was my greatest gift.

In her early twenties, Julia's long term relationship disappointedly came to end with the sad reality that her plans would not follow the course of the happily ever after with her boyfriend of five years. However, she did finish school and found an accelerated upwards movement in her career.

J: Like so many, I was faced with a harsh reality of severe peaks and valleys which would shake me to my core, and I began to lose that fire that had once fueled me despite what life threw at me. I had achieved so many things that my peers, friends or family had not at a very early age. I had put myself through college, accelerated in a career that I loved, was traveling the world, had bought my first house at 25 years old, and was thoroughly enjoying life to its fullest. But it seemed that in a matter of a moment it all changed. I had lost my job as so many did around me, and to my greater disappointment I couldn't even get hired flipping burgers, so I could no longer afford to keep my house. In addition, my parents were at odds after a bitter divorce with me stuck in the middle to mediate the conflict, and I had found myself falling deeper in a self-destructive, dysfunctional relationship. I allowed the very thing I despised watching my mother, or anyone for that matter, enduring emotional abuse and heartbreak in return for validation and what I thought was love. I became a fearful, self-sabotaging disaster! My confidence was shot. My anger and rage were through the roof although I did a great job of masking it to the world around me. I was dying inside without anyone having a clue, not even my closest friends. I became severely depressed and thought that I would never be able to climb out of the hole I had dug for myself.

Sadly, what shook Julia from depression were the horrific events of September 11, 2001. She could not allow herself to remain in that dark place of self-pity in the mist of such tragedy.

J: Luckily, I gathered enough strength to declare my intent to change my life from that point on to what would serve me better... or so I thought. I ended the dysfunctional relationship, but kept the bitterness, anger and rage, although at the time I did not recognize that I harbored all those feelings. I had yet to find a steady, well-paying job, and found myself reconnecting with an unsuspecting friend. Many years earlier, I had a significant crush on this man. We found ourselves nursing fresh wounds of the heart as a result of our unhealthy relationships, and despite my initial resistance, I quickly began a new relationship with this person from the past, although old wounds had not healed. Quickly, we were going to the extreme. After only five months of courtship, we found ourselves moving in together and owning a house together. Moving too quickly without any time for either of us to heal from our last relationships, the first years of our life together were very tumultuous and filled with friction, although we did love each other.

After a few years, Julia found herself back in that familiar feeling of having to fill that void, but this time with greater desperation to find direction because she grew more lost than ever.

J: Things started to improve in my relationship and we began to find some sense of calm and enjoyment, and eventually got married. Like too many women often do, I had hoped that marriage would change the man I married because he was now a husband, but of course it did not. At that point, I had to decide to make changes to improve my marriage, and like most, I made it my husbands' responsibility to fix himself so I could be happy. A couple we knew presented us with the opportunity to take a self-improvement workshop. We did, and as many people in relationship, I thought my husband needed it because he was the one with the issues. Of course, that was not the case. I was the one who needed to change. Thanks to the workshop, I had become invigorated, reconnected with my soul and prepared to give life. I experienced how meditation and guided imagery elevated me to a connection with my greater consciousness. With a new awareness, I understood that I needed to continue my journey and growth to find my ultimate purpose in this life.

Julia was not a practitioner of religion. She had always believed in the concept of reincarnation and the notion that we are here on this planet for a purpose.

J: I had always had a curiosity for the art of hypnosis by what I had seen in old movies, where a doctor would use a watch to put someone under and visualize experiences of the past and lives previously lived.

Julia also understood that as a future mother, she not only would provide the physical means to give life, but the emotional as well, and that everything she had within her soul, she could pass on to her child. Therefore, she had a great motivation to find more tools to guide her to continue her soul's healing, so she could give her child the best of her.

As I began guiding Julia to connect with her subconscious awareness, she went very fast very deep. By describing the journey of her soul from life to life, how she died as a human being and returned Home, and then how she journeyed back into her mother's womb in her next human life, Julia uncovered captivating details consistent with those provided by Mia, Sophia, and many other clients, achieved a deeper understanding of life and discovered her life purpose.

THE MOMENT OF DEATH

J: I'm in the desert. It's nighttime. There is a fire next to me. I'm a man, an older man wrapped in blankets. There is a young Indian woman with long, black hair and a round face holding my hand. She has ivory bones as a necklace. She is my wife. She is very young for someone as old as I am. There are Indian men standing around me in a circle. There are two young men on their knees at my feet. They are my sons. We are from the North American lands. It's not current times, there are no buildings anywhere. (Notice how both Julia's conscious and subconscious levels of awareness were active, allowing her to make a parallel between the two lives.) They are bringing me offerings of food and animal skins. The moon is full. I'm waiting for something, but not a person, to come and take me. Everyone around me is praying. I feel their energy. There is something above me, reaching out for me, a figure of some sort, light… I'm leaving my body.

THE JOURNEY TOWARD HOME

J: I'm an essence but I'm not alone. (Julia used the term "essence" to describe a soul, a spirit, a consciousness.) There is a much older spirit next to me who came to get me—a very, very old spirit.
Dr. G: What does it look like?
J: A much larger sphere, I would say the size of two beach balls. It looks a lot like radiant, blue light. A very powerful energy… He embodies wisdom—many lives lived.
Dr. G: What do you look like?
J: I'm a much smaller orange sphere, about half his size. We have entered a different dimension of some sort. We travel very fast, like light. People couldn't see us even if they tried. It's very dark. The only light is coming from us.

      Regression clients often mention that they travel "at the speed of light" after they emerge from their bodies and journey toward the Light.
Dr. G: How do you know where to go?
J: I'm being guided by this greater essence, but there is another essence with us too. I think it's someone else who passed before me. It's a female. She is a pink color, almost my size, just slightly smaller.
Dr. G: How do you know that it's a female?
J: Just feels as though she was. It's almost like we are attached to this bigger sphere. He is a Guide and the keeper of souls. I feel so peaceful!

IN THE LIGHT

J: We are coming to a brighter Light. It's overwhelming and blinding. I can't tell what it is or where it's coming from. We have reached our destination. I feel an overwhelming surge of energy! The Light is like a heartbeat almost. It's so large! We are melting into it... (Julia paused.) Now it feels like I'm becoming part of a bigger source, we all are. We are not even spheres. We are all like particles of some sort, being contained in this energy, but not existing one without the other.

Julia shared her experience of transformation from soul into spirit, as she moved beyond the Light into the River of Life.

IN THE RIVER OF LIFE

Dr. G: Do you still have an identity?

J: Yes. I still feel like I'm my own entity but I don't exist without the others. There are thousands and thousands of us, and more. It's almost infinite. And we are just floating together, but there is a bigger source of energy that is containing us.

Dr. G: Bigger than the Light?

J: It seems so. There is no limitation. It's boundless but something is containing us. Not binding us but just containing us, as if we're magnetically drawn to each other. And we are waiting for our turn.

Both Julia and Sophia mentioned souls being magnetically drawn to each other, floating like small magnets in the River of Life.

Dr. G: How does it feel to be there?

J: It's unbelievable. It feels greater than life! Indescribable... just greater than life! And it's limitless, it's eternal. We all have a purpose and we are all waiting for our next purpose. But some come from their latest lives unfulfilled. Most of us keep coming back to this place. We are all here, waiting I guess for rebirth, waiting to exist. We all have a mission of some sort.

Dr. G: What is your mission?

J: To save lives. This is what I was chosen to do, to save the lives of other people.

Dr. G: Do you see other essences that are about to rebirth?

J: No. I can't see where any of them go. We are essences within a bigger essence. There are so many of us!

Dr. G: Are you organized in groups?

J: No, but it seems that the ones who have lived longer find themselves moving toward the front, I guess. There is no line or specific order, but there are some of us who move toward a path. We move toward the center of the essence, and the rest of them float around us. (In this context, Julia calls "the essence" what I call the River of Life.)

Dr. G: What does that center look like?

J: It's like when you see the water flowing. That's what all the essences are, but there is a force, like a tide in the middle of the ocean, pulling under the stream. There is a certain number of us flowing through that stream and it's almost like we jump into it. Not everyone does. The majority are just floating and waiting. There are many that jump into this center, but comparing to the number of souls here there are few.

The tide that Julia described was what Sophia described as a whirlpool, the window between the upper and the lower dimensions.

Dr. G: Are there wiser essences amongst you?

J: It seems that the essences that have lived many lives are ready. They are older and stronger, like me.

Dr. G: How do you identify them as being older and stronger, if they all look just like particles of energy?

J: You feel their wisdom. You can just feel that they have lived many lives, and they are the ones jumping into the stream. And we are very small in this essence. We are much smaller than we were. (Julia referred to how big they were prior to entering the Light and while in the Light.) We are like particles now. I guess you can use a word like atoms, very small particles, or like cells I guess.

Dr. G: Do you communicate with one another?

J: There is no communication but we know things. It might seem like a second is an eternity, but here, time doesn't exist.

Dr. G: Do you feel lonely there?

J: No. There is no loneliness, there is no such emotion; just consciousness. We have all been here before together many times. Some never left. And we are all bunched up together. It's like when you look under a microscope, everything is moving very quickly. But it's all energy, it's all light. I see light everywhere.

THE WINDOW OF PASSING INTO THE EARTH'S DIMENSION

J: I'm in the stream, and even the stream is moving much faster than everything else. There are still a lot of us and we are waiting. It's moving faster... much, much faster... faster than any moving body of water... just moving extremely fast.

Dr. G: Is there still light around you?

J: There's still light, and it's still not my turn... Now I'm getting closer to darkness in front of me. We are starting to separate. It's getting darker and darker... Now I just see light behind me.

Julia's experience was very similar to Sophia's journey in the River of Life. Sophia went through the fast-moving current into the whirlpool of energy that carried her into the Earth's ethereal plane to fulfill her role as Spiritual Guide.

THE REBIRTH

J: It's very dark. I feel as if I'm floating going through a tunnel… Now I feel like I'm moving very slow. I'm floating in some kind of fluid. I can't see anything but I have eyes.

Dr. G: Are you in a physical body?

J: It's very small. I'm in a womb. I'm growing very quickly.

It seemed that Julia's soul had entered the physical plane and was developing as a human being.

J: Now it's my time to be born again. I'm a girl.

Dr. G: How do you know?

J: I just know… The walls keep pushing in… keep pushing… whatever it is that I'm in. Just keep pushing in at me from all areas… pushing me down and pulsing. But I can't hear anything. I just feel. I'm curled up and I'm being forced. It doesn't take long and I'm out.

Dr. G: What do you experience now that you are out?

J: Fear.

Dr. G: Did you feel any pain?

J: No pain. It was very quick, almost instant.

Dr. G: Do you hear now?

J: Not yet. Someone is holding me. I'm cold and I can't breathe. Someone is sticking their finger in my mouth. I scream! I'm crying. An old woman is holding me. She has dark skin. She is a very active woman. She is my grandmother. She wraps me in an animal skin. I'm all dirty, covered in white stuff. They don't clean me off right away. They're putting me on my mother's chest. I'm instantly calm. She is holding me and smiling.

Dr. G: Can you see?

J: Yes.

Dr. G: How do you see?

J: With my mind's eyes.

It is amazing that Julia, like many other people in this elevated state of awareness, was able to review her birth from another life. Our soul, our consciousness, is always present and aware. It doesn't matter what stage of physical development or of the conscious mind we may have attained. It seems that newborns and babies are aware of everything going on around them at the higher levels of awareness. They simply use a different apparatus to perceive the physical world. They *see* with their energy field, their consciousness, the eyes of their soul. What Julia experienced raises the question whether we really perceive reality with our sensory organs or with our consciousness.

JULIA'S LIFE PURPOSE

Julia continued to review that entire life. Her name was Francesca Robino. She was born in 1829 in an Italian fisherman's village and died in 1897. This life mirrored back familiar feelings and patterns from Julia's current life, such as the feeling of incompletion, being stuck, wanting to escape and run away, and not finding her life's purpose. Then Julia connected with her Spiritual Guide and learned about the purpose of her current incarnation.

J: My guide is showing me people all over the world starving; children dying, hunger everywhere. I need to find a way to feed them. There is hope everywhere but not enough people see it. People are consumed by selfishness. People have stopped listening to nature. They are disconnected from each other. They are disconnected from the Source. They choose to be blind. Their energy light is very dim. The physical form abuses and unbalances their essence. And most people keep unbalancing their essence until they deplete it. They are very brittle, like candles that are almost burning out. That's how they live. The majority of people are disconnected. It's sad. It's the physical form that has more power than the essence. It dims their inner light. They are just like empty bodies with a low battery, barely, barely existing. But with each life there is an opportunity to… it's hard to explain; to I guess achieve a greater level of your purpose, on a grander scale, because you can't achieve purpose with one thing, one person, one scale. There is no limitation to the degree of fulfillment and purpose… I'm here to give life, to evolve myself, to feed the hungry. I'm here to create opportunities, to create connections on a grand scale, to unify people and create hope. I will meet very powerful people on the same path, other essences I have traveled with before. We will find each other. We will find a way to teach them to grow food, no matter the state of the Earth, under any conditions. There are many everywhere, of different origins. I just need to listen more, pay attention to the ones who are entering my life because their purpose is intertwined with mine, and mine is intertwined with theirs. I have to see not with my eyes, but to be present with everything and everyone around me. I have to quiet my doubt.

When Julia came back to her conscious awareness, she shared with me how amazed she was by the information she accessed. Not only that she managed to access two of her past lives and identify the root cause of her feelings of incompletion, being stuck in life, wanting to escape and run away, but she discovered and explored the Light and the universe of Home. Moreover, she connected with her Spiritual Guide who revealed her life's purpose.

J: I had no prior experience or real understanding of this form of healing, so I had no idea what to expect. I was just hoping for some tools on how to improve my meditation skills, and I never expected to have these experiences. It is so great, that I want to continue with these sessions to access my subconscious and explore my immortality.

THE PURPOSE OF REINCARNATION—SPIRITUAL EVOLUTION (VIBRATIONAL GROWTH)

Returning to my conversation with Mia's Spiritual Master, I asked him about the speed souls travel at, and he answered that souls travel faster than the speed of light. Then I asked him how we evolve energetically.

SM: You get to grow vibrationally according to how much you have discovered and how much you have increased your energy. You grow based on the decisions you have made and the actions you have taken. What matters is how you've felt about your actions, not whether you've done good or not. If you felt everything on a high level of vibration and also helped others, then you grew vibrationally.

Dr. G: So then you grow energetically more in terms of vibration, not in terms of size?

SM: Correct. You grow in size as well, but not to gigantic sizes.

Dr. G: When you grow what do you grow from?

SM: You grow from the energy of the universe and from the energy of others. It basically depends on the type of energies you keep with you.

Dr. G: When you grow in energy from others, does their energy decrease?

SM: No because everything unfolds like a chain reaction, according to the energies you have accumulated. To give you an example, think of two identical snowballs. Imagine that one of the snowballs is placed in an environment with a very cold temperature, in snow, while the other is placed in an environment with a very high temperature. In this example, the cold represents love, meaning positive energy, and the heat represents negative energy. The snowball placed at a low temperature accumulates snow and grows in size. The snowball exposed to high temperature melts, and the heat that makes it melt is, in this example, negative energy, which that snowball accumulates. So it depends on where the snowball, the soul stays. If it stays only in a cold environment and accumulates snow, in other words love—positive energy—it increases vibrationally and in size. When the soul attracts love energy, all of the other souls in its surroundings benefit as well. They can attract positive energy and recharge from each other. In the case of the snowball placed in a high temperature environment, which is low vibration in this example, the soul decreases vibrationally and in size.

Dr. G: Can the purpose of a life, which has been set before incarnation, be changed during that life? For example can you change your purpose to achieve a greater purpose by helping more people?

SM: *You* determine your life. You have decided what kind of life you wanted to live prior to reincarnating, and you have agreed to all the possibilities of what may happen in that life. If the awakening occurs and you decide, for example, that you want to help more people, then the universe will support and assist you in accomplishing your new goal. In that moment, the purpose of your life takes a different turn.

THE REINCARNATION CONCEPT

The concept of reincarnation is a common component of Indian religious traditions and Buddhism, and it was a popularly held belief in ancient Greece and Rome. Although it is a controversial topic for Western society, lately, many people from the West have embraced the concept of reincarnation. University researchers such as psychiatrist Ian Stevenson, MD, have investigated the possibility of reincarnation in light of their patients' cases, and saw reincarnation as the survival of personality after death. Over a period of forty years, Professor Ian Stevenson studied and wrote about three thousand cases of children with memories of other lives. One interesting aspect of his work was that some of those children displayed xenoglossy, the ability to speak foreign languages to which they had not been exposed in any way. He believed that the study of reincarnation could help modern medicine better understand human development and the various facets of human behavior. Professor Stevenson published several books including *Twenty Cases Suggestive of Reincarnation.*

Psychiatrist Jim B. Tucker, specialist in pediatric psychiatry, Associate Professor of Psychiatry and Neurobehavioral Sciences at the University of Virginia, has studied numerous cases of children who remembered past lives, as well as prenatal and birth memories. He described some of those cases in the book *Life before Life: A scientific investigation of children's memories of previous lives.*

Psychiatrist Brian Weiss, MD, Chairman Emeritus of Psychiatry at the Mount Sinai Medical Center in Miami, presented in his book *Many Lives Many Masters* the case of one of his patient,

Catherine, who he managed to heal using past life regression therapy. Catherine's review of her past lives led to her healing from recurring nightmares and panic attacks. Mia's case reminds me of Catherine's case. In the superconscious state of awareness, both displayed an extraordinary ability to receive and transmit information from the universal mind, and to reveal parts of this infinite informational treasure with the help of the Masters.

Psychologist and hypnotherapist Michael Newton, PhD, described in his books *Journey of Souls* and *Destiny of Souls* the path souls travel from the moment they leave their physical bodies until their return to Earth.

The discoveries made by my clients match, reassure and confirm the findings made by Brian Weiss, MD, Dr. Bruce Goldberg, Dr. Michael Newton, PhD, Dr. Edith Fiore, PhD and many others, so many that I must take this opportunity to apologize because I cannot mention them all. Their contributions have been extraordinary in shedding a light on the mysteries of our existence, which have puzzled us ever since we, as species, have been sufficiently aware to wonder if there is life after death or death represents the end of our identity.

Chapter Seven

Human Time versus Ethereal Time

"Space and time are the framework within which the mind is
constrained to construct its experience of reality."
Immanuel Kant

TIME

Mia was still at Home relaxing and transmitting information from the
Spiritual Masters.

Dr. G: Regarding time is the future set in stone, is it predestined, or can
it be changed? Can you see what will happen in the future or does the
future vary?

SM: For us, the ones from Home, time does not exist. It's only a
human limitation, a human construct. For you, time exists because you
have created human time—linear time. To answer your question, the
future is decided prior to a person's birth. You have chosen your life
prior to reincarnation at your spirit consciousness level. You had the
opportunity to know everything that would happen, to change things,
and you approved everything. Your life is what your spirit wanted and
agreed to. Plus, once reincarnated, you have free will. You have the
power to choose in every moment everything that you want to
experience. We, the Guides, cannot make decisions about your life. We
can help you by influencing situations and bringing you opportunities,
but we cannot make you do what we want, what we consider best. We
can bring you a limited or an unlimited number of the same type of
opportunity, so that you can follow the path set by your own spirit

when you are ready. But the decisions belong to you entirely, and that's how it must be. Through these decisions, you have the opportunity to grow vibrationally and spiritually. Everyone is the creator of their own life and experiences. So, to answer the question of whether you can change the future more specifically, in one way or another, you will arrive where you need to be. We cannot estimate how long it will take you, but we do know where you will arrive.

We can compare this concept to climbing a hill. We may reach the summit by taking one of the many paths that ultimately lead us to the top. Some paths may be easier to climb and lead to the goal more quickly, while others may be more difficult, require more effort and take longer. Assuming that we don't stop or go back, no matter what route we take, we will eventually make it to the summit.

ETHEREAL TIME

Dr. G: So you are at Home, in the universe that we have given many names to: Heaven, Paradise, The Ultimate Reality or The Absolute.
SM: Yes. It's a plane of existence parallel to the Earth's.
Dr. G: What other planes of existence are there?
SM: There are an infinite number of vibrational planes of existence.
Dr. G: I imagine The Source of Life—God—to be at the very tip of this evolutionary pyramid.
SM: Chi Energy—God—is at Home also on a parallel vibrational plane. All of the planes of existence are parallel, absolutely everything is parallel, but not in the way you understand "parallel." Here's an example you can understand with your human mind because at your spirit's level of awareness you already know all of this: the past, present and future are parallel in the life of a human being. The past is parallel to the present, and the present reflects the past. But only the present determines the future, and in one way or another, all of them are connected through the present. But all these planes of existence are parallel: the past, the present and the future. It's the same with all of the planes of existence that we have at Home; they are parallel. And it's not like some people believe that you cross over bridges to get Home. You either come Home drawn by the Light, or you wander aimlessly, and it depends on where and how you wander. You don't pass through gates. You pass through other energetic planes of souls on lower levels of vibration compared to Home, until you arrive at Home. As human beings, with your analytical minds, you tend to structure everything with as much detail as possible. Many of you don't understand the infinite. The infinite is limitless, endless, without beginning and

without end. There are an infinite number of planes of existence on Earth and at Home, and all of these planes are parallel.

Dr. G: Is there a past, present and future occurring the way we perceive them or is everything happening simultaneously?

SM: From the perspective of Home, everything is taking place simultaneously because in reality time does not exist. All lives of every soul are happening simultaneously, and they are all parallel.

This explains why Mia was experiencing her previous lives (the cave man, Liz and Helen) as though everything was happening in the present. According to the Spiritual Masters, those lives *are* actually happening in the present moment. It also clarifies why they said that we evolve simultaneously through transitional lives as insects, plants, and animals.

Quantum physics is beginning to support this perspective on time. However, it is understandably challenging for us to think about time as not being linear because we see the days passing one after another, the sun rising and setting, children growing and us advancing in age. It's difficult to comprehend this concept of ethereal time in which all of our lives—past, present, and future—are parallel and occurring simultaneously.

Perhaps this example (which may not be the most eloquent) may make it easier to understand ethereal time. Imagine yourself at a water park, standing on an elevated terrace from which you can see the entirety of a big waterslide ride. From there, you can see a line of people waiting. For them the ride represents the future. You can see people currently on the slide, and for them the slide represents the present. You can also see the people who have just dropped from the slide into the pool. For them the slide has become the past. But you, the observer, from your elevated perspective can see everything happening at the waterslide at the same time. You can see all of the people and how their actions occur simultaneously.

SM: The past is linked to the present and the future is also linked to the present. The past determines the present, and only the present determines the future. What you do in the present can change the future or, in other words, determines what version of the future you experience.

THE FLOW OF OUR ENERGY AS VIBRATION

Dr. G: How does vibrational and spiritual growth occur, since all of the lifetimes of a soul are occurring at the same time?

SM: Imagine a thread stretched tight from one corner of a room to another. This thread represents the past, present and future of a soul unfolding simultaneously. When a soul grows to a higher level of vibration, it's like when you pluck the thread at one spot. The vibration is transmitted across the entire thread, from the point of vibration toward both ends.

Dr. G: Is each one of us living its present life on different *parallel lives or versions of life*, depending upon the choices each one makes in the moment?

SM: Yes. According to the choices you make, you experience nicer or less nicer versions of your life, which are all parallel. So the past and the future are parallel but in between them lies the present, which determines what version of the future you experience. Every single moment of now is very important, in the sense that it has the potential of changing the future according to the choices you make. It's the same with the universe from Home. Home is situated between the vibrational plane of Chi Energy and yours, the Earth's plane. We can change what happens to the Earth through you, the human beings.

Dr. G: Is there an infinite number of me living all the lives that I have ever lived—lives of the past, present and future—and all of my lives are unfolding simultaneously?

SM: Correct, but I have to clarify something. Whether there is an infinite or a limited number of you existing simultaneously in all of your lives depends upon what spiritual experience you, as a consciousness have. It depends upon when you were born as a spirit from Chi Energy. From a certain point of view, there is a beginning—the moment you emerge from Chi Energy—but from another point of view, at the moment you emerge from Chi Energy, you actually originate from the energy of another highly evolved consciousness that has merged with The Source. You detach from Chi Energy, which is infinite. It's an infinite cycle. Your beginning actually represents the union of other highly evolved energies with Chi Energy, and your union with Chi Energy, which will occur when you reach that ultimate level, will represent the birth of other souls and so on to infinity. When you reunite with Chi, new energies are born from your energy. It's difficult for the human mind to conceive of this because actually, what people are trying to do is to understand who God (Chi Energy) is.

Dr. G: Since we've arrived at this topic, would you describe what God is?

SM: God is all there is. God is the breath and the beat of the heart. God is infinite and unimaginable, unthinkable and incomprehensible for the human mind. God is the absolute truth. Can a limited mind understand a notion that is outside of its sphere of understanding? The limited, human, conscious mind cannot conceive of the unlimited. It's as if a human would try to swallow a mountain.

A question emerged in my mind: could we speak with The Source the way I was speaking with Mia's Spiritual Master?

LIFE COMPRISED OF AN INFINITE NUMBER OF PARALLEL LIVES

Dr. G: You've said that we choose prior to coming into the physical world with whom we will reincarnate, and what we will do once we're here. Since in the earthly dimension there is duality, both the positive and negative energy streams, can we decide, prior to reincarnating, the way in which the negative energies will affect us?

SM: Prior to reincarnating you chose and see your life. You see all the versions of your life, or possibilities or parallel realities, whatever you want to call them. Then you decide, moment by moment, which version of your life you want to live until you design your entire life. From these versions united one with another will result your life. Your life is comprised of all these versions or parallel lives you choose to experience.

Dr. G: When you design your life, do you choose all of these versions or parallel lives, or do you choose just one?

SM: It's up to you. In principle, you choose all of them because the main idea is for you to have the freedom to make choices that help you grow vibrationally.

Dr. G: In the moment of now, in this physical life of mine, do I actually exist in multiple parallel versions of my life?

SM: Basically, you are just in one. The others are only possibilities, mirrors or reflections of what you do now. All of your parallel lives or versions, possibilities or realities exist, and can be activated by changing your vibration. You do indeed have an infinite number of parallel versions of your life existing simultaneously with this life, but you are living this one, the one from now. Let me give an example. Let's suppose that you decide to move back to Europe, where you've lived before. Your life in Europe would essentially reactivate and continue the moment you will move back to Europe. After a while, if you decide to return to California, the life you had in California would resume or reactivate. Your life in California is on a different level of vibration than the one in Europe. If you decide to relocate to an entirely different country, you would activate or "step into" a version of your life in which you live in that country, which exists on a different level of vibration than the other versions of your life. In addition, your life in

California, your life in Europe, or your life anywhere else has an infinite number of versions as well. Based on the decisions you make in every single moment, you can activate different versions (levels of vibration of that version of your life). All of the lives are parallel, but very connected as in the example with the stretched thread. When you make a decision, for example, to move from California to Europe, this action vibrates, and the vibration reaches into the parallel version of your life in Europe. But actually, it's just one life comprised of an infinite number of parallel versions of your life.

Dr. G: Very interesting. Yet, although we have one life comprised of an infinite number of parallel versions of life, you know what is going to happen until the end, right?

SM: Theoretically, you know when you leave Home to reincarnate. However, you can't control from Home what version of life you will choose to activate in any moment. As I said before, we can protect you and offer you guidance, but the decisions belong to you. Every moment, with every decision you make, decides the version of the future you activate. You are Chi Energy, therefore you are creator of your own life.

In other words, before reincarnating, we design our life based on certain goals that we would like to achieve, or scenarios we would like to experience within certain parameters. If we choose to, we make different agreements with certain souls and our Spiritual Guides. In fact, we create a life plan that includes an infinite number of variables. It's up to us, since we have free will, how we choose to explore those predestined scenarios. It's up to us what connotation we give to them, and how we walk our path: feeling like victims or enjoying and learning from every situation. It's up to us to understand that we are the creators of those circumstances, and the more positive and connected with our true nature we remain, the more beautiful versions of our lives we activate.

SM: Due to free will, the possibility also exists that even though you begin your journey with a plan, you may not always complete it. This is where that conflict between the positive and negative energy comes into play, and it's also where you have the opportunity to grow vibrationally. From these infinite choices, you can either choose positivity and elevate yourself, as a soul, on increasingly higher vibrational levels, or you can make decisions that don't serve you. When you make such decisions, you either remain on the same level of vibration or, if you have gathered negative energy, you actually decrease vibrationally.

Dr. G: So reincarnation, seen from this simultaneous time perspective, is actually simultaneous, parallel existence.
SM: Correct.

IMAGINATION-THOUGHT-ENERGY: PROJECTED LIFE

Dr. G: How do we really create our life on Earth?
SM: You, as human beings, create your life on Earth by choosing and activating various versions of your life that you've already created at the spirit level of your consciousness prior to reincarnation. As human beings, you choose and activate various versions of your life with the thoughts you think, with your beliefs, with what you imagine, what you feel and the decisions you make. You basically create your life by projecting what you have imagined, thought and decided.
Dr. G: Was it really us who created the infinite possibilities or versions of our lives?
SM: Yes, you have created them yourself before incarnation. So as a human being you have infinite possibilities or versions to your life from which to choose, and you choose from what you have created before coming into your physical life. The process is very complex.
Dr. G: At one point you said that the life we live is just an illusion. Albert Einstein said the same thing: "Reality is merely an illusion, albeit a very persistent one." Also, there are all sorts of opinions and hypotheses that suggest that everything happens in our minds, and this physical reality doesn't really exist.
SM: It's exactly what you once told Mia, I heard you with my own "ears." It's the energy that you create thinking about something that you want to experience in the future. For example, you yearned to make your discoveries known to the world. You thought about it so much, you visualized yourself and put your energy into this project. You began collecting the material and started writing the book, so your book became a reality. There is nothing created without you first desiring it. But the physical life is an illusion because this physical plane is not the truth. Home is the truth. When the spirit descends from Home and as a soul enters the physical plane, it forgets about the life at Home and the significance of what is at Home. The real life, the absolute truth is at Home. That which is in the physical plane is an illusion compared to what is at Home in the sense that what happens in the physical plane is not really relevant, and is also transient. You focus on way too much and put too much energy on ephemeral, meaningless things such as the pursuit of materialism.
Dr. G: And yet, even if we were to call our lives illusions, if we are not

careful, it can cost us our energy. Everything has a real price.

SM: Right. Your vibrational trajectory during your physical life is real, meaning that the experience of human life is real. But the physical life itself is not the truth. When I said "illusion," I didn't mean it as a matter of hallucination, of perception. The process is very complex. If you didn't have dreams, desires, aspirations and goals your life would not exist. Think of the severely retarded children. They don't really have the possibility to have thoughts or desires of their own about what they would want to become in life. They are dependent on their parents and they're playing in a controlled environment. They don't make decisions about their lives. When *you* think about how you would like your life to be, when *you* dream about what you want to happen in, let's say, four years, you actually create or activate what will happen in four years. It may not be exactly what you thought, but it will mostly be what you have imagined.

Dr. G: The concepts of parallel lives or realities and infinite possibilities are being discussed in quantum physics.

SM: It's not accidental. In fact, nothing is random. An important detail about the process of creation is to remember to have patience because it takes time to create on Earth. Time does have significance in the physical plane, unlike at Home. The planet Earth was created in billions of your human years, yet many of you want your dreams to materialize immediately.

Dr. G: I think we would all like our desires to materialize instantly.

SM: Here, at Home, you could "stretch a finger" and fix everything because at Home you instantaneously create. But in the physical life that you have chosen to live, time has meaning. And it has a beginning and an end.

FUTURE LIFE PROGRESSION

Dr. G: What can you tell me about future life progression?

SM: Past life regression is a very useful therapy. Future life progression is also a very good therapy, but since the future is relative, the future life will be activated only if you decide to reincarnate and take that specific parallel road in the future. So it isn't certain that the specific life you see during future life progression will happen. It depends very much on your current life and the decisions you make in every moment. Future life progression can certainly influence a person in a positive way, especially if that person sees a beautiful life. However, if the person sees a life with many challenges, he or she should not get discouraged because it's possible for that life to not even occur at all or the way they saw it. So it depends on each person's capacity of understanding.

ABOUT MIA

I thanked the Spiritual Master for the answers he provided, and I asked how Mia was doing.

SM: Mia is relaxing. She is speaking with me right now. We went together so I could show her the Tree of Life and the River of Life. Next time you can guide her to come through the Light directly to the Tree or the River because she feels too much heat in the Light. I noticed that the concept of infinite, parallel lives is not yet completely clear to you. I showed Mia exactly how the lives can be seen from here, and I showed her your life, with how many possibilities there are, as an example. You can ask her. I will try to keep the information fresh in her memory so she can explain what I told her.

Even though I was aware that the Guides and Masters have the ability to divide their energy and be present in multiple places at the same time, what the Master said took me by surprise. It seemed that while he was answering my questions, he had a discussion with Mia as well, and traveled with her to show her various "places" at Home.

SM: There are so many things to be said to answer your questions, but the answers must be filtered through the perception of the subconscious mind, of the soul, not through the limitation of human words and hearing. We will talk soon. I wish you a pleasant day.

When I thanked him again and wished him the same, he reminded me that the *day* at Home is unlimited.

Dr. G: Mia, where are you now?

M: I'm in the Light. It's very hot here. I'm saying goodbye to Marc. He tells me to go back because I have something to show you.

MIA'S REVELATIONS

After guiding Mia back to her conscious state of awareness and suggesting that she remember all the details that Iam (Marc) had shown her, she began drawing and describing what she was putting on paper.

M: How can I explain? It's so much to explain. First, he showed me your life. This is your life.

Mia pointed to her drawing of many windows arranged in line, one after another, stretching to infinity (see the reproduction below), and each representing a possible version of my life. Parallel to these windows were an infinite number of other windows arranged in line, also up and down, leading to infinity as well.

Some of my clients have described these windows as television screens, each showing the movie of that specific version of life and each movie having the same main character.

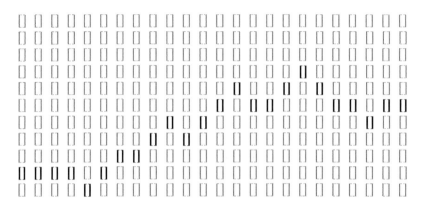

M: All of these windows are located on one plane, the plane of your life but on different vibrations. Marc explained to me that you as a spirit create your life, see it, and choose what you want to experience in your life. When you decide to reincarnate, you pass through this window (Mia pointed to the first black, bold window on the left), and enter the physical plane as a soul. Your life is actually everything you see here, all of these parallel windows together, which are possible versions of your life. This is your life, as you have created it.

Dr. G: So I have created my current life and agreed to this infinite number of versions or possibilities represented by the parallel windows. And my current life, with what versions I've activated so far, is represented by the black windows, right?

M: Right.

What activates the versions of life represented by those windows is our energy flow, which represents or vibrational trajectory. You could imagine your energy flow as a river of golden, intense, glowing energy flowing through and activating those versions of life.

M: Let's say you decide to do the good deed of helping someone. When you do that, your life vibrates and elevates you to another level, another version of your life that's in the window situated on a higher level of vibration. When you decide to do something that is not beneficial and you *feel* that you have done something bad, you descend to a window located below, on a lower level of vibration. Every window represents a different version of your life. So with every decision you make you can jump from one version of your life to another or, in other words, from one parallel life to another. You maintain yourself on the same level, increase or decrease vibrationally according to what you choose. There are an infinite number of possibilities at every step. Marc told me that the rest are just mirrors, possibilities or reflections of what you have decided to experience. He said that in fact, you live only the versions you have stepped into, that you have activated with your energy (which in the drawing are represented by the black windows). At any moment you can jump into another window, another parallel life, and continue on that new frequency.

This explanation of our life being comprised of an infinite number of parallel lives made me realize that when we change our thoughts, beliefs and feelings for the better, and, as a result, elevate ourselves to a higher vibration, we are not actually changing our lives. We are, more accurately, activating and experiencing a higher version of our life, one that matches our soul's new, elevated vibrational frequency.

I asked Mia what she knew about quantum physics, and she said that she was not familiar with it at all, that such matters held no interest for her.

M: This was the first time Marc said we will have a separate session, just me and him. Otherwise, I only remember that he took me and showed me the Tree of Life and the River of Life. He told me that when we meditate, that's where we should go: to the Tree or to the River. Then, I stayed in the Light and toward the end it got very hot. But I don't remember what was being said. I can't bring back the information, I can't remember it. Just when you tell me to say goodbye to him, I can remember what he says: "I'm glad that I saw you. I'm with you all the time. We're in contact." He told me to think of him like I would think of my Guardian Angel.

Dr. G: What does the Tree of Life look like?

M: The Tree of Life is like an extremely bright, illuminated willow tree, with energetic impulses going through its branches. The Tree and its branches have a white color, and it always sparkles. Around it it's a valley with a lot of beautiful green hills and grass like on the sports field. There is just that one immense Tree. Then Marc showed me a waterfall and the River.

I was intrigued. What could that waterfall be?

M: The River of Life comes from somewhere above, and you can see beautiful mountains around. It's like a postcard but very vivid. It's not water that flows in the River. It's a River of energy, with sparkles or impulses of energy running through it. But even though it's not water, you can still hear it as a river of water. The River has all of the colors due to the energetic impulses: blue, green… but really bright. It is really, really nice over there. The colors of the River are superb, and appear as though you're looking at a crystal. Everything is so clear. Around the Tree there is open space, but somewhere in the distance you can see the hills, the mountains. It's more of what you feel and sense rather than what you see. It's very pleasant and relaxing there.

After a few moments of reverie Mia said:

M: I can't believe I lived a life as an animal. It was disturbing when the other animal ate me. The truth is that I could feel when the wind was blowing and I could smell the blood.

I asked Mia if she was still able to see Marc (Iam) when she was at Home.

M: I don't see him but I feel him. I can't say that I see a light or an energy, but I feel that he is there. I don't see myself either. And communication doesn't happen through speech. You don't need words. You don't need to look at each other. It's an energetic connection. (Mia had clearly described telepathy.) I feel very good there. However, I can tell you that the Light can become suffocating if you're there for a while. But it's not actually light. At first, when you pass through it, you see it as light, and you can either choose to go beyond it or remain in it. I remained in the Light, and it didn't appear to be a very bright light. It was just like a sunset. However, it became very hot in there.

After Mia left, I contemplated on the principles of Ethereal Science that the Spiritual Masters have revealed to us, and how similar they are to the theories of quantum physics. Quantum Physics says that all time is simultaneous, that the future is a system of probabilities and possibilities, and describes the wave-particle dualism. It also suggests that physical reality is controlled by consciousness. I believe it is, basically, the same science but presented from different perspectives. The Masters present it in a more spiritual perspective because it's the science that actually describes the evolution of our souls or spirits, of our consciousness, of the entirety of existence.

Dr. Niels Bohr once said: "Anyone who is not shocked by quantum theory has not understood it." I feel the same way about the subconscious, ethereal science.

The Masters have suggested that there are an infinite number of possibilities for every moment of our life, which quantum physicists calls a universal ocean or sea of pure potentiality, and our consciousness decides which of these possibilities we get to experience.

Physics demonstrates that the universe is not made of solid matter; that everything, including both mind and matter is a single, universal, unified field of consciousness. We are eternal and are essentially made of vibrational energy (Chi Energy) which forms this universal ocean of consciousness.

The Masters also suggested that the infinite is a feature of everything that exists. There are infinite possibilities for every moment of our lives and infinite planes of existence. We are part of Chi Energy, which is infinite and it's found at the base of everything in existence, forming the infinite energetic ocean in which we progress as souls. We originate from the ultimate reality, the Universe of Home, which is also infinite. Ultimately, we have detached from the infinite Source of Life, God or Chi Energy. And depending on when we were born as energy, we may have an infinite numbers of lives. We also exist simultaneously in all of them.

If I had had any doubts about the validity of the information Mia had been bringing forth, that it may have simply been sprung from her imagination, they completely vanished by the end of this session. Her knowledge acquired in this physical life was too basic for her to be able to explain such complicated concepts; ones that not even science has been able to clarify yet.

CHAPTER EIGHT

Passing into Eternity

> "No one knows whether death, which people fear to be
> the greatest evil, may not be the greatest good."
>
> Plato

MIA'S ABILITIES

My next appointment with Mia took place at my office in Santa
Monica, California. Although she had completely recovered from
depression, suicidal tendencies, anxiety, fears and fatigue, and
maintained her new healthy lifestyle and ideal weight effortlessly, we
decided to continue our sessions to further research and explore the
mysteries of consciousness.

I wondered if Mia was able to go straight Home because so far,
she had only managed to access Home and the Spiritual Masters after
first reviewing a previous life. To answer my own question, I decided
to guide her straight into the Light and beyond it, to the Tree of Life or
the River of Life, wherever she felt compelled to go. To my delight, she
had no problem going Home directly. When she got there, the Spiritual
Masters joined her.

Dr. G: Thank you for coming. How are you doing? (I addressed the
Masters directly.)

SM: We are very well, thank you. We are always very well.

THE DEATH OF HUMAN BEING AND THE SOUL'S PASSING INTO ETERNITY

Dr. G: How does death occur?

SM: Every soul, every spirit decides how long it wants to stay in the temporary, physical life, and when it wants to return Home.

Dr. G: Do we decide prior to reincarnating when we will die?

SM: Yes, but once you've reincarnated, you have opportunities to change what you want to do, and that would cause you to enter or activate other versions of your life. Thus, you can change when you want to leave your human life. When souls decide to leave their physical lives, they take all of their energy and their bodies become lifeless. They leave the physical plane of that life for good, entering the ethereal plane of the Earth. Then, they go Home through the Light either directly, or after a period spent between the two dimensions, of Earth and Home. When people die, they feel liberated as if the weights from their shoulders, or more accurately from their souls, have been lifted. They are attracted by the Light and feel so much joy and love that they don't even think about who they've left behind. They go into the Light and then beyond it because that's where their world is, their permanent Home. When they enter the Light, they are cleansed of all the low vibration blockages or energies they brought with them, which are then transformed into positive energy. All of the worldly emotions disappear, and they enter Home as pure, positive energies. They are welcomed with much love by their Spiritual Guides and all of the other loved ones; by all of us at Home.

Dr. G: Do souls take their human memories with them?

SM: When a person dies, the memories of absolutely everything that human being lived—the memories that are stored in the human brain— are taken by the soul and stored at Home, in the Akashic memories, at the Tree of Life. They belong to their spirit, their greater self. The spirit has access to all those memories at Home anytime it wants. Also, that soul will be able to access that life's memories in its next lives if it does a regression. To give you an analogy related to your current technology, think of a computer, which has a soft part and a hard part. The hard part represents your greater self's memories, the memories of the entire existence of your spirit—your Akashic memories. The soft part is what is stored in the human brain, the human life's memories. You cannot access that backup of hard memories from all those other incarnations unless you, as a soul, come Home. That's what you do through past life regression.

Dr. G: So after every life, when we return Home, we download the files of our memories, of what happened during our life into the external drive, called Akashic records. All of those memories and experiences represent energy, and by collecting them life after life we progress energetically as eternal beings.

SM: Correct. And I hope this helps clarify why we don't remember what's at Home when we take on a new physical life. Once you reincarnate to Earth and you don't have access to the necessary techniques to come Home, you have no conscious memory of who your soul or spirit really is, and what else it has lived. You don't have Akashic memory. You have only soft memories, not hard. But when you find the energetic balance between the spiritual and physical planes of existence, it's exactly like you've put the hard and soft parts of a computer back together... And that's why initially, until you grow spiritually and open your mind's eye, you only have access to the soft memories, the memories of your current physical life. Then, when your soul begins to awaken, when you begin to come Home consciously and access your other lives, it's like putting all the parts of the computer together. You align your human self with your higher self consciousness.

WHAT HAPPENS WITH THE SOUL AT HOME AFTER PHYSICAL DEATH?

SM: The soul is welcomed by us, and you have seen what happens in the greeting hall in Mia's regression. There are actually more halls the soul passes through, where we get to see how much it has evolved spiritually during its human life, whether it needs to return to live another life, and so on. We decide together what needs to be done: will the soul remain at Home for a while, or will it prepare for a new incarnation, in which case it would begin the "training," so to speak. There, it sees what unfavorable decisions it made, what should have been done instead, what should be done in a future incarnation, so on and so forth. In human time, this process would seem to take an eternity, but for us time doesn't exist, and everything happens according to... his will.

Dr. G: You mean God's will, Chi Energy's will?

SM: Yes, who is basically all of us, all of our energy at Home. But in the greeting hall, our energy that forms Chi is somewhat limited because that area is the gate between dimensions.

Dr. G: Is the greeting hall, this gate between dimensions, located in the Light, or is it beyond the Light, toward Home?

SM: It's beyond the Light on this side, toward Home. The moment you exit the greeting hall and the other halls, we take you around so you remember that you're at Home. This process doesn't happen instantly; it takes a while in human time.

It seems that "the last judgment" some people fear is actually an evaluation of the progress we made during our human life, which leads to the decision of the level of vibration we will be on as we enter Home.

Dr. G: Not all souls go directly to the Light after leaving their physical lives, right?

SM: It depends how you leave your physical life, whether at the moment of death you leave behind the negative feelings and energies or take them with you. If you leave that life reconciled, or perhaps wander for a while between the two dimensions and manage to come to terms with the idea that your physical life is over, then you leave everything behind and move toward the Light, toward Home. After you return Home, you can choose to go back, to reincarnate, and resolve the unsolved problems if you want. But if you leave angry and don't want to forgive not even when you are between the two dimensional planes, then you return Home on a lower vibrational level. As a result, when you reincarnate, you will be more vulnerable to negative energy.

WILL WE RECOGNIZE OUR LOVED ONES AT HOME AFTER DEATH?

SM: Yes. You will recognize them but it will have no relevance. You will have detached from your human sentiments.

Dr. G: What does that mean? Does it mean that we become indifferent?

SM: No, not indifferent, because you still feel intense love, only equally for all the energies here. You just aren't subjective or biased in your love anymore. The same love you felt for the person you loved the most in your human life you feel for everyone here.

Dr. G: That really sounds like… heaven.

WHAT IS RIGHT AND WHAT IS WRONG?

Dr. G: Is there good and bad, right and wrong in your opinion?

SM: No. Here, at Home, everything is done by mutual agreement. All decisions are made together, and everything is evaluated according to the experience that was accumulated through the sharing of ideas. The experience is, in fact, energy. There is no good or bad, right or wrong, no matter what. Everything is experience and there are no positive or negative results. What really matters is not what you did, but how you feel about what you've done. What you feel raises or lowers you vibrationally, and your energetic evolution and how much love you've gathered is all that matters.

Dr. G: What happens to a soul that has returned Home and has done terrible things on Earth, let's say killed other people? Will that soul be punished somehow?

SM: It won't be punished but that soul will understand its own experience. It decides by itself what will be best to do. Most of the time, these souls return to Earth to repay their debts or, in other words, atone their "sins." In fact, the Light through which we enter to get Home performs an analysis of the life you have just lived, and you get to examine and understand your own actions. That analysis is basically an expression of the Universe that is impossible for you not to understand. Then, *you* choose whether you want to return to Earth to repair or redo something, or go back and do something else. As I've told you, nothing is imposed on you. Everything depends on you, on what you want to do. *You* create your own experiences.

WHEN AND HOW IS IT DECIDED HOW MUCH WE HAVE EVOLVED IN A LIFETIME?

SM: At the end of your life, after you return Home, we establish a balance, an average, based on which it is decided whether you grew or decreased in energy. You don't grow very much, but you do increase or decrease in energy according to the feelings of love that you had or not. As a human being, you can vibrate on a high level of positivity or you can draw down toward negative energy. These fluctuations represent your vibrational variations. Basically, when you leave your human life and get Home, we do the sum of all the elements of positive vibration.

Dr. G: So the evaluation is done at the end of, not throughout our life?

SM: You do influence your current life by what you do, by trying to increase vibrationally as much as possible, but the sum is done at the end of your lifetime.

Dr. G: How is it decided whether twin flames, those evolved souls who divide their energy into multiple parts and incarnate in the same timeframe into multiple people, have increased or decreased vibrationally?

SM: At the end of their lives the sum of their positivity is done, but for them the chances of decreasing vibrationally are minimal considering their level of evolution. It's almost impossible that none of the twin flames increased vibrationally or that all of them decreased. And if one of them did well, all of them will be fine at Home.

HUMANITY'S PERCEPTION OF DEATH

Dr. G: Why do we suffer so terribly when our loved ones die?
SM: When a person dies, the news of their death affects their loved ones at the conscious mind level. The people closest to the deceased suffer terribly. The problem is that the pain and grief they accumulate are not positive energy, and as they succumb to pain, they create and accumulate more negative energy. Therefore they feel exhausted, sad, depressed and lack enthusiasm for life for a while. Although they have been informed about this decision at the subconscious level, they aren't able to consciously access that information. The suffering is due to the fact that the death of human being is misunderstood or misinterpreted. Only the physical body dies. The soul, with all of the memories of that human existence, all of the energy of love, and all of the experiences accumulated in that life goes Home rebecoming a spirit. The spirit is immortal. The physical life is temporary, the spiritual life is eternal. That person continues to live in the existential universe of Home, where all of you will return sooner or later. The soul who returned Home is very happy that it has returned, and we are all happy for that soul. We greet the soul with great joy.
Dr. G: But when someone we love dies, for us, as human beings, it's very difficult.
SM: You must consider that, for example, life for elderly people can be very challenging. Perhaps you will understand the heaviness of your body when you reach a mature age. When physical death occurs, the soul feels total liberation, which you understand only when you experience it. It's a moment of joy! I've never understood why you, human beings, cry when someone returns Home. You should celebrate with joy! Death represents only a transition from one dimensional plane to another.
Dr. G: We're actually grieving for ourselves because we won't get to see our loved ones again in physical form and enjoy their presence.
SM: But you get to talk to them and be with them, if you choose, every night when your body is asleep! When you're asleep, you, as souls, come Home because Home is your real life, but you just don't remember these things consciously. And you can also talk to them in the state that Mia is in, or during meditation.

Death is not, as many people think, the end of identity. Death represents the passing from one level of consciousness into higher levels: from the level of the conscious mind to the level of the subconscious—the soul mind—and, after passing through the Light and entering Home, into the superconscious mind state—the higher self, the spirit state. Through death we experience a more expanded, more pure version of ourselves.

SM: Death represents the transition from the physical universe into the nonphysical, of Home. The moment you die, all you do is close your physical eyes and see through your soul's eye, stepping out of the telluric (physical) plane and entering the ethereal plane, and then at Home. From the energetic and spiritual point of view death does not exist. It's just waking up to your true nature and identity from the illusion that was your physical life. When a soul decides to return Home it's a very good thing because sometimes there are very big barriers at the physical and soul level. Therefore, the soul prefers to come Home and start a new physical life instead of decreasing energetically.

People who go through near-death experiences get to see what death really is, just like the past life regression therapy clients. Their lives are changed for the better by those experiences because they gain a new perspective of life and death.

SM: People who have near-death experiences basically enter the Light and come Home. We greet them and talk to them, and if they choose to return to their bodies and continue their lives, they go back. Some of them remember what happened here and what they talked to us about, but not all. Anyway, you should rejoice and celebrate when someone dies because they have arrived at Home, and they are free of pain and problems. At Home everyone is very well. We are all well and happy. And Home is infinitely more than what you imagine Paradise or Heaven to be.

IS CONSCIOUSNESS A PRODUCT OF THE BRAIN?

So if our consciousness doesn't die when the body dies, then is consciousness a product of the brain? Is the mind a result of brain activity or is the human brain a receiver of consciousness? This is a dilemma that scientists continue to research. Most scientists assume that the brain is what produces consciousness. However, various clinical research regarding cases of near-death experiences suggest that it may not be the case.

What we, for some reason, fail to understand is that consciousness is eternal. It is not born at the same time with the physical body and it does not die when the body dies. This is a new paradigm that will gradually replace the old one. But since this concept is new, many resist it because most humans do not like to be coerced out of their habitual belief systems and traditions. New discoveries are made each day and what we take today as an absolute truth could be completely overthrown tomorrow.

But even so, are we really at the forefront by suggesting these seemingly new concepts about human consciousness? The Greeks, the Egyptians, the Romans, the Hindu and Buddhist traditions, as well as various religions believed that all people have the duality of physical and nonphysical. They believed that a part of the human being—the nonphysical part—detaches from the body and transcends the physical, ephemeral life, and that nonphysical part is eternal. They called it "psyche," which means soul in Greek language.

Research regarding near-death experiences (NDE) in cases of fully monitored patients during surgery shows that some of the patients were able to describe, upon revival after clinical death, what had happened in the operating room, what the doctors and their medical staff had discussed and done, and what kind of surgical equipment was used. In clinical death the patient's heart and brain are completely stopped, having no electrical activity. Science considers that these patients had absolutely no way of knowing what happened during their surgery. The experts in neuroscience believe that the mind, the consciousness, is the result of brain activity, and say that you cannot have experiences or memories if the brain does not function.

After establishing that the experiences described by the NDE patients after revival had actually taken place while their brains were not functioning and their hearts were stopped, it was concluded that those patients had indeed perceived and remembered what had happened in the operating room while they were clinically dead. These findings led to the conclusions that consciousness cannot possibly be the product of brain activity, and that those patients had perceived and processed what happened during surgery not with their brains, which were not functioning, but with their consciousness. These cases begin to prove that consciousness survives after the brain stops functioning. As a result, modern science is beginning to realign itself with what ancient civilizations and religions took as a fundamental truth for millennia. As it says in the Tibetan Book of the Great Liberation, "Matter derives from mind not mind from matter."

Reports of near-death experiences are startlingly consistent. After spending some time observing what is going on in the operating room, these patients generally see a bright, blinding light that attracts them. They float toward it, and there, they feel overwhelmed with wonderful feelings of peace, unconditional love, joy and rediscovery of their true selves. All the negative feelings and pains disappear. They are welcomed by loving beings of light and sometimes even relatives that have transitioned before them. After communicating with those loving beings, they return to their bodies to continue their human lives. Now that you have read the experiences of my regression clients, doesn't this sound familiar?

Near-death experiences prove that consciousness can have experiences out of the body. When the body is brought back to life by the medical team, the consciousness—the soul—returns into the body, bringing the awareness of the experiences it had outside the body into the brain, where they are stored as memory. If the soul decides not to return into the body, the human being dies or, if the body is on life support equipment, that person remains in coma.

And if there are still doubts, what is most fascinating is that patients who are blind from birth, who went through NDE experiences during surgery, while in clinical death, could *see* for the first time in their lives. Could *see*... just like sighted patients during NDE, and could report accurate visual memories of what happened in the operating room. How could someone who is blind from birth see under any circumstances? They saw with the eyes of their consciousness—their mind's eye. The same process takes place in case of blind patients when they connect with their higher states of awareness in hypnosis. They too begin to see in spite of their eyes not functioning, and to live experiences they never thought possible. Our soul—our consciousness—doesn't need the brain in order to think and retain information, nor the eyes to see, the ears to hear and sensory organs to sense. When we stop having a physical body, we continue to exist and have experiences as intelligent, eternal, energetic beings.

People in hypnosis have similar experiences and see the same things as the NDE patients. They go through the same emotional states when they extend their awareness from the physical body and reach the Light. The major difference between the NDE patients and people in hypnosis is that during hypnosis the person is in a state of relaxation, while a person in near death usually goes through shock, injury, cardiac arrest or surgery. But the concordances of the experiences they recall are remarkable. They all enter the same state of release from the body and operate from a higher state of awareness—the subconscious awareness—reaching high vibrations that allow them to take the same path toward the Light and Home.

So then what is the conclusion? That our consciousness is the result of the brain activity? Or that in fact we think with our soul, our eternal consciousness, and not with the brain? I believe there is a partnership between consciousness and the human brain. The soul (our subconscious aspect) can think, perceive and retain information, communicate and have experiences without the help of the brain. It can feel without having sensory organs and see without having physical eyes. The consciousness will continue to exist after the human being dies and the brain ceases to function. But the soul, the consciousness, needs the brain and the human body in order to live physical lives, to create in the physical plane, and progress energetically and spiritually. The brain is a receptor of consciousness and a vehicle through which consciousness creates more positive energy to evolve. Our human brain and human life help in the process of evolution and expansion of our consciousness. We cannot create in the physical plane and evolve unless we are incarnated as souls in physical bodies that have functional brains. On the other hand, a human being with a functional brain cannot function without a soul, a consciousness that powers it.

Since the Spiritual Masters have graciously answered all of my questions, I realized it was time for me to bring Mia back to her conscious state of awareness.

SM: Mia is at the River of Life. I initially brought her to the Tree but she told me she was going to the River.

After saying my goodbyes to the Masters and bringing Mia back, she did not seem to recall the information the Spiritual Masters and I have discussed.

MIA'S REVELATIONS

M: When you started guiding me toward the Light I felt as though I was flying over water. Then I started to go upward. Do you know the feeling when you fly in an airplane and you see the clouds beneath you? That's exactly how I felt, that I was above the clouds and I was heading toward the sun. After passing beyond the Light I admired what was around. I just relaxed mostly. When I get Home, I don't care where I am or where I go because I know nothing bad can happen to me. I know that once I pass through the Light I am very, very safe. It's interesting that ever since I've started this therapy with you, I have no fear of death. No fear. Perhaps the only thing I should be afraid of is how I will die, with or without suffering, but not even that scares me anymore.

People who use past life regression to review their transition into the nonphysical typically manage to overcome their fear of death.

Mia had experienced what it means to die and how to get Home. She had discovered what awaits us all after the so called death.

M: Before starting working together, I was very afraid of death. When I came to you for our first session, I really wanted to see what it feels like to die. Ever since I was a child, I was curious about what happens afterward. I wanted to know whether people have some kind of "magic power" to come back to Earth or Death, cloaked in black, awaits us. But now that I've experienced life after death several times, I can tell you that it's wonderful. It's just amazing!

People who have had near-death experiences feel the same way about death, expressing this same perspective.

M: You wouldn't even want to stay another second in the life you're living. You just want to go. You don't even want to look back!

CHAPTER NINE

Secrets of Healing

"If you want to heal your body you must first
heal your mind."
Plato

Mia returned for another session excited to tell me that since we last met, she felt so pervasively happy that she'd often ended her days tired from the exuberance. "I just want to shout how happy I am!" she told me.

Mia also shared that she had realized she felt most connected with the gypsy life, of all the lives she had seen, because of the simplicity, freedom, joy and amazing love she experienced during that life. Deep down in her heart she believed she was the same this time: a simple, happy, loving and humble woman who enjoys the simple things in life.

She also was very excited to tell me that she had seen her physician, and the precancerous, cervical lesions she had, caused by papillomavirus, have completely disappeared. Just as Plato said, healing the mind leads to healing the body.

We shortly began guided relaxation and after I directed Mia to the Tree of Life or the River of Life, she connected with the Masters who were glad to answer my questions.

ENERGETIC, SPIRITUAL BALANCE

Dr. G: Iam, you have previously referred to "energetic, spiritual balance." Can you explain this concept?

SM: The purpose of reincarnation is to evolve energetically and spiritually. Many people have every material thing they desire, but can't find inner peace and happiness because of an energetic imbalance. You can have everything you want in life as long as you reach and maintain this balance; as long as you are a positive energy. Being a positive energy means that you have a high vibration, love unconditionally, help others, and look at life optimistically. As a result, you'll succeed in attracting everything that's available in the physical plane, everything you want, including the finances.

Dr. G: How do we reach this balance?

SM: Spiritual balance is achieved when your conscious, subconscious and superconscious find and rediscover each other. Your decisions and goals must satisfy both your physical being with its conscious mind and your spiritual essence—your soul and spirit.

Dr. G: Can you give me practical examples of how a person can achieve spiritual balance?

SM: Spiritual balance, which leads to optimum physical and mental health, is achieved when you set aside or stop being driven by worldly desires and perceive everything with the eyes of your soul. Why do you, as humans, want to have so much? Do you eat with seven mouths? How many beds can you sleep in at once? You can only sleep in one. Why do you need more? The moment you realize that your purpose on Earth is to live happily, you will feel fulfilled spiritually. And when you reach spiritual balance everything will come to you as a reward because the soul rejoices in the goodies that this existential plane has to offer. When I say "goodies," I'm referring to the satisfaction of coming Home consciously for the purpose of remembering who you are and progressing spiritually. I'm referring to the satisfaction of living comfortably, to the satisfaction of your senses, of experiencing the pleasures of life, and so on. The energetic balance is achieved when people detach from negative thoughts and feelings; when they learn that the human thoughts and feelings of hatred, anger, blame, fear and harming others are to be released. It's achieved when people manage either to transform the accumulated negative energy into positive energy or to detach from it. There are many temptations in the physical world. As a result, you can fail to reach balance. Spiritual balance is so simple to attain, and yet so difficult because people are driven by earthly desires which mask low vibration energies that their souls, sometimes, even unwittingly attract.

It's so pleasant and intense for souls to live physical lives because here, at Home, we don't get to experience some of the pleasures we can experience in human form. And it's easy for souls to lose themselves in those worldly desires. And then, when they free themselves from their physical bodies, some of them realize that their human lives were just a waste of time so to speak, although time does not exist here. They realize that they should have worked on more important things, such as increasing their energy. But sometimes it's too late and they must reincarnate. Who doesn't wish to become one with Chi Energy?

Dr. G: Do all the souls want to reunite with The Source?

SM: Yes. It attracts us energetically. We all tend to reunite with Chi.

DISEASES AND THEIR CURE

Dr. G: How would you explain, from an energetic perspective, human diseases caused by viruses and bacteria?

SM: Sickness is not always caused by low vibration energies. The energetic body emanates energetic waves, which are sometimes of a higher and sometimes of a lower vibrational frequency. When the waves have a lower frequency, the immune system becomes weaker and the physical body is vulnerable to catching a virus or bacteria. When the energetic body begins to vibrate with a higher frequency, the physical body gets rid of those microorganisms.

Dr. G: How can you cure the more complicated diseases?

SM: What kind of diseases are you referring to? Bodily diseases or soul' sicknesses, meaning spiritual illnesses—the illnesses, traumas and unresolved issues that your soul brings with it from other lifetimes?

Dr. G: First let's talk about bodily diseases such as the chronic ones. What would a person need to do to cure them?

SM: You can cure the bodily diseases only by curing the spiritual ones. There are many aspects but generally speaking, you can heal them by replacing negative feelings and negative energy blockages with positive energy.

Dr. G: How can you replace negative energy blockages other than by replacing your negative and limiting thoughts and beliefs with positive ones? What else can you do?

SM: What you can do is always remember that it's because of love that you're alive. You can always offer love to yourself, to your body, and to those around you, and in this way you can acquire the positive energy you need to heal. In addition, your Spiritual Guides and the protective energies can always help you, as long as you accept them. The positive energy that they speak of is nothing but an immense love that gives you a wonderful feeling of wellness. It's also important to think more before speaking because many times, through words one brings low vibration energies. Prior to speaking, people should consider that regardless of what happens, only love wins.

Dr. G: So no matter what, it's better to have a positive and forgiving attitude. In other words, the ego must be left aside.

SM: The ego is negative energy.

Dr. G: It's part of the conscious mind. It's the false or illusory self.

SM: Herein lies the problem and from here stems the solution. The ego of the conscious mind represents negative energy, which comes into conflict with the positive energy of your soul—your subconscious mind—creating an energetic imbalance and inner turmoil. And it all depends on how well you maintain that positive energy. You can increase it over the negative, or you can allow the negative energy to overpower the positive and the entire production of hormones and chemicals in your brain is affected. It all depends on how well you organize or balance your energies.

A very eloquent case, which confirms that healing is the discovery and realignment with the true self, belongs to Professor Ben. We will continue the conversation with the Masters after reviewing the first session of this truly life-changing story.

PROFESSOR BEN'S JOURNEY OF HEALING AND SELF-DISCOVERY

Ben was a professor and department director at a European university who had traveled extensively for his work and conducted research in addition to teaching. When we first met, he was 47 years old, married for twelve years with children. Though he was outwardly successful, he had struggled with depression, anxiety and sleep disorders for fifteen-twenty years.

Prof. B: The strength of my symptoms has fluctuated over time but some aspects of depression are always present: heaviness throughout the day and a sad mood that I have to fight against. But I can't find a reason for my sadness. I have so much that I should be happy about, but I constantly feel anxious and low. Both my wife and I think it is some sort of chemical imbalance, but medication hasn't made a difference. I've tried treatment with three different therapists during particularly low periods, last time for about eight months. The psychiatrist prescribed antidepressants such as Paxil and Prozac but they didn't help. I often have nightmares that I can't remember, and sometimes I wake up with a heavy suicidal feeling that eventually fades. I also have uncomfortable thoughts because of not knowing what's wrong with my life: "Am I doing the right thing?", "Am I at the right job?", "Am I in the right house?", "Am I married to the right woman?" I'm not sure if I'm making the right decisions.

Ben continued with how he became open to subconscious exploration and regression therapy.

Prof. B: A friend of mine recommended a book to me, "Many Lives, Many Masters" by psychiatrist Bryan Weiss, and I read it in one night. I have always been open to the idea of past lives, even though I'm a Christian, but I never thought about how past life experiences could affect the subconscious in the present life. I was fascinated and intrigued. I felt a bit nervous but I made an appointment to see you, to see if you thought regression therapy might be an option for me. I hope so. I'm just so tired of feeling sad.

Professor Ben was eager to change his life and improve his health. After many years of psychotherapy and medication, he still felt so overwhelmed by his chronic depression, thoughts of suicide, anxiety, and sleep disorders that he began drinking too much wine at night. He was ready for a change. We decided to begin with regression therapy and analysis to find the root causes of his issues, knowing that once we found the real sources, the symptoms would ameliorate and then disappear. I also decided to work on optimizing his subconscious and conscious thinking by using the same techniques that led to Mia's recovery from her lifelong depression, suicidal tendencies, anxiety and fears.

PROFESSOR BEN'S LIFE AS A WOMAN

After guiding Ben in a deep state of relaxation, he had difficulty entering the Light because he was afraid of it. Many people overwhelmed by anxiety and depression fear the Light. If you'll remember, Mia, as Joseph, was also afraid to get into the Light. This fear doesn't come from our true self, of course; it comes from our illusory self. To help him enter the Light, I continued to relax him while removing his fears and doubts. When he was finally able to enter the Light, he viewed a fragment of a woman's life; a strong, tall woman in her twenties. While admiring the view from a rocky area, Ben, as this woman, suddenly felt threatened and extremely frightened by a man who was approaching her. After the regression, Ben described how he related to this scenario.

Prof. B: It felt very familiar, very sudden and so terrifying, like what I feel when I'm scared in my nightmares. I felt like I was pushed off of something, as if I was high up and someone came behind and pushed me. I don't know what happened, if I fell. The energy didn't feel sexual, didn't feel threatening that way. It felt like hate, and it happened so suddenly! In my ego, I haven't realized what hate I have caused. I wanted to know what I did to this person who hated me because I felt powerful, really strong. Why would someone really hate me like that? There is usually a reason.

I guided Ben to focus on his future, to image himself being positive, confident and healthy, in control of his thoughts and feelings, happy and content with his life. I suggested that he think in this positive and empowering way every time he thinks about himself. However, it was challenging for him to visualize the positive aspects of life. He felt stuck. This is also very common for people overwhelmed by depression.

Prof. B: It almost feels like positive thinking is inviting something bad to happen. It's not healthy, I know. But it feels like if you start to think everything is good and positive, that's when something goes wrong and you weren't expecting it; you weren't prepared.

As you may have noticed in Mia's case as well, people with depression and anxiety have a hard time understanding the concept of positive thinking because they have lost hope and basically operate from negative belief systems.

We will continue with Professor Ben's second session after clarifying with the Masters how various lives of a soul influence one another.

HOW DO A SOUL'S LIVES INFLUENCE EACH OTHER? SPIRITUAL DISEASES

SM: The previous lives, as you perceive them from the human time perspective, determine the vibrational level on which you enter the present life, and the present determines the next life you will live. If you grew vibrationally in the life you've just completed, you would return Home on a higher energetic level. When you reincarnate, you would begin that new life on the increased level of vibration. If you didn't succeed in reaching the vibrational level you had intended, we would have to decide together whether you would reincarnate or remain at Home for a while. If you decreased vibrationally, you would remain at Home for a while, and would get a little bit of, how would you say, "an admonishment?" Of course, in a loving and constructive way, and afterward you could reincarnate into a life of your own design. As I mentioned before, the more you grow vibrationally in each life, the healthier and freer from diseases and problems your future lives will be.

Dr. G: What exactly happens during past life regression therapy when the clients experience past lives that represent the sources of their symptoms, issues and diseases?

SM: When you guide people beyond the Light to the source of their issues, they access their Spiritual Guides, but not consciously so that they can tell you they met with them. But they do, and their Guides show them their lives that the Guides decide they need to see and understand in order to overcome their challenges. It's with our help that people see what happened in parallel, past lives.

Dr. G: I know that the Guides won't let you see anything other than what is relevant or important for your progress.

SM: Correct, and to tell you frankly, we could actually let everyone see all their lives and absolutely everything, but it's not always relevant. For example, when you try to help someone overcome a phobia, it's a waste of human time to shuffle through countless lifetimes until you come across the ones that are relevant. We choose what needs to be seen because the goal is the recovery and spiritual growth of the client. It makes no sense for them to see things that aren't beneficial for their growth, such as when they were less evolved, as all of us were, not always doing things they could be proud of. There is nothing to gain by the client accessing such experiences.

Dr. G: I now understand why people in regression typically don't see lives of great personalities who have influenced humanity. Their negative egos might grow and that is not the goal of seeing those lives.

SM: That's right.

Dr. G: So the past lives people review in regression are their own past lives, not others?

SM: Yes, the Guides will show you only your lives. Anyway, in case you get to see a life that is not yours, you will *know* it's not your life.

Dr. G: Please correct me if I'm wrong. The already-lived lives of a soul continue to exist, and that soul continues to live in those lives. During regression, the client connects mentally and energetically with who he or she was in that parallel, past life.

SM: That's correct.

I know it's difficult to imagine how a soul continues to exist in all its lives. Maybe the following comparison will help. A soul is a river of energy going through different lives on different planes of existence, just like a river on Earth would pass through different cities, towns, villages or regions until it empties into a sea or an ocean. It's the same river, the same soul, flowing simultaneously through all of those locations, through all those parallel lives.

Dr. G: Can a person influence or change the past life that they access during regression?

SM: No. A parallel, past life that a person accesses through regression is actually influencing their present life. These influences manifest through issues like fears, anxiety, depression, weight problems, addictions, chronic pain and various diseases. And they are also reflected in the relationships with certain people. But the person in regression cannot influence or change the parallel, past life because of the construct of time you have created, and the history that must flow forward. You, on your plane, don't have a way of influencing or changing the past because we don't allow it. For example, if you can mentally transpose yourself from your current year's plane of existence and see a life from the beginning of mankind, you cannot change that year or period. But that year or period can change your current time.

Dr. G: What exactly do you mean?

SM: Well, for example, Mia saw a life as a cave man, whose main concerns were finding food and survival. In that life, he knew that if he couldn't find food he would die. By reviewing that life, Mia came to understand that the conditions of the previous, parallel life were no longer valid in her present life. She realized that it's safe to eat in normal quantities because she will have food every day. Therefore, Mia made progress and managed to eliminate her excess weight. Her present life changed its course. Moreover, the fact that after reviewing that life she accessed us here at Home so we could explain to you what is really happening, is a step forward toward uncovering the subconscious, ethereal science that you are presenting to the world. In this sense that parallel, past life, the caveman life, is influencing the present world. In this way the past can change the present.

Dr. G: What else would be beneficial to do for clients to regain their health?

SM: For their cure and recovery you can help them see their parallel, previous lives. In this way, you make them aware of why exactly they have their current challenges and diseases. In addition, in order to get healthier you can help them elevate themselves vibrationally by teaching them how to come to the Light and Home, optimizing their conscious and subconscious thinking, and motivating them to choose positivity at the conscious level. If it's a matter of physical disease, you succeed in helping them cure it by keeping them in the Light, where the low vibration energies that caused the disease are removed. If it's a matter of trauma, whether it occurred in this life or in a previous life, the secret is that the client needs to remember it. You have to take them back to the scene of the trauma, so they can become aware that the harm is over in order to keep it from continuing to torment their soul. They have to resolve the problem and stop running away from it because they have put it aside and lived with it, without resolving it. The negative energy that's behind the trauma nourishes itself with the energy of that client's soul. By facing a problem you either diminish the trauma or transform it, just as you can transform negative energy into positive energy. However, what happens at the client's soul level is their own battle, which they have to fight in order to elevate themselves vibrationally.

It is incredible how past lives can have such a dramatic impact over our emotional, mental and physical health. The following past life reviewed by Professor Ben revealed the root cause of his suicidal thoughts and chronic depression. We will continue the conversation with the Masters after visiting this life.

PROFESSOR BEN'S LIFE AS BRIAN

Four weeks passed before Ben returned for another session. He was already beginning to have more positive thoughts and this time, he had no trouble accessing the Light. He saw himself as a thin teenager who had run away from home and was spending the night alone outdoors, in a place that seemed safe and familiar. He felt weak but not scared.
Prof. B: I hope my family will come find me here. I don't feel scared, I feel hurt. I'm watching and waiting for them to worry and come for me… Now it feels like it got darker than before. It wasn't dark at first, and I felt like I'd be found but it's too far at night, and it feels so much scarier. I keep thinking about a knife sticking into my heart.

Shortly, Professor Ben was able to ascertain the real reason he was sleeping outside.
Prof. B: My name is Brian. My heart hurts. It's so tight. I had a misunderstanding with my parents but I love my parents. I'm from a happy family and I'm just like a normal teenager. I just got mad, so I got dramatic, and now I'm outside and they didn't come to get me. I feel like I have a younger sister. I don't think bad things happened to me. I feel like I should be more scared to be by myself outside than I am.

Then Professor Ben, as Brian, tried to explain his heart pain.
Prof. B: This is probably not a health problem, just something that really hurts me; hurts my feelings so badly. It's the fact that my parents

love my sister more than they love me. Her name is Susie. I can't see her face but she has pigtails. I see the way they look at her while she eats. There is so much love there. I love them and they're not bad people. I just know in my heart that they don't love me the same. It's as if they don't see me. I don't know, maybe I'm adopted. I feel a lot of emotions. I feel like I'm shy, like I want them so much to see me. They are not mean to me. They just always focus on my sister. Like when I ran away, I thought they would worry and come find me but they didn't. They figured I would just come back whenever. I want them to love me so much! But maybe I'm a foster kid. I feel like they're good people who took me in. It's hard to watch how they love their daughter and I just don't have anyone like that.

Then Ben, as Brian, saw himself in his thirties, in a sunny home office sitting at a desk. He had a mustache, and hair "that flipped up in the back," just like when he was a teenager.

Prof. B: Through a glass door I can see a small yard and a hedge. I'm married and I feel lonely and sad. I have no one in this life. I think...

Ben started to cry. He later said that he was overwhelmed by the familiar feeling of deep sadness that washed over him. He pondered and then said: "I know why I'm in this life."

Prof. B: My wife is not home. I'm thinking of killing myself. Things happened and I'm just so sad, and this feeling never goes completely away. I just don't know if I want to keep suffering through the same thing, never feeling like the loneliness would go away. I know I love my wife but that doesn't help.

The session became very intense. Ben was crying out loud.

Prof. B: I don't kill myself today but I'm thinking about it because I realize that nothing is ever going to make it better. I get some peace thinking that suicide is an option. My mom may have died when I was little, and I'm thinking about her too. I'm blaming her and that makes me feel really guilty. My wife is coming home soon. I feel peaceful thinking that suicide may be an option.

After a few moments of silence Ben opened his eyes and fully returned to his conscious state. Brian's life seemed to be the root cause of Ben's thoughts of suicide and depression.

Prof. B: That was just amazing! Maybe that's why I feel suicidal sometimes when I wake up. Then the sun comes out, I have some coffee and it fades. It's the same feeling. It's so interesting because last time I didn't see it this clearly for this long. But I felt so different as Brian than I did as the woman. Is that normal? As the woman in our first session I felt strong and powerful. In this body I felt very sad, and kind of thin, and not strong. You think you would feel kind of the same but I guess not.

Ben felt that Brian eventually killed himself, which was later confirmed by the Masters through Mia's connection. Brian had lived in the early twentieth century and was indeed adopted.

I wondered how exactly Ben's soul brought Brian's depression and suicidal feelings into his present life. To clarify my question I asked the Masters to explain this process. We will continue with Professor Ben's third session after their explanations.

HOW DO SPIRITUAL DISEASES FORM?

Dr. G: What is the process by which you bring certain symptoms, medical conditions and issues from a past life but not others?
SM: When you reincarnate to the physical plane you are vulnerable to low vibration energies. Due to the challenges you had with them in previous lives, you retained traumas caused by those negativities. In order to increase your vibration, you have to overcome those traumas and vulnerabilities. So you bring illnesses or diseases with you to this life as opportunities to grow spiritually.

What a beautiful definition of illnesses: opportunities to evolve spiritually! The Spiritual Masters see the positive side of everything. This is something we should learn as well.
Dr. G: So you come into your next incarnation with the desire to overcome your vulnerabilities and elevate vibrationally. You design a life that will bring you the opportunities to face your fears and hopefully overcome them.
SM: Correct. At the spiritual level, you know that when you come into the physical realm and develop as a human being you are vulnerable, and you will attract a specific type of negative energy. As a result, you fight your own battles and when you prevail, you free yourself from that or those low vibration energies and the symptoms disappear. Your illnesses heal and you have a better life.
Dr. G: You've said that there are no accidents, but I'm still going to ask you. Are there accidents that have not been planned at the soul level?
SM: No. Basically, the conscious mind is supervised by the subconscious. The decisions of what will happen to the human being are made at the higher levels of its consciousness.
Dr. G: What you just said made me think of what Albert Einstein said: "The field is the sole governing agency of the particle." In other words,

the physical being is governed by its nonphysical aspect: its intelligent, electromagnetic field—its consciousness, its soul, its spirit.

SM: Correct. The two worlds, the one from Home and the one from Earth attract low vibration energies. It's the attraction that physics describes between positive and negative energy. Both positive and negative energies need positive energy to survive. Positive energies recharge themselves in the Light, but the low vibration energies can't enter the Light and Home because they can't vibrate that high. They are attracted by the light of our souls and energetic bodies when we are on Earth, so they impact Earth's plane of existence. To evolve spiritually, and, as a result, heal your illnesses, you have to transform the negative energy you accumulate or create on Earth into positive energy. At Home, your higher selves decide with our help how vulnerable each of you wants to be to low vibration energies once you reincarnate. It's at the spiritual level that you decide whether you will have "accidents" or not, spiritual illnesses or not, or if you will allow low vibration energies to influence you or not. As I have said, there is no accident in the Universe.

Dr. G: Can you cure any disease? Of course, I'm not referring to the terminal stages of cancer or other similar conditions, when the physical body is already irreversibly damaged.

SM: The conscious and subconscious mind of the physical organism, and the positive energy that occupies that organism, with the life experience accrued in its current and previous lives, can resolve any illness or disease. The healing of illnesses represents vibrational growth and spiritual evolution. From the spiritual level you can maintain your weight and manage your illnesses, including cancer.

THE BENEFITS OF MEDITATION AT HOME

Dr. G: How much can you increase your vital, positive energy by entering states of deep relaxation or hypnosis, like Mia is doing right now?

SM: These meditative states can greatly increase your positive energy by connecting with the Light and bringing the Light into your body. They can revive you as a spirit and physical organism. But it's very important for you, as souls, to extend from the body after you fill your body with Light, enter the Light and continue meditating there, and then come Home. Although it's much easier for a soul to reach the Light, get Home and contact its Spiritual Guides with the help of another person who knows how to facilitate the process, it's doable alone as well. In principle, people with your knowledge and techniques are necessary because the person's conscious mind often blocks the subconscious, and interferes with accessing that which is beyond the material world.

Dr. G: When I meditate or practice self-hypnosis, which is actually the same thing, most of the time my conscious mind falls asleep; it shuts off.

SM: When you fall asleep, you shift into a higher level of awareness and you, as a soul, come Home. That higher level of awareness doesn't surface consciously. As a result, you don't recall what happened. But regardless, your higher self is always aware and in control of what happens with you.

During meditation or hypnosis one can keep both levels of awareness active. The conscious mind can explore the subconscious universe, and become aware of what the soul or spirit does. There are many studies that show how extremely beneficial meditation is. Neuroscientists have found that people who meditate shift their brain activity from the stress-prone areas of the brain to the calmer areas, reducing the devastating effects of stress.

SM: It would benefit all of you to practice meditation, access the Light and Home consciously, so you can understand and perceive what is here. You have many questions that cannot be answered unless you see for yourself with your mind's eye. You have to *feel* how it feels to be in the Light, and to pass beyond the Light. You have to see the Tree of Life and the River of Life, and travel with us in "time" to see multiple lives, if you wish. And you can personally access at Home whomever you choose, including Chi Energy.

Dr. G: That sounds very exciting. The secret is to remain conscious during meditation.

SM: Definitely because otherwise you are all coming Home every night, or at least you should. You're just unaware of what happens when you sleep.

I was beginning to realize that our different levels of awareness are energies of different vibrations, which almost seem to have their own personalities. The higher, greater self is pure, positive energy. It's very wise, embodies unconditional love and positivity, and possesses all the experience, knowledge, wisdom and love accumulated from living physical and nonphysical lives. It's our God-like consciousness. The soul is the mask of the spirit in the ethereal field. It can pick up, in our world of duality, disempowering and misaligned beliefs that lower us vibrationally. And lastly, the conscious mind, which is limited to our physical reality, is basically an amalgamation of beliefs collected throughout our current human life, and only a part of these beliefs resonate with the higher self. The alignment of the conscious and subconscious levels of the mind with the higher self consciousness is one of the main keys to healing.

SM: All human beings have the ability to come Home, to access information from other lives and see with their third eye. But it's important to practice, so that you can rediscover and master these abilities. Meditation in the Light is very beneficial. It's possible that some of you can't stay in the Light very long and might fall out of it at the beginning. It's also possible that some of you have the sensation that the Light is too hot, it rejects you or pulls you back. After you learn to meditate in the Light and want to come Home, pass quickly through the Light and go beyond it. Your Spiritual Guides will greet you. But once you're here, you'll realize that you don't actually need anyone. You'll realize that you already know what to do and where to go, since you are at home.

THE EFFECTS OF VARIOUS COLORS OF LIGHT

Surrounding ourselves during meditation in different colors of light has different effects.

SM: Each color of light is used for something different. White light is the one that heals. Golden light is used for relaxation and for coming Home; for the detachment of the subconscious from the conscious mind. Orange light is for relaxation in the physical plane without traveling Home. Violet light is for wisdom. Blue light that tends toward dark blue or violet can be used to support the well-being of the body. Green light is for the relaxation and to fall sleep.

Dr. G: What about red light?

SM: Red light exists but it's not ours.

Dr. G: Is it not a positive energy?

SM: Red light can be transformed into positive energy if the soul is clothed, if it's surrounded with white light. But if it comes toward an unprotected soul it can have destructive effects.

HOW CAN WE PROTECT OURSELVES AS ENERGY?

SM: First of all it's important to *feel* love. Not erotic love, but unconditional love for everyone. It's essential to think positively and to avoid being negative under any circumstances. Every negative thought and feeling, each negative word lowers you vibrationally, and you attract more low vibration energy. When I say not to have negative thoughts, I refer to not being intentionally mean, not being unforgiving or critical, not succumbing to worries, fears, despair, sadness, hatred or anger; to not wishing others harm, not blaming others, not being envious, not talk about or focus on negative things, so on and so forth. All of these negativities will result in the blockage of the flow of positive energy in your bodies. It will lead to an energetic imbalance that gradually manifests as symptoms and emotional disturbances, and, over time, as illnesses. Another important aspect is to try to detach from ephemeral, material goals. It's also important to envelop your body in white light, and to see yourself, in your mind's eye, as beings of light to help protect and heal yourself.

POSITIVITY AND HEALING

The most important thing that can help us heal our lives and prevent the development of diseases and struggles in life is to be positive at all costs, both consciously and subconsciously.

1. THE POWER OF THOUGHTS. POSITIVE THINKING

First of all, it's important to become aware of what type of energy we produce with our thoughts, words and feelings. Producing positive energy strengthens our electromagnetic field, while producing negative energy weakens it, creating blockages in our energy flow. In time, these blockages will manifest as symptoms and diseases. We can't expect our lives to improve if we don't change first. When we improve our thinking and change our life perspective, our lives instantly reflect the shift toward positivity. Essentially, our conscious and subconscious thoughts, beliefs and definitions can be our best friends or our worst enemies. As Buddha said, "Nothing can harm you as much as your own thoughts unguarded."

In order to create the life we desire we have to consistently focus our energy on our goals. We have to direct our thoughts toward what we want to experience, not toward what we don't want because our energy flows like a river in the direction our thoughts and attention go. The more time we spend focusing on the negative, the more we experience that low vibration.

An effective technique to create the life we desire is to visualize each day where you want to get in life, tap into the feelings of already being there, and take steps in that direction. Essentially, by putting our energy into our vision, we activate that enhanced version of our life. Just to be clear, I am not promoting the idea of material acquisition as the end goal. We all know plenty of people who are financially wealthy but are unhappy. Many of them lack the most important things in life: love, happiness, inner balance or good health. We have also met people who are happy and content with their lives, and are not rich in material terms. It's because from the perspective of our higher selves, it's not the material things that we really desire, it's the spiritual progress. This means it's the feeling of pure, selfless, altruistic love that we want. It's the clarity, joy, harmony, happiness, safety, and freedom that we really desire. These are the feelings we should wish for and perpetuate, related to the material things we dream of, that will ensure us high vibrations.

To heal ourselves and improve our lives we have to stop being negative, angry and critical because in fact we are harming ourselves. At the subconscious, the soul level we experience exactly the same energy. "You will not be punished *for* your anger, you will be punished *by* your anger," Buddha said.

We should also let go of beliefs that limit us, such as: "I am not smart enough, attractive enough, competent enough, educated or wealthy enough." We should not compare ourselves to other people because everyone is at their own distinct level of evolution. They live the lives that they have created, and are confronted with situations that can help them progress on their spiritual path.

2. POSITIVE LANGUAGE

Every word we speak has an energetic charge. Therefore is essential to speak in a positive, compassionate, non-violent way. Repeating positive affirmations is a very useful tool for ingraining healthy beliefs that result in feeling better mentally, emotionally and physically. It may be difficult to accept, but we really are responsible for everything that is happening to us.

3. RENOUNCING THE VICTIM MENTALITY

There are no victims, there are only creators. This is a concept many people have trouble understanding and accepting. It comes from the lack of faith in oneself, from not understanding who we really are.

Whatever we see from our human perspective is only the tip of the iceberg. It would save us a lot of turmoil to have more confidence in the wisdom of our higher self, our eternal consciousness. Regardless of how bad or tragic a situation might appear from our human perspective, it can lead to spiritual growth. In fact, specifically what is happening isn't as important as how we feel about what is happening, because our feelings determine our vibrational trajectory. As Buddha said, "Pain is certain, suffering is optional."

4. THE CORRELATION BETWEEN OUR PATTERNS OF THINKING AND THE WAY WE FEEL

Neuroscience reveals a clear correlation between our thoughts and the production and release of associated neuropeptides into the blood stream from the hypothalamus. They carry the information to the cellular level and are responsible for our emotional states. (Hypothalamus is a small area of the brain that directs a multitude of important bodily functions). Positive thoughts determine positive feelings, negative thoughts lead to negative feelings.

Feelings can be wonderful teachers. Professor Ben discovered during our third session how much is there to learn from feelings.

PROFESSOR BEN'S LIFE AS HENRY

Two weeks after he experienced his life as Brian, Professor Ben returned feeling much better. He had great news to share with me.
Prof. B: My suicidal thoughts and those feelings I had waking up sometimes in the morning are completely gone! The pain in the heart area that I felt as Brian persisted for another week before it disappeared completely. When I was in Brian's life, I remember thinking, "I know why I'm seeing this life." It just swept over me. I realized that Brian's feeling of self-pity was so familiar because that's how I've been waking up for years, sometimes feeling suicidal. And there was never a real reason for it. (At least not a reason that Ben was aware of consciously.) It's why I thought it was chemical depression that needed medication. And then, after the session, poof! The heavy suicidal feeling went away! I also didn't have any nightmares and I don't feel that depressed anymore. I feel much better. I've also reflected on my feelings as Brian, and one thing that has struck me is how I felt such great empathy for the boy. His pain and love felt so pure, and I wanted to love him and help him. Yet I felt more frustration than compassion for the adult Brian who had feelings of self-pity mixed with depression—those feelings that were so familiar to me in this life. He appeared to have a sunny life and loved his wife, so why couldn't he get on with things? Things happen. Many of us have painful childhoods, but it seems such a waste to not work with what you have. Just like me. I also had so much to be grateful for, but couldn't break

free from feeling sad and sorry for myself. It made me impatient with myself.

Ben was excited to start a new journey of remembrance. After guiding him into relaxation and directing him to the source of his symptoms, he saw himself as an older man, a grandfather. He had "kind, really sweet eyes," and was wearing "preppy clothes, like loafers and a plaid shirt." However, what Ben saw around him didn't make sense to him.

Prof. B: I'm standing in what looks like my grandparents' house. It's made of brown wood, has a small staircase and a fireplace.

Dr. G: Does anything look different than your grandparents' house?

Prof. B: There is a sunroom that used to be stacked with magazines when I was little. I see two reading chairs there. It's more like a library. Also, when I was a little boy, there was a garage back behind the house and a tree, and they aren't there. Part of the front of the house looks different too. Also, there are photos on the mantel. I have grandkids... My grandkids love me and I love them. My wife died recently. I'm thinking about whether I should move or stay in the house. I'm not sad at all, I feel very strong. I'm just wondering if living here will give me enough to do to fill my day.

Then Ben, as Henry, found himself walking down the street toward the library.

Prof. B: I love this library. I come here a lot. It makes me happy. I like the shiny floor with dark patterns and the smell. There is a back door. Sometimes I leave it open. I know people are there. They let me in because I come here a lot. Now I'm looking at the librarian at the desk. She is laughing. She has a beehive hairdo and horn-rimmed glasses on. She is kind of young, maybe in her thirties. She has a tiny hat. She is very sweet to me. I'm thinking I'll go out of the library just to walk a little bit. People say "hello" to me. Sweet town! It feels very rich, an old-fashioned town. I see a boy on a bicycle with shorts on. I'm speaking to him. He's got bowl-cut hair. It's nice. I'm walking down to the church. I think I'll sit here for a while and remember my wife.

When I guided Ben to the next important event, he noticed that he was in a hospital bed.

Prof. B: There's a nurse approaching on my left, now standing by my feet. She is sweet. I feel pain sliding on my heart! My hand and heart hurt. There is a light coming all around me, white with gold light... My hands are different. They are older and thinner. I know I don't have thick hair anymore. The nurses are so sweet to me. They call me "Mister Henry." Now I feel like I'm supposed to go home but I don't know how... Now I'm not in that building anymore, I'm back outside my house. This was a good life. I was a good man. But there was something I wanted to do and I didn't do it. I wanted to move, I wanted to sell the house. But I like my town.

Then, I guided Ben to the last moments of Henry's life.

Prof. B: I'm back in that hospital room and I see I have a white sheet on me. I'm in a single bed. There's a silver handle, like a handicap railing to the side on the bottom… I know I've died in this bed but I don't know how. I don't know if I left in my sleep or because of my heart.

Dr. G: What were the lessons you learned, and how did you do in that life?

Prof. B: I think this is what I was feeling when I went back to the house. This was good, this was kind, and there was love. But I didn't take any risks. I don't know if that's a bad thing but I feel there were things I wanted to try but didn't because I wanted to be safe. I think I wanted to write a novel. I think I never even told anybody. It sounds very pretentious and I'm not a pretentious person. But I feel like I was a good father.

Dr. G: What is the connection between your current life and Henry's life?

Prof. B: In my current life I don't feel the steadiness that this man feels. I think he really sees other people and he likes himself. In this life I feel different. I relate more to his other feeling about maybe not taking risks or putting it out there. That's more of what I feel. But I don't have that calm or steadiness, with that kind of wisdom. It would be nice to have them, wouldn't it?

After regression, Ben said that Henry's life was very intriguing to him.

Prof. Ben: The house I was living in seemed to be my grandparents' house.

Dr. G: Could it have been a house that looked like it?

Prof. B: I don't think so because it was the same town, the same library, the same church.

Dr. G: Could Henry have lived in the same house before your grandparents lived there?

Prof. B: As far as I know my grandparents built that house.

We were puzzled. I suggested that Ben research when his grandparents' house was built, and if anyone lived there before them.

Prof. B: It's so interesting that my regression experience is all feeling. I'm fascinated how things have been presented to me in such an orderly way. The things I've learned and what I felt while being in these incarnations! Feeling that Brian felt so weak and so sorry for himself.

He never learned, he never accessed his power because of whatever happened to him when he was little, being a foster child. It was so sad that he never got over that. And now I went into Henry's life and it was right here. (Ben pointed to his heart area.) He was so strong and so loving. He just looked around and everybody loved him, and he loved and appreciated everything. It was this love and strength! I think he figured out his strength. He knew he is God. He had God inside of him. But he never *did* anything, he just lived that way.

Professor Ben left the session determined to tap as often as he could into the wonderful feelings of strength, steadiness and love for life that he learned from Henry that were completely unfamiliar to him, and to perpetuate that loving emotional state.

Ben later found out that his grandparents did indeed build their house in the 1940s.

THE MYSTERY OF HENRY'S HOUSE

Mia was still at Home, relaxing. Returning to my discussion with the Spiritual Masters, I asked Iam to elucidate the mystery of Henry's house.

SM: Ben's grandparents built the house he remembers from his childhood. In fact, they modeled it after their grandparents' original house, and their grandfather was Henry.

Dr. G: Between what years did Henry live?

SM: From 1839 until 1902.

After I explained to Ben what the Spiritual Master said about Henry's house, he explored the documentation about the property his grandparents' house was built upon, which his family owned for many generations. The findings were remarkable. The original house built on that land was indeed built by Ben's great-great-grandfather, whose name was Henry. Henry owned that land and lived with his family in the original house. Ben found records on Henry's life that matched the information the Spiritual Master provided. In the 1940s, on the same property, Ben's grandparents built another house after the model of Henry's house. This is the house Ben remembers from his childhood. Ben wasn't aware of the original house that existed on that land nor did he ever hear anyone in his family speaking about his great-great-grandfather—Henry.

About sixty years after completing his life as Henry, Ben's soul returned to the same family. Ben can truly say that he was one of his own ancestors. He spent time during his childhood in the same town, on that same property where Henry lived his life. Henry and Ben are human facets of the same soul, the same immortal consciousness. Henry had a very positive outlook on life, lived in the moment, and enjoyed the simple things that his life had to offer. His beautiful and peaceful life was a mirror of his feelings, and his feelings were a mirror of his thoughts and beliefs. Henry's inner peace, strength and wisdom became a powerful lesson for his own soul in another life—Ben's life.

FEELINGS AS INDICATORS OF OUR VIBRATIONAL LEVEL

Studies conducted at the Institute of HeartMath show that the electromagnetic field produced by the heart correlates with our emotions. Positive emotions have a positive effect on the electromagnetic field produced by the heart, while negative emotions disturb it.

While our feelings are a result of our thoughts and beliefs, they are also indicators of our vibrational level, which matches the vibration of the energetic environment we are in at the soul level, and the energy flowing through us. Our senses interpret the vibration of the energy passing through us as emotions and feelings. If a stream of positive energy passes through us, we feel good, if a stream of negative energy passes through us, we feel bad. These vibrations influence us at many levels, including our biology, determining changes at the cellular level.

As I have mentioned before, studies show that there is a close connection between what we feel and our immune system's ability to respond and protect us from diseases. When we feel stressed, the number of immune system's cells (T cells) decreases, along with the body's ability to fight disease. When we think positively, feel good, calm and relaxed, the number of immune system's cells increases, along with our immune system's ability to protect us from diseases. This is mind over the immune system, also known as psychoneuroimmunology. Everything happens in a chain reaction: positive beliefs and thoughts lead to good feelings, good health, positive experiences and a beautiful life. Negative thinking leads to negative feelings that can result in illnesses and obstacles in life.

What else could we do to improve our health? We could perpetuate a loving and peaceful emotional state regardless of what is going on around us, and stop leaving our happiness in other people's hands. We could also very easily change our emotional state through laughter. Laughter stimulates the release of endorphins and serotonin "the happiness hormones" that give us a sensation of well-being. Meditation, in all its versions, provides similar benefits by helping practitioners attain a state of peacefulness and tranquility. Negative thoughts and stress have an opposite effect. They stimulate the release of catecholamines, the "fight-or-flight hormones," and the body reacts accordingly.

Are you depressed or anxious? Then it's time for you to become extremely serious in redirecting your thinking toward positivity, including your subconscious thinking. The highest rate of suicide is due to untreated depression. It's very important for people with depression to remember that they are valuable, that they deserve to live happily and their lives are worth living. It's important to remember that they are loved, and they are never truly alone.

It's also essential to follow the discipline of a healthy diet and to stop taking refuge in habits that lead to imbalance. Excess food, cigarettes, alcohol and recreational drugs will never fill the inner void. We also need to take care of ourselves emotionally by loving and forgiving ourselves, as well as loving and helping others. Spending time in nature, practicing physical exercise or just going for walks help release the stress and regulate the activity of our body's glands and organs. As we nourish our body, we should also nourish our soul and spirit. It's also very helpful to pursue whatever makes our lives joyful and exciting. "Life must be lived as play," as Plato said.

5. THE OPTIMIZATION OF THE SUBCONSCIOUS BELIEFS

It's very difficult to accomplish any major behavioral or health improvement goal without the help of our subconscious. The optimization of subconscious beliefs requires replacing negative patterns of thinking with positive ones through hypnotherapy. Even listening to audio recordings designed to help optimize the subconscious beliefs (motivational, hypnosis or guided meditation recordings) is very helpful.

I resumed my conversation with the Spiritual Masters asking their opinion regarding the efficiency of this type of audio recordings I give to my clients.

SM: They work a hundred percent. People who listen to them come Home. Through these recordings you confer directly with the subconscious, which is nothing other than the soul, and essentially remind the soul about the things it knows need to be done. You basically help the soul realign itself vibrationally, which means return on the level it needs to stay on because sometimes, the conscious mind becomes so strong and negatively-oriented that it overwhelms the subconscious and suppresses its information.

Dr. G: Many people don't realize how efficient these techniques are.
SM: Because people are skeptical. When they can't touch something they get scared. They're afraid of the unknown. I know this because I've practiced what you call hypnosis myself while being incarnated. Yes, this is a very, very old science.
Dr. G: I know that the Romans and Greeks had temples of healing where they were basically using the same states of deep relaxation. I assume not only them.
SM: Of course you know because otherwise you wouldn't have chosen to continue practicing it in this life as well. You've been practicing it for a very long time… What you, as human beings, experience and feel in hypnosis surprises or maybe scares you a little at first, if you are not accustomed to the sensations you experience during meditation. But then, you begin to like it because you realize that you're able to access Home, the place that is mentioned in all of humanities' civilizations and religions. It's about rest, relaxation, rejuvenation and accessing information. Here, you are no longer stressed by any worldly thoughts. It's a feeling that human beings forget to live. Coming Home is essential for your evolution and progress both as spiritual and human beings. And your spiritual evolution is the essence of life for which you return to Earth.

CHAPTER TEN

The Gift of Healing

"The one who love touches does not walk in darkness."
Plato

Before returning to the conversation with the Spiritual Masters through Mia's connection, let's review Professor Ben's following session. It turned out to be a very surprising, one-of-a-kind session that would uplift his soul and significantly influence his recovery.

PROFESSOR BEN'S HEALTH IMPROVEMENTS

Two months had passed since our first session. Professor Ben made such a great shift in his recovery process that I went speechless while listening to him. I admired his determination to do the subconscious work necessary to correct the emotional and mental imbalances that had almost destroyed his life.

Prof. B: After seeing Brian's life, I never got that morning suicidal feeling again. I've struggled with that my whole adult life and now it's just gone! I also don't have nightmares anymore. I sleep very well, and the depression and anxiety are gone too!

Professor Ben's case is another powerful example of how the subconscious mind exploration helps people recover from depression, anxiety, nightmares and suicidal thoughts in just a few sessions.

Prof. B: When I told my wife the strange feeling I had while reviewing Henry's life, that I was in my grandparents' small town, she immediately said: "Sure, that makes sense. You've always hated little towns and never understood how anyone could live there. It seemed that Henry's feelings showed you how content and happy people can be living anywhere because of an inner strength you also felt." And when I try to recapture the feeling of being Henry during my morning meditation, it makes me cry. All those emotions, that love right here (Ben pointed to his heart area), that strength and steadiness make me tear up! Henry looked around and *saw* people. He saw his nurse, saw the kids on the bikes, talked with them and appreciated everything. He really saw what was going on around him. That's what I want to feel every day. I've learned so much just from feeling! It's so intense! That's why I try to bring it back. I think it was shown to me that I can feel that love and strength, which was unfamiliar to me, but it isn't so much anymore. I've tapped into it a lot since then. I feel so much stronger, more settled and not anxious. That anxiety about "Am I doing the right thing?" "Am I at the right job?" "Am I in the right house?" "Am I married to the right woman?" You know... it's just gone. It only gets better.

It is impressive how this alternative, complementary therapy uplifted Professor Ben's life. This approach increases our self-awareness by putting us "in the shoes" of another human facet of our higher, greater self—the one who experienced the original trauma—in order to reflect back to us very familiar feelings and to help us understand why we have them in this lifetime. It can also help us reconnect to the positive, empowering feelings we had in other lives so we can perpetuate them to become more balanced. It's really a self-discovery process, and it makes us aware that our consciousness, with all its levels of awareness, is responsible for our health and the way we feel, and ultimately, for our life.

Inevitably, this therapeutic approach makes us recognize the existence of our higher, greater consciousness, and gives us tools to help maintain ourselves, as energetic beings, on high levels of vibration. It helps us shift our focus from sadness and negativity toward positive feelings and healthy beliefs. In spiritual terms, it helps our souls awaken.

Prof. B: I feel good being by myself now. I never really enjoyed being alone before. I'm even thinking of taking a trip by myself and I feel excited about that. I'm craving more alone time, which is very unusual for me. I'm craving time in the morning to be quiet, and time outside to sit in my back yard with a cup of tea. I never had that before. I was always uncomfortable, busy in the brain and worried. This is very exciting. It feels really good! I still remember how it felt to be Henry, so full, centered and loving. I pray to be able to really see people all day long like Henry did: my kids, my wife and my students. I'm really looking at them and really seeing them now. I'm spending more time with my kids, really listening to them and playing with them. I really enjoy it. I'm seeing things I overlooked before. I'm enjoying nature... My days are better.

Very pleased with Ben's progress, I initiated the process of guiding him in deep relaxation to access the Light. As I directed him to the roots of any remaining symptoms, neither of us expected what was about to happen. The following situation was something I never encountered before.

PROFESSOR BEN'S LIFE AS A ROMAN SOLDIER

Prof. B: I have sandals and a gladiator outfit. I'm a Roman man, but I'm not a big man. I have a white garment on and sandals that strap around and tie at my legs. I feel as if I'm an important man a long time ago. I'm trim and I feel very healthy. I'm pretty young, maybe in my twenties. I have light blond hair.

Dr. G: Where are you, inside or outside?

Prof. B: I'm inside but I can see outside. It feels like a political meeting place. The walls are made of stone. There is a dirt road and there are wide steps leading down to it. I don't see other people, I'm by myself right now.

As Ben accessed the next important part of that life, he noticed that his knees were hurting.

Prof. B: There are trees, like a forest. I feel as though I'm denser, maybe more muscular, older I guess. I have bad knees. I'm wearing something brown. There are others here. I feel like we're going somewhere to fight. It doesn't feel angry. It's just what we do. Maybe we've paused in the forest but we're on our way somewhere else. I feel as if I've walked a long, long way. I feel heavy. I don't know if there is armor on me or I've got heavy boots or shoes but my knees are aching. They're just bad, like I have arthritis.

Dr. G: How old would you say you are?

Prof. B: I can't see myself as clearly as before. I'm older, and feel as though I'm right at my prime but on my way out of it, if that makes sense. I'm not an old man. I feel in charge in some way. I feel like we're going to conquer someone. It's not anger or like we're defending ourselves. We're just going a very long way to get to the place on the map that we try to conquer. It's just what we do. This is a long, long walk; a long way.

Dr. G: Do you have any horses?

Prof. B: I was just thinking that because I felt like I was wishing for horses. I was wishing that I was on a horse. It would be easier. Maybe there are only a couple of horses, and I'm not on a horse because I feel like I'm making a point; that I'm the leader of this group, and I'm walking with the men and giving the horses to somebody else. No, there aren't many horses, just two or three.

Dr. G: What kind of weapons do you have?

Prof. B: They're clunky. I have on something brown, almost like a dress or smock with an armor on top of it; maybe like a breast plate and a sword. We don't have helmets, I feel bare-headed. It's not a battle outfit. It's what soldiers wear when they're traveling. Maybe when we get to where we're going, we'll have more on… We're going through the forest on our way. It's nice and we are almost at the edge of the forest. I don't think I've seen this kind of trees before. They have white bark with spots and they're kind of thin. I feel like this time we have a long way to go. There's a road to get to the other side of the forest. We will be on that road for a long time, and it feels like we are going toward the sea.

After I guided Ben to the next important event of that life, a very unusual thing happened as he was trying to speak. While still lying on the couch, Ben's body suddenly arched as though energy was passing through him.

Prof. B: I feel like I'm buzzing everywhere. My whole body is buzzing. I don't have a soldier's…

There was silence. When I asked Ben what was going on, he finally spoke almost crying.

Prof. B: I don't see, I just feel. Oh… I just know. I feel like I met Jesus or I saw him. I just felt this extraordinary, oh… don't know what, if I can… just feeling close, or seeing, or feeling love, but it was this Jesus energy that just washed over me. But I don't see anything… I don't know why I'm not seeing. I'm just getting feelings. I don't have my armor on. I feel like I may have been in a group of people who were baptized, who have walked into water. And I have like a smock on. I feel like someone else baptized me as part of this group. And I wasn't… I just… (Ben began crying.) I feel like I didn't know Jesus. We crossed paths and he touched me and changed me. There was a… I'm feeling this incredible energy! I feel this light and this energy…

Ben's body arched again. After a minute or so, the energy flow began to reduce in intensity.

Prof. Ben: I want to have this same feeling I'm feeling right now in this life. The energy is fading and I feel different. I feel good now. I won't go back to where I was.

Dr. G: Did you know Jesus?

Prof. B: I just crossed paths with him. I don't know if I followed him. I saw him, I see… and I felt strongly, so powerfully how it felt for him to be near me, but I don't know what happened after that. I'm feeling like I can't go back to where I was, and I think I was a pretty powerful person. I don't know if I stayed here, I don't know if I followed him, but I know I wanted to be close. I'm coming out. I'm leaving that body.

I asked Ben to describe what he was seeing or feeling and no answer came. Therefore I guided him into the Light and beyond it, to the Tree of Life. When he got there, I asked him to call on his Spiritual Guide or Guides.

Prof. B: The Guide is telling me that in this life I'm strong like this gladiator or warrior. This man was a strong man and a good man, but he was using his strength in a wrong way. He was learning a lesson that I need to learn too. It's a lesson I can use in this life because he realized that he was less strong and less powerful when he crossed paths with, and was touched by Jesus. He realized how much more power was in that. He was a natural leader. He just needed to be leading in a different way.

Dr. G: How is your Spiritual Guide communicating with you?

Prof. B: This is strong. I don't hear but there's a clear sentence in my head. A clear thought that feels intuitively very true.

Dr. G: What else would you like to ask your Guide?

Prof. B: I don't really have a question. I just have a lot of gratitude. Things will happen as they happen. I'm trying to thank my Guide.

I asked Ben to inquire about his present life purpose.

Prof. B: I feel clearly a strong love and a "be patient" and "it will be revealed," but still, I felt this before that is not time yet for me to know. It seems very general; to develop this sense of personal power, to make it stronger and use it for good. That's what it feels like, that my power isn't there yet. I can't use it in a big way, for a big space until I make it stronger.

Then I guided Ben back into the Roman soldier's life to see his death and transition.

Prof. B: I have brown sandals. I have on something brown, almost an olive colored cloth. It's belted around my waist and maybe over my shoulder too. I don't feel that much older. I'm in my thirties, forties. I have some grey hair but not like an elderly man. I'm outside on a dirt road.

Dr. G: Are you alone?

Prof. B: I think I've dreamed this. It seems very familiar, like I had some dreams about it. There's a road and there's this loop up to the right. There are some homes and short trees along the way. I feel like I'm with a group of people walking down the road. We are not walking now although we have been walking. We are sitting on the edge of some stones. We're having something to eat, some bread and olives. There aren't many of us; maybe five, maybe seven. I feel that there are women, not only men; a woman or two. We're Christians. We're going somewhere to start a little church. Jesus has died and it's after he... we feel a task to go and... look what happened to us!

After a long pause Ben continued.

Prof. B: My right arm hurts a lot at the shoulder. I have a strong feeling that someone has cut it off. I'm feeling the irony. I'm not in a place where I will be killed but I think that I'm being killed because I'm a Christian, and it's by someone who is like what I used to be. And I'm feeling the irony...

I guided Ben to the last moments of that life.

Prof. B: I'm in a round circle. It's low, not like a coliseum but it's an arena with seating. A few men who seem important are watching from the left. I feel resignation, not fear. I think it crossed my mind when I was eating on the road that this was likely to happen.

Dr. G: Are there others in the same situation?

Prof. B: It's just me. They may have gone before or follow after me, but right now it's just me. I feel like my arm has been cut off, and I'm on my knees but still upright. I'm not afraid. I feel ready to die. It's okay... There is somebody in front of me. This is what he does. He has a sword and a round shield, and this is what he does. And I'm so glad it's not what I do anymore. (Ben smiled proudly.) I feel powerful. I feel that powerful Jesus energy again...

Ben's voice became to tremble as his eyes teared up.

Prof. B: I feel very lucky that I've served like I was supposed to... Now I'm looking at my body. I feel like he cuts my head off but I don't think it matters. I was already gone. I feel that heart pain again... It's odd.

As I began relaxing Ben, the heart pain slowly reduced in intensity.

Prof. B: It's almost gone. I think my name is Steven. I got a new name.

And then there was silence again.

PROFESSOR BEN'S REVELATIONS

After the regression, Ben described his experience obviously amazed and touched by what just happened.

Prof. B: It was very intense! I'm getting used to how this works. A lot of it is feeling, and when you let yourself feel it, all of a sudden it's as if something washes over you, and you kind of see it but it's never clear. It's very interesting. I realize where I am and what I'm feeling. I can't look around, which is kind of frustrating because I want to. I just get impressions but I'm not really seeing… The feeling of Jesus's energy was physical! My whole body was buzzing. The energy was really, really strong and wonderful! It kept going and going… As this Roman soldier I felt that power, that feeling of being a really strong person, a very masculine kind of feeling. I felt like a strong man all the way through being executed, a powerfully built man, like a leader. It's like knowledge. And then, I was in that small arena with some important people on my left, and I was on my knees but my back was straight. There was a Roman in front of me with a sword and a shield and I was thinking of the irony, just such a weird thing to think, that I used to be that man and I was so glad I wasn't; that I was who I was later and I had that life. I felt for him. I got the irony that this is what I used to do, and I was so glad I wasn't that man anymore. After you asked me what happens and I said: "I think he cuts my head off but it doesn't matter because I'm not in my body," I felt that overwhelming love again, a kind of joy and peacefulness coming through me. Then I said: "I think I've changed my name to Steven." It came across my head. I'm overwhelmed and uplifted by all of this…

Ben didn't say much else. He left the session astonished by this amazing experience.

SPIRITUAL MASTER' CLARIFICATIONS REGARDING PROFESSOR BEN'S LIFE AS ROMAN SOLDIER

Returning to the session with Mia and the Spiritual Masters, I inquired about Ben's regression.

Dr. G: Ben saw a life during Jesus's time, at least that's what he deduced. He saw himself as a Roman soldier marching with the legions. Then he felt that he was baptized not by Jesus, but by someone else, and Jesus was also there. Is this true?

SM: He was right. He was a soldier in the Roman legions by the name of Romanus who was baptized by John the Baptist.

Dr. G: Amazing! When he was baptized and when he died, Ben felt a powerful flux of energy and love passing through his physical body that caused him to arch on the couch.

SM: Yes, because Ben manage to connect not only with his life as Romanus, but with his higher self as well—with his spirit consciousness—which connected with, and channeled Chi Energy.

Dr. G: So Chi Energy came through him, which represents God's energy, and includes the streams of positive energy and all the high vibration souls?

SM: Yes. We are all Chi Energy, the energy of love. Chi is all of us and all of you because in each of us and each of you is Chi Energy. When Ben became a channel of energy, Chi Energy flowed through him.

Dr. G: How did Jesus heal? Was he transferring Light and Chi Energy to people who needed healing?

SM: Yes, exactly. This power exists in all of us. You can all connect with Chi Energy and have this power of healing by believing and opening your subconscious. Basically, you'll just be allowing Chi Energy—God—to work through you.

Dr. G: When Jesus was healing people, was the Light and Chi Energy he was transferring to them cleaning their energetic and physical bodies of low vibration energy blockages?

SM: Yes. Chi Energy was entering their human bodies as a current of energy. It was cleaning the body from head to toe so that all the negative energies fell away. That's how people were healed.

Dr. G: Before Romanus was beheaded in the arena, he realized how much he had changed for the better. "I'm so happy I'm not that man anymore," he said.

SM: Yes because he, as a soul, had found the Light and saw his life from a different perspective.

Dr. G: The moment Romanus died, he felt that extraordinary love and thought he had changed his name to Steven.

SM: He didn't change his name to Steven. It was just another life of his that came suddenly to his mind.

Dr. G: When was Jesus born and when did he die?

SM: Jesus is part of the Alpha and Omega just like Krishna, Buddha, and Muhammad as well as others. That is all you need to know for now.

      The Spiritual Master's answer surprised me. It was the first time he had veiled his response, which made me think that there must be important details about Jesus's life that we don't yet have access to. His reference to the highly evolved souls caught me off guard as well.

Dr. G: So Jesus, as well as Krishna, Buddha and Muhammad are highly evolved souls who have not yet reunited with Chi Energy, right?

SM: Right, they haven't reunited with Chi. Actually, they've chosen to not reunite with Chi.

Dr. G: So they are all on the same levels of vibration with Chi Energy,

yet have chosen to remain on those levels without reuniting with God?
SM: That is accurate. They made this decision because after you merge with Chi Energy you detach from Chi as new, small energy and begin the cycle of spiritual evolution all over again. They've chosen to remain on the highest levels of vibration so they can reincarnate with their advanced consciousness, with the knowledge they possess, and with all of their energy.
Dr. G: Does Chi Energy—God—incarnate as a human being from that ultimate level of advancement?
SM: Extremely, extremely rare.

PROFESSOR BEN'S FINAL RECOVERY STEPS

After another four weeks Ben returned to talk. Three months had passed since our first session.
Prof. B: I feel great! Life is really good! I have so much to tell you. I've been reflecting on the past lives I've seen and the lessons are brilliant. Also, amazing things have happened since our last session. Sometimes, when I reflect on what I can remember, the energy washes over me again. It has happened several times. One time, I was driving my car and it came on so strongly. I remember thinking, "Wow, do I need to pull over?" because I was reflecting on our session, and I felt that amazing love energy again. My head and throat started tingling, and I felt as if my hair was standing up, that kind of thing. This happened often for about a week or two after I last saw you. It almost feels like a gentle confirmation of my experience, like "Yes, this happened to you. Yes, you should be thinking about this." The part I keep remembering is when I was in that small arena with the Roman soldier in front of me with a sword and shield. I remember thinking of the irony that I used to be that man, and I was so glad I wasn't anymore. I felt so much empathy for that man. I also remember having this sudden thought of "Oh my God, I met Jesus!" In that part of the life, I thought I couldn't see, and there was an amazing body energy going on that kept going... I don't know if it matters who I was in that life, except that I was part of the movement that awakened and spread the love energy. It's a lesson; you are awakened, but now how do I use that?

Undoubtedly, Professor Ben's connection with his higher nature was increasingly becoming stronger, making him reflect on his life purpose.
Prof. B: I remember doubting if my wife was the right one for me, but then I felt my Guides say, "Love her, she is good for you!" Since I've

been having sessions with you my wife and I have connected in a different way. This experience had such a profound impact!

We are so caught up in our lives, with our families and jobs that we don't even find the time to acknowledge that there may be a part of us that needs attention. And when we feel or hear it, we try to silence it with medication, alcohol or recreational drugs. And then one day we wonder why we've developed chronic diseases, why we feel depressed or anxious? Or one day we wake up realizing that something is missing, and it's not money or material things. We wonder why do we feel empty inside, or why can't we find happiness?

Prof. B: I was drinking too much wine thinking it would help me let go. But even when I was self-medicating with wine, things happened in my life and I was never able to let go of them. However, after seeing my life in Jesus's time and the other lives, I've felt encouraged to meditate and pray more because I felt there was a real reason I saw those lives. Then I began to feel like I'm getting better, so I started wondering, "If I feel that I'm learning why do I still need the wine? Why am I using it like this, sitting up and drinking wine at night?" And in my head I heard the words, and it was very emotional for me: "You are so hard on yourself." It was very loving: "You are so hard on yourself. It's okay, it's okay, don't beat yourself up." And then it said: "This is how much we love you," and I felt the love energy again. It wasn't as overwhelming as what I felt in the life when I saw Jesus, but I felt it, and it went through my body. And I heard: "We love you this much!" and I felt so much loving energy. And I perceived the thought in my mind: "When you love yourself this much, you won't want to drink anymore!" It was very much like being shepherded. "Don't try so hard. You *need* it (the wine) right now because you don't love yourself yet." It felt like, "Let us do our work, let us help you with our part. And when we get you stronger, and you learn to love yourself more like we love you, it will be easy." And it was exactly true. I didn't stop that day. It went weeks longer, but I got stronger, and I started feeling so much happier and excited about life and everything. Then one day I just said: "I'm done!" And since then, I have no desire for it. I have totally quit. My friends were confused when I stopped. I told them, "I just don't want to drink. I don't drink anymore." Now my energy levels are high and I've realized that I don't need to dwell in my fears.

My heart expanded to see that Ben was going through such positive, profound changes.

Prof. B: I often remind myself to "Quit worrying. You are too hard on yourself!" I have times when I just love my day, and then I have days when I think, "Shouldn't I be doing something to follow the path that was shown to me?" Then I would feel a very gentle suggestion saying: "Work on this (letting go of discomforting feelings) and don't worry about what's out there and your life purpose yet. You need to calm yourself. This will come."

What a wonderful accomplishment! Professor Ben didn't change his job, his wife, his house (although it crossed his mind) in order to experience a better life and overcome his depression and other health challenges. He simply had to change his own thoughts and beliefs. He had to reconnect with his greater self and relearn certain lessons. By changing himself, his health and life improved.

Prof. B: I think part of what I've learned from our sessions is feeling how great it felt to be strong in those other lives, and to feel love in an intense way. Now that I know how that felt, I need to feel it today too. In the morning, I'll think that I want to feel like Henry, to really see people around me, and see life, and feel powerful, dense love all around my heart. If you've never felt it, you don't know what to ask for, you don't know how to try to tap into it. That's why sometimes I'm talking to people that need this change and say: "Please look into this therapy, try this. This takes some time as a mental process, and then as a feeling process, but it's amazing."

For too long Ben had invited and perpetuated the energy of anxiety, self-pity, sadness and depression into his life. Reviewing these parallel, past lives helped him make new choices about how he wanted to feel in his current life.

Healing begins from the soul level. The body is a mirror of the soul. When the subconscious wounds are healed, the physical being feels the relief as well. But in order to heal, we need to increase our awareness and vibration and align ourselves with the higher levels of our consciousness. There are people whose early-stage cancer has been resolved by modern medicine, but then they developed another form of cancer because the real cause had not been resolved. The wounds of the soul were not healed. Many of us are looking for the "easy" way out, however no medicine will remove the root cause. No medicine or surgery procedure will heal the wounds of our souls.

Prof. B: I'm feeling really lucky! I just wish people would look into this because what they seek it's not "out there, somewhere," like I used to think. It's a feeling of wellness and contentment...

Dr. G: ...that comes from within.

Prof. B: Exactly. Trying to go somewhere else, changing the job or the house or the relationship because you want to feel different is not the answer. "Why am I not content and happy?" It's all just here. (Ben put his hand over his heart). But I think you need some kind of guidance to remember and feel it… And you know, it seems like there has been a sequence to what I've seen so far. Brian's life, with the feelings of sadness, depression and suicide… and then those feelings totally disappeared after seeing it. It was like: "Let this go. This is not you." Then Henry's life and the sense of being someone who really felt his power, his love for life so strongly. That was such a powerful feeling that I hadn't felt in my whole life. I had always been searching while feeling a little bit empty and frantic. But I wanted to feel about life like Henry did. I think that's what I've been building in this process, trying to feel more of that power. And then the Roman soldier's life I saw, this big leap to do something worthwhile, this incredible love… It was like having a glimpse of what the Christ energy felt like. It was amazing… The therapists I went to see before didn't know what was really wrong with me. They would give me medication and help me think through a lot of things, but with them it was never like: "Done! Feel awesome! Love life!" I want to tell them that if they have patients like me, maybe this regression analysis is something they could suggest for them. It's like you could go twenty years to psychotherapy and you would get this much of it, (Ben measured a small increment with his thumb and index finger) but through regression the relief was powerful and instant. It felt like poof, wow! That's how it felt.

Dr. G: Psychotherapy has its own therapeutic value because it addresses the conscious mind. In regression therapy and analysis you access subconscious memories and your soul's deep-seated beliefs and feelings. After that, you can analyze them as they surface in your conscious awareness. It's the power of personal experience versus information and knowledge. First comes the reliving of the subconscious memories or experiences through feelings, and then comes the conscious realization aspect. "Heart, teach my mind!"

Prof. B: That's the difference: it's feeling it! The psychotherapist asked me to meditate. I would meditate and hyperventilate because I didn't know how it should feel. He said, "You need to be calmer." And my question was "But how do I stop the anxiety? How do I make things stop?"

The soul, the subconscious, teaches valuable lessons to the conscious mind, just as Professor Ben has experienced the therapeutic value of his lives as Brian, Henry and Romanus. Through regression therapy he was guided to release the sadness, anxiety and depression. He also learned the true meaning of deep meditation. Modern medicine attempts to treat these types of disorders through medication and talk therapy, but after trying everything that is recommended, many patients discover that for them none of this really works. By relying so much on medication and ignoring the subconscious mind, this approach really forces people to redirect their focus inward. In my opinion, the medicine of the future will have very little to do with medication and very much to do with focusing within. It will have a lot to do with rediscovering and using our innate healing abilities by reconnecting with our higher nature, the Light and Home. The vibrational frequency of our energy determines our physiology and everything we feel and experience.

Prof. B: I've been wondering what this will mean for my life. I mean, Henry was so loving and centered, and he really saw everyone around him. I didn't feel it before in my life and that was good for me to feel. But he didn't *do* anything with that feeling. Same with the Roman soldier. He was saying, "I don't know what to do now. I can't go back to where I was. I'm different. I don't know if I follow Jesus..." That's kind of how I feel. Everything is different now, but what am I supposed to do with it?

Dr. G: Romanus found a way. He built churches with other Christians.

Prof. B: Yes. I guess he did use his power. At the end of his life, he was so happy because he had felt of service by helping spreading the word and building churches. So now I don't want to just say, "I'm so much happier, so much stronger, so much more loving. I love my kids, and it's so much fun to be with my wife and family, and my work is so much better," and I just sit there with it, like Henry did.

This loving, balanced and peaceful emotional state is our natural state of being. By being connected with our true nature—the flow of positive energy of the universe—all the people around us benefit, without us realizing it consciously.

Prof. B: I already feel such a difference with my kids. What will that mean for them to go through these years with a father who's loving and patient, instead of a father who is depressed, and was not even sure if he wanted to have kids? That has to be a huge difference, including for everybody that they will touch in their lives.

Professor Ben was now experiencing a higher vibration version of his life. He changed the energy in his body by improving his thoughts and feelings, which led to his healing and changing the energy in his house. He had become a source of positive energy in his environment causing a chain reaction. The change in him caused a ripple effect, like when you skip a stone onto a pool of water, except it is a pool of energy. Raising our own vibrational frequency forms energetic ripples that touch the lives of the people around us, raising their vibrational frequency as well. Each of us is a thread in the infinite tapestry of life impacting the other threads, and in turn, they impact others, and so on.

Prof. B: I feel very thankful for this change and for my kids. They seem so much more loving and happier. I feel so much energy, so much love of life. I don't remember feeling this as an adult. I used to feel this a long time ago, as a child. I feel like I was born again, like I was given a second chance.

Through this therapeutic, self-discovery process Professor Ben has received one of the most precious gifts anyone can receive—the gift of healing.

I gave Ben the opportunity to directly address you, the readers of this book, and the following is what he wanted to say to you.

Prof B: I remember feeling nervous about accessing what I thought of as "the spirit world" or "the other side," since I was raised as a Christian. It conjured ideas about opening avenues for the devil or evil spirits to get in. Looking back, my experience could not have been more opposite from my concerns. It was filled with love and peace. I think God used this path to reach me and heal me. These three months of recovery were a positive, loving process, in which I felt guided to reflect on the lives I've experienced in order to find the lessons for my current healing. I feel so thankful to God and Jesus that I have had these powerful, amazing, life-changing experiences. I feel happy and peaceful, and I'm no longer afraid of my life, but instead look forward to every day. I not only, finally, feel like my true self, but also have noticed what a difference the changes in me have made for my family and my work.

Professor Ben's journey of healing was truly remarkable. In those ancient times, Ben's soul had taken part in the movement that elevated humanity's collective consciousness in such an amazing way. And here Ben was, about 2,000 years later, breaking the barriers of time, space and human limitations, to be touched again by the same movement, by the same love energy, in such a direct and powerful way through the regression process. Ben needed to have this personal experience, to *feel* the love in order to heal, and remember that he is a part of that same energy, that God is in him as well. What a difference firsthand experience makes as opposed to what can be learned from the knowledge exposed by others.

Ben reconnected with his higher consciousness, learned to love himself thoroughly, and achieved peace of mind and emotional balance. His health was restored with no medication, and he began enjoying his life as never before. What we call "the past" has changed his present.

What Ben does from now on will decide his "future," which will be as bright as he makes up his mind for it to be.

Ben has sent you through this book the same message his soul learned twice directly from Jesus—the message of the power of love and positivity. Love saved the same soul in both lives (as Romanus and Ben), and gave Ben his life back. Perhaps one of the purposes of Ben's life was to share his story with you, to show you what love can do; to prove through his own experience that love is all you need, that love truly heals everything.

SPIRITUAL MASTER'S INSIGHTS REGARDING MIA'S SPIRITUAL EVOLUTION

When I returned to my conversation with Mia's Spiritual Master, he shared with me that he took Mia to the River of Life, and told her to call on whomever she wanted to talk to.

SM: She is speaking with one of her soul mates.

Dr. G: It's very interesting that you can both talk to me and to another soul at the same time.

SM: It is essential for all of you to come Home because you wonder about this things and ask me all of these questions but you can only fully understand the answers through personal experience. This brings comprehension at a much higher level. It doesn't help much if you ask me certain questions and your human mind cannot conceive or understand the answers. Mia sees what is here, but when she gets out of this state she forgets most of it. She can't cognitively process many things we discuss. It will just take a while because she doesn't yet have the capacity to understand everything. But she is starting to perceive. Through her work with you, she has begun to understand her present difficulties, and she is now aware of the unfavorable decisions she has made.

After saying my good-byes to the Masters and bringing Mia back to her conscious state, she described what she remembered from her journey Home.

MIA'S REVELATIONS

M: This time I spoke with an ex-boyfriend whom I cared for very much. We only talked about our friendship, not our grievances. We took a walk in a tropical paradise that had such a beautiful sun. It was an elevated area from which we could see bluish-green, crystalline water. You could walk down to it but we didn't. The vegetation was exotic, extremely beautiful and vividly colored. It was very beautiful there.

As you are probably noticed, even though Home is a nonphysical universe, it can be perceived as a physical, Earth-like realm and it feels very real.

M: Initially, I went to the River of Life. I love it at the River. It's really beautiful at the Tree of Life, but for some reason I like it better at the River. It looks exactly like a river of water, but it's not actually water. It's a river of energy made out of the flickers of souls. It's very interesting and beautiful. But there's no one around or I don't know how to perceive others yet... You know what is the weirdest thing? It's like a debate inside me. My conscious mind refuses to believe that I can do these things. It's as though it's too hard for it to comprehend what is going on. I *know* that I'm living these experiences, that they either really happen or I dream them. You tell me that I speak, that I am there, and you record all of the sessions so I can listen to them. What's on the recordings coincides with the images in my mind, but it's still hard for my conscious mind to believe that this is really happening.

Mia had accessed latent abilities that we all have, and they were surfacing in her conscious awareness. We are all equipped to perceive what is beyond the physical, to connect with the Light, communicate and exchange information, and we do it all the time. We shift every single day and night into our higher levels of awareness. But most of us are simply unaware of this. In fact, most human beings experience continuous discordance between the conscious and subconscious aspects of the mind.

The conscious mind is not only the analytical, reasoning faculty, but also the critical part of the mind—the egoic mind. It is a construct based on beliefs and perceptions, and it's limited to the physical reality. It wants to be in control, to understand, analyze and categorize everything, and it shapes our definition of reality. It is formed in childhood according to the education and cultural beliefs we received, it's molded throughout the years, and will cease to exist when the physical body dies. Since it was created in childhood, the conscious mind is not aware of what happened to us before it formed, and will not know anything after the physical body dies, when the soul—the subconscious—returns Home, carrying with it all the information (energy) we have acquired in this life.

Additionally, the conscious mind doesn't know what happens during sleep except when we become lucid during dreams, when we become observers at the conscious level of our soul's experiences (process called "lucid dreaming"). The conscious mind is just a tool that helps us function in this physical reality. It has a tendency to not accept as "real" anything it has not experienced directly (which includes anything that happened before it was formed, and what happens when it's not fully present, such as during dreams). That's why it's so difficult for this part of the mind to accept the concept of past lives, future lives and parallel lives, or the fact that we have the ability to access Home and communicate with whomever we wish while outside of its "jurisdiction." It tries to deny or discredit the experiences we had while in higher states of awareness, since it was not in full control there and in different moments it wasn't even present. Thus, it's understandable why Mia's conscious mind had difficulty accepting what she can do in the subconscious and higher self states of awareness.

Many of our problems arise from the discordance that comes from the controlling, egoic, skeptical aspects of the conscious mind, struggling against the wisdom, experience and positivity of the subconscious and higher self. It's up to us to decide which part we want to nourish. When all the levels of the mind become positive and vibrate in unison we achieve inner balance and peace. This balance is reflected in our lives as the healing of diseases, happiness and harmony, and experiencing the reality we desire.

THE MYSTERIES OF CONSCIOUSNESS

To help Mia better understand her experiences in the elevated state of awareness, I shared with her the analogy the Spiritual Master had given me during one of her previous visits Home.

Dr. G: It's as if when you have a computer that isn't working properly anymore. Before it completely crashes, you save your files in an external drive where you've been storing the information from all of your other computers. When you purchase a new computer it has no personal information in it, right? As you start using it, you download information from the internet (for example) and you save it to this new computer. This process is analogous to developing your conscious mind by acquiring and storing information from the ocean of people's thoughts and beliefs (the internet in this example). But your new computer still wouldn't have any information from your old computers, meaning from your previous lives. That information is stored in the external drive, which is at Home. It is what people call the Akashic or ethereal memories or records. In order for you to access the information stored in your external drive, you have to connect your new computer to the drive, from which you can then download and store the data on your new computer. To complete the analogy, the information you store in your new computer (brain) is usually what you will remember consciously when you come out of hypnosis. Hypnosis is the process by which we connect with the higher levels of our mind.

M: When I enter the state of relaxation or hypnosis, and pass through the Light to get Home and be with my Spiritual Guide, I know where I am, but I don't remember what you discuss with Marc. At the same time I feel very relaxed.

Dr. G: When I talk to him, the information he gives me comes from a different external drive—*his* drive, his higher self or spirit consciousness. In this case, it's as if you've connected your new computer, your brain, to someone else's hard drive. I have access to him and his external drive through your computer. I have access to the knowledge he chooses to share with me from his external drive, but this knowledge is not going to be stored onto your computer. When my conversation with the Spiritual Master ends, he disconnects his drive and takes his files with him. Good thing I record everything! When you come back to your conscious state of awareness, you download into your computer (brain) your own files with the memories you acquired on your own while I spoke to your Guide. For example, at the end of this session, you brought with you the memories of your visit with your friend, your soul mate. You have saved these new files in your brain, and now you can access them whenever you choose to. But you won't be able to access the information the Spiritual Master shared with me because it was never saved to your computer. We can also run different programs on one computer at the same time. That's what may be happening when Iam talks to me and simultaneously has a different conversation with you as well.

M: That's a great analogy! It makes everything easier to understand.

There is another important aspect. In early childhood, when we begin downloading the information we choose from internet, the vast ocean of information (basically people's beliefs and definitions in this example)—some of the information may contain viruses. Negatively-oriented and disempowering thoughts and beliefs are just like computer viruses, and our computer (brain) begins operating from these negative belief systems. The more of these viruses we have or the more powerful they are, the more they disturb the entire functioning of our computer (brain) and manifest as depression, suicidal thoughts, anxiety, phobia, insomnia, nightmares and diseases. In the worst situation, those viruses can even crash our computer, resulting in suicide.

Hypnotherapy basically helps clear up people's computers (brains) of viruses (negatively-oriented belief systems), and download healthier information—positive and empowering ideas. Some people like to use the term *Informational Medicine*.

M: When I come back to my conscious state, I feel extremely rested. I feel very happy, and I can't tell you in what an incredibly positive way this therapy has changed my life.

Mia had done a wonderful job of being willing to do whatever it took to actively participate in her recovery. Client's attitude is crucial because many people expect doctors and therapist to work miracles on them without making any effort of their own. Mia had reached the stage in which she was a conscious participant in the creation of her experiences. She was not just carried along by the waves of life anymore.

MIA'S TRANSFORMATION

M: When you have that self-awakening, you leave aside those things that most human beings run after, such as money. Money isn't a priority for me anymore. And I'm not interested in looking great. It's just a matter of soulful contentment if I look in the mirror and I like what I see. And those around me seem to perceive me in the same way. It's a matter of attitude and the energy that I'm exuding.

The majority of people who have had near death experiences, who entered the Light and spoke with their Spiritual Guides or relatives that had passed on before them, report experiencing the same transformation that both Mia and Professor Ben have described. Their priorities in life have changed, their understanding of life is more profound, and they now treasure those things that money cannot really buy.

M: The way I feel it's just fantastic! Not only do I feel optimistic, but I feel inner contentment and joy. I think I've reached inner balance. If someone says something negative I would just laugh as if they were joking. In the past, when someone said something negative to me, it would stay in my mind and I'd get upset. Now I take it as a joke. It doesn't even register that the person was trying to be serious. And I've noticed that even if something "negative" happened to me, it was for my own good, and it had to happen to me for me to become stronger. And I've noticed that, in fact, everything has two sides: a positive and a negative.

Every situation in life is basically neutral and we always have the option of choosing whether to perceive it from a positive or a negative perspective. We are the ones who assign meaning to situations, and according to our perception, we experience different emotional states. Mia, for example, had chosen to perceive a "negative" comment with a positive perspective, and she experienced good feelings—a positive outcome for her. If she had chosen to take such a comment as an offense, that would have led to negative feelings. We are fully responsible for our state of being, and consequently for our health. As Buddha said, "Every human being is the author of his own health or disease." Once we attain inner balance, we no longer see things from a negative perspective.

M: But it's a subconscious habit because I don't do it consciously. And my conscious mind had the tendency to say that I'm totally irrational.

Our negative ego will always think that it's not good to be relaxed and happy, that we should stress and worry about all sorts of life scenarios. The only way to get out of such disempowering patterns of thinking is by perpetuating positivity. The common denominator of the two worlds we belong to, the one from Earth and the one from Home is positivity. We achieve inner balance only when we choose positivity at all costs.

M: Only the thought of my Spiritual Guide, of what I experienced in that regression when I was his wife, gives me an unusual state of calmness. I can't even explain it in words. It seems that nothing bothers or upsets me in this life anymore. I feel very good. I feel happy and joyous, and it's as though everything works out better for me. I'm sincerely telling you that if I hadn't ended up on your couch to guide me in hypnosis, I wouldn't be alive today. I had reached rock bottom. I was hanging on by the last thread. You have performed a miracle on me. I feel extraordinarily well, confident in myself and overly optimistic to the point that my conscious mind says that maybe I'm being irrational! This whole transformational process is incomprehensible for my conscious mind.

CHAPTER ELEVEN

Following the Footsteps that Lead Toward Home

"Anyone who becomes seriously involved in the pursuit of science becomes convinced that there is a spirit manifest in the laws of the universe, a spirit vastly superior to that of man."
Albert Einstein

On her journeys Home, Mia, guided by her Spiritual Master traveled to the Tree of Life and the River of Life, and also saw a Waterfall. From these descriptions the question might reasonably arise: "What significance do these energetic "places" hold? The River of Life consists of nonphysical energies that are on their path toward reincarnation. Many of my clients have seen themselves traveling along with millions of others in the River of Life, in nonphysical form. Some of them have noticed, as they were exiting the River en route to their new lives, the "doorway" of communication between the upper and lower dimensions. They have described it as a whirlpool, tornado, spiral of light or spinning cloud of light.

The Tree of Life is an energetic "structure" where in the higher-self state of awareness we can consult with the Spiritual Guides and Masters. But what is the Waterfall? It seems to be made of energy, but what significance does it have?

A few weeks after our last meeting, Mia returned for another session. She continued to feel very good. Also, since I last saw Mia, I have had two more sessions with Julia who was very excited to tell me that she was pregnant. Julia was the interior designer who wanted to discover her life purpose, and who had previously reviewed lives as an American Indian man and as an Italian woman (Francesca) living in a fishermen's village. During the first of these two new sessions, Julia discovered the Waterfall and communicated with a very large and wise energy. It had been hard to determine whether the Waterfall and the large energy were the same or not. Our second session raised even more questions. I was glad that Mia had returned so that while she continued to explore the universe from Home, I would have the chance to clarify my questions with the Spiritual Masters.

Here is what happened in the first of the two new sessions with Julia.

JULIA'S EXPLORATION OF HOME

After attaining a state of deep relaxation, Julia went directly into the Light and beyond it, Home, where only positive energies coexist.

J: I see vibrations of green light, like ripples in water that are surrounding me. I see the silhouette of a face, a light… Now I see vibrations of red light.

Dr. G: Is that red light surrounding you or emanating from you?

J: I'm not sure. They're really soft, very faint glows of light, combinations of red and green, but in rhythmic waves and almost a milky color, yet distinct. Now I see vibrations of energy of some sort, very different from before, almost like sound waves, like they're being spread out… Now I see not water but just colors kind of falling into a umm… kind of a vacuum, sucking the colors into a hole. But it looks how water looks falling down a waterfall.

I realized that Julia was describing the Waterfall. I asked her what she looked like in that moment.

J: I'm not even in the same form of an essence, as before, but almost like a mist. I'm part of the mist. The mist is like clouds in a sense, but of vibration, some kind of energy. I'm like some kind of matter but with no defined shape. I can't see much of a form. It's almost like particles just vibrating in place. I see movement of colors everywhere. It almost feels like I'm moving in water. And now, I've come to a… some kind of a Source Energy that is not bright like the other ones. This energy is there but it's as if I can't get to it. It's not acknowledging me either. I have to say it's almost like it has its back to me. It's very large. I can't really tell because I feel like I'm at its base looking up.

I was intrigued. Julia seemed to be traveling in the River of Life toward this very large Energy Source after she had just seen the energy that looked like the Waterfall. Both seemed to be very large, so

could it actually be the same energy projecting different forms?
J: It's getting very dark. It reminds me of a rock… It's getting much brighter now. This is a very peaceful, flowing energy in front of me, very angelic. It's a movement of golden light, almost the gold color you see in fire, in sparks. It's like sparks of gold electricity, and it's right next to me, almost at my side but slightly above me. Now it looks more like a star… I lost it! I don't know where it went! I'm calling it back. It disappeared for a second. It looks a lot like a star, it's very strong. It's an essence but it's evolved, and it's a different shape.

Julia meant "a different shape" than the other Spiritual Guides she had seen in our previous session. It seemed that this large Energy Source that Julia was trying to engage in conversation was able to change its shape, the intensity of its light, and could even become invisible.

JULIA'S CONVERSATION WITH THE LARGE ENERGY SOURCE

I encouraged Julia to ask questions about her life purpose by sending them telepathically to this Energy Source, and to quiet her mind in order to perceive the answers.
J: It's definitely one of my main Guides. He says I have many Guides. He is saying I'm meant to find ways to feed the hungry. (Julia used the term "he" for lack of a better term since energies are androgynous.)
Dr. G: What kind of hunger is he referring to?
J: Famine. I see images of children crying, skin and bones, reaching out —a lot of despair. He is showing me pictures, images, diseases…

In this higher state of awareness people receive information in different ways. Mia had demonstrated the ability to telepathically receive information, see clearly, hear and transmit unaltered the information she accessed. Her conscious mind did not interfere at all. Julia received information both as images, which she described to the best of her abilities, as well as blocks of thoughts. I asked what the Energy looked like now.
J: He is still that star. Now he is taken the form of an angel. He is just these big wings. He is not keeping a single shape.
Dr. G: How can you accomplish your life purpose?
J: I have to stop being afraid. I have to trust people. My purpose is to help those people. He is saying that the people I'm meant to change the world with, that I'm meant to feed the people with, are already in my life. Situations are already unfolding but I have to be patient. I need to stay committed to one thing and listen to my instinct. That I already

have the answers I'm looking for, but I don't see them when they come because I don't trust. He is saying I still have too much fear and I disguise my fear with impatience. I need to practice quieting my mind, to stop trying to control the outcome of things and just let things happen. You are a Guide as well.

Dr. G: You are a Guide as well?

J: No. He is telling me that *you* are; that you were right.

Taken by surprise that the Energy Source was talking about me, my mind went instantly blank and instead of asking, "What was I right about?" I asked if Julia's purpose was connected to mine.

J: You're supposed to teach me to channel, to be more open. Our lives have crossed before. There are similarities in our purpose. You're a vehicle for many. You haven't evolved to your ultimate state yet, and you still have doubts as well. You still hold back. You doubt so you don't risk completely. Once you stop being afraid, you will acknowledge who you are.

My mind froze again. Not knowing exactly how to react I redirected the conversation.

Dr. G: Is your Guide talking only about literal famine or is it a metaphor for spiritual hunger?

J: It's connected but it's my spiritual connection more than theirs. I can feel in my heart that I'm meant to reach out; that I'm meant to create hope, to feed the hungry, to be their Guide. That's why I always feel empty and incomplete. I never risk enough to do anything of significance. Although I do touch the lives of people in my life, it's not my ultimate purpose because I'm made for healing of some sort, spiritual healing I guess. He is telling me I'm supposed to do some kind of healing with my hands as well. He says the wealth I'm seeking I will find sooner rather than later, and I'm assured to give it away to help heal, to help feed and shelter the hungry.

Dr. G: Can you please ask why souls choose to reincarnate into lives like those of the people in very poor areas where they starve and barely survive?

J: Souls who choose to reincarnate that way understand that they are an essence of an elevated spirit. They are here to teach compassion and gratitude, to teach humanity. My purpose is to expose others to compassion and humanity, and lead them to a higher sense of self. My journey is not to be made alone. I'm meant to be accompanied by many. That's how I'm meant to teach others, so in return they can teach others as well.

I have many times asked my clients the same basic questions to help them discover for themselves the answers. In addition to this process being helpful for the client, it is also an opportunity to track the consistency of information received from different Spiritual Masters and Guides. As you may have noticed, Julia accessed versions of the same knowledge Mia brought forth on various occasions. Next, I asked if souls live forever.

J: They continue and some reach an evolved state, but there is no "forever." There is no concept of time. There is only an evolution of the soul's Energy Source.

Dr. G: What exactly does it mean to be an evolved soul?

J: I guess it's like my Guide. He is an evolved Energy Source who is no longer following a pattern of existence and nonexistence. He is not in the flow anymore. He is with and of all other Sources, and he can still choose, but he is not in the flow.

What Julia meant by "no longer following a pattern of existence and nonexistence" is that this Energy Source is not reincarnating anymore. He had reached the elevated state that no longer requires rebirth and spiritual growth through physical life experience. The "flow" Julia referred to was the cycle of reincarnation.

J: He is not part of the flow anymore but I'm still part of the flow. He is an evolved Energy Source, still very much part of the same overall essence that all of us are. But he has an evolved purpose—he is a Guide for the other souls. The Guides are extensions of souls in a sense, always connected with The Source of All That Is. But not all souls become Guides. There are souls who continue their spiritual evolution without choosing this elevated purpose. The Guide's consciousness is more elevated because they exist at the same level of consciousness even if they choose to take a physical form. That means that even when they are in the physical form, they are still awake. Yes, beyond comprehension.

Thanks to the Masters I already knew what Julia meant. The Guides and Masters, as well as all of the other evolved souls, can choose to reincarnate with only a part of their energy while the other part can remain at Home, existing at the same level of consciousness— the higher self level. So they can choose to continue guiding other souls when part of their energy is reincarnated. If they decide to, they can even guide the incarnated part or parts of their own self.

Julia continued revealing that there are many Guiding Sources but not many others above their level of progress. I asked her what the ultimate level of evolution was.

J: I guess what people call God. That's the only way I can describe It. He says that we're all part of God, together and separate. There is no dimension to It. God is more than essence. It is infinite. It is both part of the physical and the nonphysical, like both worlds combined. Everything physical and nonphysical is It.

Dr. G: What does God look like?

J: It doesn't have form. It is beyond that. It is whatever the physical mind can dream up, but the mind can never capture what It really is.

Dr. G: What is the purpose of life in the physical form?

J: To create, to learn, to experience, to live and to die. We are only a small fragment of life in the universe, and its energy flow keeps existing, just not in the form that we know.

Dr. G: Can souls die?

J: A soul is energy. It never disappears but in the physical form a soul can disconnect and deplete. The soul can, in a sense, almost die within the physical form. Lack of faith or a detachment from oneself is a detachment from the soul. The soul can detach from its physical form. The body doesn't necessarily die, but the soul depletes until it's almost nothing. Those humans are just empty.

Dr. G: If the soul depletes, can it, after the person dies, reach the Light and get Home?

J: That soul will have very weak energy. They're not able to reach their Guide or connect with the higher state of being in order to choose to go back into the flow and come back again in a physical form. Some of those souls just linger between the physical and essence.

Julia referred to the souls who don't go to the Light after their physical life ends—those that float in the ethereal field between the two dimensions. Some of them will eventually find a way to get Home helped by other souls while others will have their positive energy depleted or contaminated. They will probably end up in lower dimensions of existence where they will continue their process of evolution from that lower level of vibration.

J: There are those evolved souls who guide all of us if we are paying attention and listen—if we are open. They're guiding us daily when we choose. But they can't help if we're not open. They can hear our requests and guide us to manifest, but if we're not open and we don't listen, we will never see. We have to be open to receive. And they don't guide just one person, they guide many. So they're more receptive to those who call, who are open and willing. Sometimes you don't realize you're open but most people are to a certain degree. The Guides help us by sending messages through thoughts, dreams and the manifestation of desires. People like to call it luck. It's not luck. People like to call it coincidence. It's no coincidence. The Guiding Sources are part of the universe. People call it "universe responding to their desires."

JULIA'S INSIGHTS

After returning to her conscious state of awareness, Julia described her experience in this session.

J: There weren't any words. There were images, and then I felt as though he was just answering through me. We were kind of intertwined but I could still see him. It was this very strong gold light, like a star radiating out; a very solid and very old energy.

Dr. G: So it was a large energy?

J: Yes. It was a different kind of big energy compared to what I've seen before—like a larger kind of orb. This was different. It didn't have that same faint glow as the orbs do. This was just very powerful, very radiant, a very solid color, almost like the gold color in fire. It was a solid energy that looked radiant, like it pulsed. And I could feel my hands absorbing a lot of that energy.

Julia made me wonder: a large, very powerful, old, strong, wise, pulsating energy of a solid golden, radiant color that had the ability to become invisible and change form, with which Julia merged, and from which she was absorbing energy. What or who was this energy? It was an unusual description. None of my clients had described their Spiritual Guides or Masters this way. Was this energy the same as the Waterfall or was it something else?

J: When you were asking me about the ultimate being, I labeled it God because that's the word most people like to use. But It is beyond that. It was very interesting, very unusual, just like infinite space. There is no definition one way or another. I kept seeing images of both life and death together, earth and water, and fire and air. Those were the representations. It is everything, all in one. It is everything and It is nothing. That's why all these images were coming to me, but I couldn't define It because there is no definition. It is infinite. That is the only way I could describe It.

JULIA'S CONVERSATION AT THE TREE OF LIFE

During the second new session, I guided Julia directly to the Tree of Life and asked her to describe it.

J: I see beds of flowers surrounding a massive tree. But it's not a tree the way we know trees, made of wood and with leaves. It's just light, little veins of light coming together to make the Tree. I don't know where it ends and where it begins. It's almost as if there are veins of light, and it is life within them, streaming through them like how blood cells flow through our veins. It's all light. It's massive and has lots of branches. The glow of the lights makes it look like a tree with lots of leaves, but it's not. There are no leaves, there is no trunk, there is nothing. It's just in the shape of a tree made of little veins intertwined, thousands and thousands and thousands of them. And in each vein there are hundreds of thousands of different little lights equivalent to a life.

Dr. G: Now mentally call on your Spiritual Guides.

J: How do I call them?

Dr. G: Just call them mentally, "My Guides, I would like to talk to you."

J: (After almost a minute of silence) I see them.

Dr. G: What do they look like?

J: Just orbs of energy, orbs of light. There are seven or eight.

Dr. G: While you're talking to your Guides I would like you to recharge your energy with God's energy that is all around you. Just allow yourself to be in His energy fully and completely, and absorb it into your essence.

I did not know what this request would trigger. It was actually the first time I had formulated my direction in this specific way. What I meant was for Julia to relax and recharge her energy with the positive energy—God's energy—that I know is everywhere at Home. I didn't know that this request would open the door to a path I never even thought existed.

Dr. G: Also, ask your Guides if it's possible to call Mia's Spiritual Master as well.

I had never spoken with the Mia's Guide with the help of any other client, and I wondered if it was possible.

J: He is here. My Guide is at his right.

Dr. G: Please ask Mia's Spiritual Master if he would be willing to answer a few questions for us. And thank them for coming.

There was silence. Usually, Iam responds immediately with a greeting. Was this hesitation because Mia and Julia had different ways of perceiving information or were we speaking to a different Master?

THE CONCEPT OF LOVE

Dr. G: Let's begin with the concept of love. What's happening when we fall in love? Why do we have those strong feelings for each other?

J: Falling in love is not what you think it is. It's not without intention. It's the renewal of a connection that existed long before, in many lives over. It's the reincarnation of the connection between souls, and it doesn't happen by accident. It's a soul connection. Souls are connecting and reconnecting. The minute that you make the contact it ignites, but it is more than just what humans know love to be. It's more profound and is much more on the spiritual level. Some people mistake that soul connection with a notion of what they believe love is because they want to be in love; with what their perception is, their understanding of love is, what their desire is. But that is not the true connection.

HOME

Dr. G: Could you please describe the universe we come from, our souls' home?

J: It's not a physical world, it's nonphysical. It's evolved and very well organized. It's a rhythmic balance of life's Source Energy. The sensations you experience are calm vibrations and balance. Home feels like you are the puzzle piece that found its fit, serenity and completion within your soul. Like you are a plant that found its proper garden and can now grow for all the benefits the Earth can give. Here you are safe, you are protected and sunshine is upon your face. You can only be beautiful. The vibration is simplistic, untainted, flowing, rhythmic, balanced and organized. The vibration levels all vibrate together. And there are no in-between steps, no stages, just greater degrees of connection.

Dr. G: What attributes do souls who reach the highest levels of evolution have?

J: It's difficult to describe. You're the holder of the rhythm. You become the rhythm through which all the other energies flow. You become the vessel that everything flows within. It's the ultimate elevated state.

Dr. G: They really are Light Keepers, aren't they?

J: That's what I was talking about. They became more of a Source that sustains all other energies and life sources. They become the fiber-energy that holds it all together and keeps it in existence.

Dr. G: Do you keep your identity as you get closer to the Source?

J: The closer you get to the Source, the less individual identity you have. Essentially, you're reaching out to wholeness. Once you become part of the Source there is no identity, no definition and it's eternal.

Dr. G: Please describe to me the River of Life.

J: It's like how the brain is, with many routes and turns. All essences—vibrational energies—flow together in the River of Life.

Dr. G: What else is at Home besides the Tree of Life and the River of Life?

J: Those are just forms in which you understand and interpret the connection between souls. There are many levels of vibration and evolution, and there are different passages, depending on where you flow from one "place" to another, where you go on your path.

Dr. G: What about the connection with our Spiritual Guides?

J: The connection with the Guiding Sources is always available but the human mind chooses not to see it. The mind gets blinded. It becomes impure, it denies, it forgets. So even though vibration will always exist, the level of vibration weakens when that happens.

Dr. G: Please talk to me about accessing previous lives.

J: Previous lives are the keys to fitting pieces of the puzzle together. Each piece helps complete the picture and has a goal linked to it. With each piece comes a learning experience, a lesson learned or a lesson that needs to be relearned leading to spiritual evolution. At Home you know everything. You know your direction and your purpose. But it's not decided *for you* when you go back to evolve and raise your vibration. *You* get to choose another opportunity to go to the next step; to go back to learn what you didn't learn, to evolve and master the next vibration. But you can also choose to forget because the human form is influenced by many things, and then you keep coming back trying to learn the same thing. It is possible to never achieve what you are trying to accomplish.

Dr. G: Are there places where souls can study, learn, create and experiment besides the physical form?

J: It's not like science laboratories. It's just a state of being. The physical life is the experiment. Part of your soul's purpose is to rediscover what you already know, and to create. You are part of the experiment. In a way, it's how you are writing your book. You inherently already possess the knowledge, but you require other vehicles to confirm it, like how a scientist has to prove what he or she already knows. You, in essence, are conducting your own experiment to confirm the knowledge, but you possess it within your consciousness. This is why we make contact because the time when humans used to know and trust is long gone. We are here to remind, to evoke and to guide to the place that once existed for you. The human mind at one point did not doubt. People knew within themselves with complete certainty, and allowed us to just be the vibrations that flowed through them. Things changed and humans are now clouded by the physical world around them. Our role is to present opportunities so they can see, but like I said, the physical world is an experiment and some choose to see and others not. Souls keep coming back, and they keep going out for the purpose of mastering their lessons. Unfortunately, just because they make that choice doesn't mean they will succeed…

However, humanity is waking up again. It's time! Spirituality will evolve again.

After a short pause Julia told me that the Guides were no longer there. As I guided her back to her conscious awareness, I realized that in a way this amazing conversation has been different than the ones I usually had with the Spiritual Masters through Mia's connection. Was it really Iam we'd been talking to?

JULIA'S INSIGHTS

J: First, I saw beds of flowers in a path. When I got to the Tree there was this massive energy form which was branching out. It was unbelievably massive! There were like little veins, all white. Everything was electrical. You know when you see blood cells flowing through veins in science videos? That's the way it was, but it was all energy, thousands and thousands and thousands going off like little branches, all over the place. It was unbelievable. And when you asked me to call the Guiding Sources, it was me in the center, and I was surrounded by a group of orbs. And when you called my Guide it came, and there was another big energy there. And this was the Guiding Source we were talking to.

"A big energy?" We had spoken with a big energy during our last session as well.

J: It was very clear. As you started talking and engaging him to answer your questions, it was as if they were spinning me and getting me closer and closer to him. And then he was me and I was him! He was slowly embracing me, bringing me to him. I felt as though I was spinning, and the next thing I saw was him spinning and coming around behind me and just merging. And the whole time he was communicating, I felt this pulsating vibration as if I was floating, as if I was in really intense vibration. It was rhythmic, like a pulsation. It was amazing and unusual.

I was even more intrigued by what Julia described. What or who was that large energy? Mia never described anything like that. I was certain that this strong, pulsating energy was not Mia's Spiritual Master. Last time we also talked to a very large, golden, pulsating energy. Was it the same energy? I knew that it was a positive energy. I had no doubt about that. As long as you are Home, beyond the Light, you are completely safe. At Home there are only positive energies, no matter who you access, and you would receive accurate information. Much depends on you and your ability to accurately understand and interpret the information presented to you. But who was this large, pulsating energy?

SPIRITUAL MASTERS' UNBELIEVABLE REVEALING

I was very glad that Mia returned for another session so I could get the chance to ask the Masters to elucidate this mystery. I directed Mia toward the Light and beyond it, to the Tree of Life or the River of Life wherever she wanted to go, and she quickly connected with the Masters. I expressed my joy at being able to speak with them again, and I asked if it was indeed Iam I had spoken with during the last session with Julia.

SM: No, it wasn't me. Did they say it was me?

Dr. G: I told Julia to call her Guides and after they came, I asked them to call you.

SM: I wasn't there.

Dr. G: Can you please take a look or call on Julia's Guides to find out who it was? Julia described it as a large Energy Source, much larger than the energies of her Guides. Her Guides had positioned themselves around her, and carried her toward that large Energy. The Energy enveloped her until they became one. During the entire time we spoke, Julia felt a rhythmic pulsation.

The Spiritual Master's answer came as a complete shock.

SM: Yes, indeed, I see it. Her Guides carried her close to Chi Energy.

I was speechless. My mind went instantly blank. It took a while to wrap my mind around this absolutely astonishing information. It never crossed my mind that such a thing would even be possible. I had a hard time finding my words.

Dr. G: It was Chi Energy? God?

SM: Yes, indeed. She was carried and passed through Chi Energy. I see it.

I couldn't believe it. I hadn't read anywhere that there was any technique to guide one to *directly* access The Source. And I might never have known that this energy was God Itself if I hadn't asked Mia's Spiritual Master. I asked him one more time to make sure I understood correctly.

Dr. G: So then who did I speak with? With Chi Energy, with God?

SM: Yes.

Dr. G: That's unbelievable. I received very interesting answers to my questions. I had the feeling it wasn't you because the communication was somehow different. This is extraordinary!

SM: Chi Energy is basically the energy that we all aspire to become one with.

Dr. G: I feel honored.

SM: You are very blessed.

I was completely taken by surprise. I had no idea that my request would actually bring God to our meeting. My request was taken literally by Julia's Guides, and they carried her to God so that she could be in his presence. In my mind I recalled my request: "I would like you to recharge your energy with God's energy that is all around you. Just allow yourself to be in His energy fully and completely, and absorb into in your essence." I had formulated my request this way because in my mind God is the highest evolved consciousness and ultimate healing energy. I didn't actually think that accessing and communicating directly with God was even possible. An idea emerged in my mind. Could I possibly repeat the results? Could I lead other souls to The Source with the same technique? While part of my mind continued processing the information, I again addressed Iam.

Dr. G: The first time you showed Mia the Tree of Life and the River of Life you also showed her a Waterfall. What is that Waterfall?

SM: It's Chi Energy, God.

So the Waterfall Julia had discovered during our previous session was Chi Energy as well. Could it have been the same energy that we communicated with during that session?

Dr. G: Julia saw herself going toward a Waterfall of colors. Afterwards, she saw a large, powerful, golden energy bright like a star, which had instantly become devoid of light and then bright again. We engaged it in conversation. Was that golden, angelic energy the same as the Waterfall, as Chi Energy?

SM: Yes, it was. It was Chi Energy you spoke with.

Dr. G: That's incredible. Julia felt that it was a very old and highly evolved energy. At one point she said that it was one of her Spiritual Guides.

SM: Yes, because Chi Energy can be everyone's Spiritual Guide.

Dr. G: Before seeing the Waterfall, Julia saw vibrations around her. I don't know if they were emanating from her or if they were coming to her. She saw green and red vibrations in circular waves.

SM: It was simply her own vibrational frequency. They were emanating from her.

Dr. G: What impact did these sessions have on Julia from your perspective?

SM: They certainly had a positive impact on her. They helped her grow spiritually, understand more, and open her soul towards what's at Home.

Julia later told me that the sessions we had together in which she had such profound experiences of euphoria gave her a level of peace she never knew before. It gave her great comfort to finally make a different level of connection with herself and even her unborn child. Up until that point she was still at odds with her sense of spirituality because she could never allow herself to connect with her soul, what she now knows is her elevated consciousness. She would always find herself deferring to some *rational* or *logical* explanation of having constant series of coincidences at critical moments in her life, and resisting this greater energy that guided her. After our sessions, there was no question for her if there truly is a Source that guides her because she has seen and connected with It. As a result, even her skeptic self no longer doubted.

Julia's journey of exploring her subconscious universe had cleared up a lot of her personal unknown and it has been a gift to be reassured of some of the subconscious truths. She has received a sense of clarity regarding her purpose, and can now more easily trust her inner guidance. She now knows that when things happen almost magically, it's not a coincidence.

SM: The fact that Julia managed to get in such contact with Chi Energy is a wonderful thing. You will succeed in communicating with Chi Energy again, which is... I cannot begin to tell you how blessed you are because guiding people the way you do to access Chi Energy had never happened before in the history of mankind.

I couldn't find my words. I felt as though I stepped into a different reality in which connecting consciously with The Source was actually possible. Guiding other people to experience what God, The Source of Life is instantly became my goal. Even though I had a hard time getting my thoughts together, I continued asking questions.

HOW IS THE UNIVERSE OF HOME STRUCTURED?

Dr. G: How would you describe the infinite universe we, as souls, come from, so that a human mind can understand?

SM: I'm not sure you can understand if I tell you in words. You understand when you are here. Home is not a world that fits the patterns and settings of any science or religion. It's beyond the rules and settings made by humanity.

Dr. G: So as you've said before, it's an existential universe located beyond time and space that is very difficult to perceive with the human mind and senses.

SM: Correct. And what is at Home doesn't have earthly sentimental implications either. Everything is completely altruistic. Here is The

One without beginning and without end, Alpha and Omega, God, Chi Energy, The Creator, The Source of Life. Here we are all, in a sense, Gods because we are all Chi Energy. A description does not exist that the human mind can understand. And it's probably not yet allowed for humans to perceive what is here.

Dr. G: What do you like to do most there?

SM: It's very difficult for me to describe in words in a way you can understand. You have a completely different notion about free time. Here there are no rules, no limitation, no time, no numbers and no speed. Here, we are not humans in physical bodies concerned with filling our time and staying busy. Here there is no time, and there are no rules that would be similar to the earthly justice because everything is in perfect harmony. But we all have a role. For example, what I do is give my agreement for those who want to reincarnate and help them grow spiritually. And also, when someone decides to return from a physical life, I must know about it. But that doesn't mean I'm the only one who knows. Everyone at Home knows, not just Chi Energy or me, or those from that soul's plane of existence. We all know, and we all rejoice when someone returns. I don't have control over what happens on the levels above me, above the Masters, but I have control of, and know everything that happens with all the spiritual energies up to my level of evolution. I know everything about them: when they decide to reincarnate into physical lives, what they do there, and when they return Home either temporarily or permanently.

Dr. G: When you evolve to the next level, what would that level be?

SM: I can choose to either reunite directly with Chi Energy, or to remain on that high level. But when you reach a very high level of evolution, it doesn't depend on you anymore when you advance to the next level. You don't decide when you reunite with Chi Energy. Until you reach that high level, yes, it depends on you. Chi Energy decided that, for now, I'm still needed here on this level.

Dr. G: What attributes or functions do the highest evolved spiritual energies have at Home?

SM: Their functions are to maintain the organization and hierarchy we have here, so that Home doesn't collapse; to maintain the mode in which the universe of Home functions.

Dr. G: Can you tell me a few words about the highest evolved souls?

SM: Buddha, Jesus, Krishna, Muhammad and the other highly evolved energies on their levels, are teachers that promoted the teachings about God at the level of human consciousness that existed in their times. There was not that much openness toward the world from Home in their days. They are truly extraordinary evolved energies, and they represent the consciousness of love. They continue to exist, in this moment, as Buddha, as Jesus, as Krishna, as Muhammad in those respective lives, in planes of existence that are parallel with your current life. That which their souls represent is simply impossible for the limited, conscious, human mind to conceive and understand, or for your mind's eye to see.

Dr. G: To get an idea of the size of these highly evolved souls, please tell me, if one of them, let's say Krishna, wanted to reincarnate and divide his energy into as many people as he could, into how many human beings could he reincarnate on Earth?

SM: He could reincarnate into all the people on planet Earth and he could still have energy to reincarnate on other planets.

Dr. G: That's amazing. What can you tell me about the concepts of heaven and hell?

SM: Heaven and hell, which are so deeply implanted in the human consciousness, do not exist outside of you. The state of bliss and love that you sometimes feel is the heaven, and the moments of despair and depression are the hell.

Dr. G: Is Home the closest thing to the heaven we dream of?

SM: It's a kind of heaven but that word is too limited. It's *Home*. The word heaven cannot define what Home is. It cannot describe the magnitude of this infinite universe. It's *Home*.

TRUE LOVE

Dr. G: Let's talk about love.

SM: The concept of love is understood incorrectly in your time. Love is not what you believe it to be, as you define it in the physical plane because many of you are driven only by worldly pleasures. You see the love through your human eyes, not through the eyes of your soul. Look within a person, not at their physical appearance. True love, pure love is unconditional, which means you love without asking for love in return. Every single lifetime teaches you good lessons. Every life is a great opportunity to learn to love unconditionally. Even if someone hurts you deeply, beyond human feelings you have to offer love. That is the kind of love that we have here, at Home. People in love have a connection not only in the physical plane, but also beyond the earthly dimension. It's a connection at the spiritual level. It is possible that the love people feel for one another has come from a previous life where they were unable to be with each other. Therefore, they may have decided that in this life they will go beyond what happened before. Often, feelings of abandonment are rooted in scenarios in which one of them died earlier. If those two people find each other in the physical plane, they have the chance of overcoming the previous life's barriers. Usually, people who have a connection at the energetic level are drawn to each other and feel good in each other's presence. There are people whose souls vibrate on high energetic levels, and there are people whose souls vibrate on lower levels. There are people with whom you have connections at the energetic, spiritual level, and those who just pass through your life. The energy is very powerful when twin flames or soul mates find each other. Each person you come in contact with teaches you a lesson of life. The most important consideration in relationships is to open your eyes and receive love, affection and everything that is good from that person. And when I say to open your eyes, I'm not referring to your physical eyes because those you already opened in the moment you established the friendship. I'm referring to the mind's eye. Let your soul receive whatever the friendship can offer; the memories to be remembered with love, and view those who have hurt you with forgiveness and unconditional love. To love is the most important thing you can do.

MIA'S INCREDIBLE EXPERIENCE

Dr. G: What is Mia doing this time?
SM: She wants to see what Chi Energy is, so I'm going to take her there.
Dr. G: You mean you're going to take Mia to God?
SM: Yes. She is curious to experience God. Although she is not yet at those ultimate levels of vibration, Chi Energy will welcome her because Chi Energy doesn't put limits or barriers.

I was very… I don't even have a word to describe what was going through my mind as these unbelievable situations cascaded over me in less than half an hour. My mind was barely keeping up with this amazing and unexpected new possibility that presented to me and my clients.
Dr. G: Great, let's do it! I would like to ask you both to describe this experience to me. First I would like Mia to describe everything that she perceives as you get there.
M: We're going to the River of Life and we've entered the "water." I'm asking Marc to stay with me. We're in the River and now I see the Waterfall. It's like a magnet that draws us.

This was very similar to Julia's experience. Julia felt as if she was going through water before she arrived at the Waterfall.

M: It's such a state of well-being, joy, lightness and laughter! But it's not really a Waterfall because there is no mountain it's falling from. It's just like a majestic artesian fountain. It's very tall and it seems to have a lot of water. But it's not water; it's energy. And it beautifully changes colors. It has all colors but now it's predominantly violet… I'm still in the River, but it doesn't wet me. I just feel the pleasant sensation of being in water. We are drawn into Chi Energy… It feels like electromagnetic impulses, like tingling sensations.

Dr. G: Ask Iam what those impulses are?

M: He says they are the energy of God. We're inside! We've been pulled into the Waterfall… It's a complete feeling of ecstasy, very difficult to explain, a feeling beyond words; a sublime and supreme love, a happiness that you rarely experience. A feeling of complete fulfillment, of gratification, a constant feeling of ecstasy… I also feel an implosion and explosion at the same time. (Julia described that feeling as a rhythmic pulsation.) It's really amazing! Now it looks like a spiral of all the possible colors and I'm carried up and down. It looks like a kaleidoscope with all the colors and forms. It can take any form and color, there is no limit here. I feel like I'm carried up and down by the breath of the wind but there's no wind in here. And all these sparkles of colors of light have geometric forms but they're so small, like sparks of fire. And I'm even smaller than them, maybe a hundred times smaller, and I see everything with a superb intensity. I feel the energy like a heat wave that carries me up and down. But somehow I don't hit any of those sparks of light. They appear to be in free fall, and none of them hit each other. Everything is perfectly organized.

Dr. G: Please ask Iam what those sparkles of light are.

M: They are the energy of all the spirits who have merged with Chi Energy, and are now part of God. Visually, everything is so powerfully illuminated in diverse fluorescent colors that it simply takes you beyond reality. It's extraordinary! Now it looks like a light that's transparent and opaque at the same time. It's always swirling, it's in constant movement, like it's pulsing. (How amazing! Julia used the same words *"swirling"* and *"pulsation."*) You feel like it's an energy inside of you that somehow disperses your "energetic body" and causes you to explode in the light. You become like an explosion of love. You become one with God. And you feel and experience God's love.

Dr. G: That is amazing.

M: God is asking me, "What do you want from this life?" I tell God that at the moment, I feel so pleased and satisfied on all levels that I think He offered me more than I deserve in this life.

Dr. G: What did God say?

M: He is laughing. He is asking me, "Are you sure there is nothing you desire?" I answered that I don't have any material desires, and spiritually I feel happy, so what more could I ask for?

Dr. G: That's beautiful.

M: I could say that here, you reach the state where you no longer desire anything. Everything you think of or desire is instantly satisfied. You don't feel like you could want anything. You're not thirsty, you're not cold, and you're not hot. You don't feel anything except a state of bliss and complete fulfillment. You don't even want to be with anyone. It's all at maximum bliss. It's a feeling very difficult to describe in words... Now I see some small white particles like they could be snow, lots of snow. I miss snow. But they're not cold and they're all coming toward me! And I'm so small. It's superb, it's fantastic! I feel that I'm one with God! I don't want to leave.

Dr. G: Mia, I would like to talk to Iam. Iam, could you please describe Mia's experience from your perspective?

SM: Mia is having an extraordinary experience. Chi Energy welcomed her, and enveloped her in love, and made her feel not only unique, not only special, but *one* with God. The sentiments she feels are difficult to explain. They are feelings of total ecstasy. Such an experience is very hard to describe. It's a feeling that you want to live forever, and you never ever get tired of. Mia is like a bottomless cup that you try to fill with water, but no matter how much water you pour into it, you will never fill it up. That's how she basically feels. And at the level of the mind's eye it's an explosion of unimaginable colors, like a spiral of all colors. These colors ultimately transform into immaculate white.

Dr. G: Iam, could you please describe what you feel in Chi Energy as a spirit?

SM: The beauty that you feel on the spiritual level is magnificent. It's beyond the power of perception of a human being. There is no greater pleasure than to unite with Chi Energy. As a spirit you feel far beyond the human senses. It can't be described in words. It has to be experienced to understand it. This is actually your challenge as human beings, to find a way to access Home and Chi Energy; to find this state of absolute bliss that you can take with you, and that will help you heal emotionally and elevate vibrationally. We are all Chi Energy. Chi Energy would not exist without you, without me, without all the human beings' souls, without Buddha, Jesus, Krishna, Muhammad and without all the souls of the higher dimensions... Now Mia has to detach because she is not yet at this level of vibration.

Dr. G: Thank you very much for this incredible experience and for everything.

SM: We love you all! Goodbye.

The extraordinary experience both the Spiritual Master and Mia described is called in Hindu philosophy *the state of Nirvana*. It is described as being achieved through the union with the Brahman (God). To be honest, I never thought that one could experience this ultimate state of being in human form.

MIA'S REVELATIONS

After I brought Mia back and gradually collected herself, she had just a few words to say. She was visibly moved by this astonishing experience. How could one not be?

Both Mia and Julia had traveled through the River of Life to get to The Source, which both perceived as a very large Waterfall of colors. Both had felt, while being inside of God's energy, a rhythmic pulsation, and described that they had become one with God.

M: Being in God's energy is something that you cannot even imagine. It's very difficult to describe those extraordinary feelings. Those are feelings you don't get experience as a human being... There was complete silence and tranquility like in deep meditation. The colors I saw were amazing, fluorescent and simply indescribable. I can't find the words to describe this experience... Tomorrow I will be like new. In my case, the idea of *God* has changed. I no longer have that religious indoctrination about God. I feel so blessed, it's extraordinary!

CHAPTER TWELVE

Home, the Ultimate Reality

"The only way you can conquer me is through love
and there I am gladly conquered."
Krishna

The next appointment with Mia took place almost exactly one year from our first appointment. Her progress from our work together was remarkable. She continued feeling balanced, happy and confident. Her depression, suicidal thoughts, anxiety, fears and fatigue had been completely gone for about seven months. Even her precancerous cervical lesions have disappeared. She was easily maintaining her ideal weight and a healthy lifestyle. Shortly, after guiding her to go beyond the Light to the Tree of Life or River of Life, I was able to talk to the Spiritual Masters directly, asking them to clarify certain aspects of parallel lives.

PARALLEL, SIMULTANEOUS LIVES. OMNIPRESENCE

As the Spiritual Masters have previously described, the previous lives, the present life or lives, and the future lives of a soul (as they are seen from our linear time perspective) are all parallel. Also, for the current life of every person on the planet there are an infinite number of possibilities, versions or alternatives, called *parallel lives* or *parallel realities*, which are also parallel and encompassed in one infinite plane. We basically shift from one version of life into another, as our vibration increases or decreases according to what we feel.

Dr. G: Iam, please correct me if I'm mistaken. When my present physical life ends, I will continue to exist in this life and in all the lives I have ever lived, which are, from the ultimate reality's perspective, occurring simultaneously. Is that correct?

SM: Yes.

Dr. G: So somehow, the energy of my spirit is *spread* (and I'm not sure if it's the right word) in all of my lives?

SM: Yes, and yet, the moment one of your physical lives ends and you come out of it, you return Home. You *are* at Home, but at the same time you exist in every single life of yours because you are a flux, a flow of energy. It's a concept that the human mind has difficulty perceiving. It's a characteristic souls have as Chi Energy, called omnipresence. In every moment you are living in all of your lives, which are parallel. And each life, and every moment of that life happens *right now* because actually time doesn't exist.

Dr. G: So for example, in Leonardo da Vinci's life he exists at the same time as Leonardo the baby, the child, the teenager, the adult, and as Leonardo in every moment of his life. But that life exists with the decisions Leonardo has already made.

SM: Right. And when you decide to reincarnate, you add another life. You can stop this cycle of temporary lives when you remain at Home. The lives you've lived up to that point continue to exist occur simultaneously. This reality is difficult for me to explain and maybe even more difficult for you to understand. You ask: "How can I, after coming out of a life be at Home but at the same time continue to exist in all of the lives I have ever lived?" The answer is "Because time does not exist, omnipresence exists." Each one of you is omnipresent.

It's a paradigm that is indeed difficult to imagine and understand. Quantum physicists use different terms, saying that consciousness is non-local. The Spiritual Master was right when he questioned if our conscious mind, limited to our physical reality, can even comprehend the concept of an unlimited universe, in which there is no time, space, number, beginning, end or limit. However, at the highest level of consciousness we are all familiar with these concepts, which characterize our own energy.

Dr. G: In other words, after I return Home and decide to reincarnate I enter another life that actually *already exists*?

SM: Exactly. I couldn't have said it better myself.

Dr. G: So I have already designed that life. It already exists and, moreover, I'm already functioning in it?

SM: That life is already sketched out but it's not active. When you step concretely into that life as energy, as consciousness, then you activate it. To give you an analogy, it's as though you have a daisy seed. You know what kind of seed it is, how the plant is going to look, yet you don't have the actual plant. You only have the seed. That is what your next life is: a seed. In order to have the plant, the daisy, you have to put the seed in the soil, water it, and it has to have light.

Dr. G: So only the lives you have already lived are active—the previous lives and the present life. The next lives exist, but they are not activated.

SM: Correct. And the present life and the previous lives stay active eternally. The next lives exist, but aren't activated because you first have to decide whether or not you want to reincarnate and live them.

THE SPIRIT AS AN ENERGETIC TREE

Dr. G: It seems to me that the spirit is a living energetic organism that is incarnated in infinite planes of existence, is evolving simultaneously as souls and physical beings in all of its lives, and is aware of all of those existences simultaneously.

SM: Yes. That's the spirit's energy.

Dr. G: I envision the spirit evolving simultaneously, in all of its lives, as an energetic tree with many leaves, and each leaf representing a life.

SM: You could not have described it more beautifully. And when you go in regression to access a parallel life from your past or future, you are actually *living* in that life. Your conscious and subconscious aspects of your mind extend from your current physical body and actually go into that parallel life.

Dr. G: So basically, through regression or a progression therapy the conscious and subconscious levels of our consciousness form a bridge between our current life and the parallel past or future life that we explore for the purpose of accessing information.

SM: Correct.

Dr. G: I see the spirit as this energetic tree with all of its lives unfolding at the same time, and its vibration in all its lives determines the overall vibration of that spiritual energy.

SM: Exactly. And the water the tree needs in order to grow represents spiritual knowledge and Chi Energy. You said it perfectly.

Dr. G: And when the wind blows and the leaves touch each other it's as in regression or progression when we access information from another life, from another plane of existence.

SM: Right, and when you grow vibrationally another leaf falls.

Dr. G: What happens to the life represented by that leaf?

SM: That life disappears, in the sense that it becomes much more difficult to access it through regression because you're becoming highly evolved as a spirit. At that point, you've already lived infinite lives and you're getting closer to Chi Energy. When all of your leaves fall, you merge with Chi.

Dr. G: How is that life more difficult to access?

SM: You need much more meditation at your conscious mind's level. It becomes more difficult to access that life because it remains at Home akashically, spiritually. You've probably noticed that there are lives some of your clients can't access. That is the reason.

Dr. G: As I understand, you as Guides and Chi Energy are able to see and know everything that happens to us, and you can access anyone's life. Who records everything that happens with us here, in this physical plane and everywhere else?

SM: It's the capacity of memory of Chi Energy within everyone that records everything. Everything works on Chi Energy. We're all made of the same Chi Energy "structure." We, at Home, can access any information and we can see absolutely everything at the Tree of Life and the River of Life. And Chi Energy—The Source—obviously holds all of the information as well.

HOME: THE TREE OF LIFE, THE WATERFALL AND THE RIVER OF LIFE

Dr. G: How would you describe those "places" where the universal mind with the souls' memories—the akashic memories—can be accessed? Some people in meditation or hypnosis perceive them as a library, others as a tapestry room, others as multiple computer screens, and so on.

SM: Those are images created at the human mind's level. There is nothing tangible or physical here.

Dr. G: Is there only one Tree of Life?

SM: There is only one Tree of Life and one River of Life.

Dr. G: How would you describe the Tree of Life? I understand that the River is a river of spiritual energies, but what about the Tree? And also, does the River nourish the Tree? Are souls passing through the Tree?

SM: On one side is the Tree of Life, in the middle is Chi Energy—The Source—and on the other side is the River of Life. Also, there are an infinite number of dimensions in which we exist at Home. When souls return Home after completing their physical lives, they pass through the Light and become pure again. Then, they pass through the Tree and deposit their life memories there. These memories can be also accessed from the River but they remain in the Tree. Then, if they choose to reincarnate, they enter the training program and then into the River of Life from where they pass into the earthly dimension. If they don't choose to reincarnate right away, they remain at Home in the dimensions they belong to according to their levels of vibration. The River does not nourish the Tree. Chi Energy is connected with both the Tree of Life and the River of Life. Basically, it's the energy that unites them. The new energies born from Chi Energy enter the River, and from there, they incarnate. Chi Energy can be perceived as a waterfall or spiral of colors but at the same time can be visible or invisible.

Dr. G: When you pass from the Tree into the River do you pass through Chi Energy?

SM: No, you don't.

Dr. G: When highly evolved energies who have reached the same levels of vibration as Chi Energy reunite with Chi, do they enter Chi Energy from the Tree of Life?

SM: Yes, they enter from the Tree of Life into Chi Energy.

Dr. G: So on the one hand, highly evolved spiritual energies enter Chi Energy from the Tree of Life, and, on the other hand, new energies are born from Chi Energy that enter the River of Life. Is there a balance between how many energies are being born from The Source and how many merge with It?

SM: No.

Dr. G: So in this infinite Universe of Home, there are infinite levels of vibration and infinite planes of existence for all energies that pass beyond the Light?

SM: Exactly, which means that we are not all in the Tree or in the River. We are in our dimensions. You may try to limit, to imagine what is here, but there is no image, no color, no time, space, numbers, limit or separation. The only thing that exists is this special energy—the energy of life—in infinite dimensional planes, protected by the energy that is perceived by those who come Home as "the Light." We, the Guides and Masters, are in our own dimensions. And those of us who decide to reincarnate, enter the River and from there into lives.

Dr. G: Do we study at Home?

SM: You have in your minds the notion of study, work and absolutely everything as a clearly defined notion. Here, study doesn't exist in the terms of picking up a book and reading it. It's simply meditation. You learn from Chi Energy what it means to become an elevated spirit. Although you don't have the same levels of vibration as Chi Energy, you can enter Chi and learn unconditional love. What is at Home is not seen with physical eyes. It's felt with the mind's eye. Why would we need sight when we're not physical, when we're pure energy? We and you are all the same energy that has special properties. It can take whatever color you can imagine. It's physical from a certain perspective and not from another.

Dr. G: What exactly do you mean?

SM: If you think about steam, sure it has molecules, but can you hold the steam in your hand? No. Even though you can feel it, you cannot keep it in your hand.

Dr. G: So although some people may perceive the Tree of Life as being a physical tree, it's actually an energetic tree.

SM: Exactly. And it's the same with the River. And there is no boundary of the Tree of Life or the River of Life. And another thing: the Tree is named as such because that's how it's seen and interpreted by you, since on Earth there is such a thing. But the Tree doesn't truly have the form of a tree. Mia and all the others who have seen it have not yet reached the level from which to perceive it as it really is.

Dr. G: And I suppose the River doesn't have the form of a river, either.

SM: No, it doesn't.

GOD, THE SOURCE OF LIFE

Dr. G: How would you best describe God?

SM: Do you want a description like a photograph? What people seem to want is to have a photographic-type image of God that they can frame and hang on the wall. It's impossible to limit God into a drawing or a picture. What can I tell you? God, The Source of Life, is absolutely everything. Look into the depths of your soul and find that feeling of complete comfort, that feeling of altruistic love, that candidness, that gentility. Everything that represents good and beauty in you and in everyone else around you is God. God is the comfort that you need to warm you up when you're cold, to cool you off when you're hot, to calm you down when you're nervous; to wipe your tears when you are crying and to ease your pain when you're upset. It's everything that represents goodness and kindness. If you need an image, imagine a waterfall or a river of rainbow colors, colors that would flow one into the other. Or picture the white's purity of the snow or the calmness of the infinite blue sky. We are all part of God, part of God's energy. Each of you might see God in a different way, depending on how you want to see God. Some may wish to see God as an all-powerful man while others as a person dressed in white linens sitting on clouds and judging, but those aren't accurate descriptions. God is all of the good that you perceive in you and around you. And God is none other than The Source of Life—Chi Energy—that each of you carry. We are all Gods by virtue of being part of God's energy. We all come to Earth to incarnate again and again, so that when we reach God's levels of vibration we can reunite with It.

Dr. G: How does the reunion with God occur?

SM: When you become such an evolved positive energy It attracts you like a magnet until you merge with It. You cannot resist God, nor can you say that you don't want to reunite with God. Such desire doesn't exist. You become one with the Source and wish to remain there. Then the process of creation starts over. While highly evolved positive energies reunite with Chi Energy, others are being born from Chi. The end becomes the beginning.

Dr. G: I don't know why but I picture God as a sun from which new energies radiate out, energies that will eventually return to God.

SM: It's an analogy. The sun, which is energy, is created by God and the planet Earth would not exist without the sun. You feel its warmth and somehow you make an analogy between the rays of the sun and the love of Chi Energy. It's actually a very pleasant metaphor.

SOPHIA'S EXPLORATION OF HOME

Before continuing the conversation with the Spiritual Masters and Mia, there is another amazing session that I would like to share with you. Sophia, who in our first session uncovered some of her experiences as a Spiritual Guide, returned to continue exploring her true nature and accelerate her spiritual growth. She was excited to tell me that our first session changed her perception of reality and of herself. This allowed her to understand people and human relationships from a higher perspective. She could recognize, without judgment, which people could see beyond human limitations and material things and which could not, and she was able to understand what type of challenges they faced. Furthermore, she learned to distinguish between what she or her soul wanted rather than her negative ego.

Sophia was also very happy because she met her *soul mate* and they were already planning to get married. The first time he held her hand she felt his vibration, and that has been an incredible experience for her. In that moment she realized that he was *the one*. She seemed overjoyed about the turn her life had taken.

Knowing that she could easily connect with the higher levels of her consciousness, I decided to somehow guide her to The Source without her knowing where she was going. I wanted to prevent her conscious mind from interfering with the information accessed by her subconscious and higher self. I didn't know exactly how I was going to achieve this, but I decided to try. I first guided Sophia into the Light. As soon as she got there, she began describing her experience.

S: I feel very good in the Light. I look like light, like rays of light. I know I belong here. It's my home. I'm going to stay here for now.

Dr. G: Try to change your color.

S: I can't change into any other color. I'm just white light.

Dr. G: Can you change form?

S: Not much. I can change from a cloud of light into rays of light.

Then I instructed Sophia to go beyond the Light and enter the River of Life.

S: I'm in the River. It looks like a huge line of bubbles of light, and I can actually see their faces. They are all smiling. They are like me, they are my family. They are all in front of me and it feels like they've been waiting for me. They are many, I would say hundreds of lights. They are welcoming me. It's very nice. My Guides are here too. I see my three Guides—the older man and the two women. They're telling me that what I create is very beautiful and important, and that they will always be around. I just need to listen.

An idea came to mind. I told Sophia to ask her Guides to take her to the Tree of Life but in my mind I asked her Spiritual Guides, and mine, to take her to The Source instead. I didn't know if this would work. I've never personally tested how well the telepathy that our souls use for communication works between us and our Guides. But I believe that experimenting is one of the keys to uncovering our abilities and to learning more about our true nature.

S: The older Guide asked me if I'm really ready. I think I am… So we're going away from this place, far away really fast and everything is getting white... There is a column of light in front of us. It looks like a column of many, many strings of light. It looks like strings of gold and white light connected, but I don't see where it comes from or where it goes. It doesn't look like a tree! I can also feel it… I feel the light, and I can go inside of it!

Judging by the tone of her voice, Sophia was very surprised by what she was seeing.

S: There is so much energy going through this column of light! It's very pleasant. It's going through me too. It looks like a stream of gold and white light or energy. It goes all the way from the top down and from down up. It goes through my body too. It's such a beautiful feeling!

Dr. G: What do you look like?

S: I'm like a cloud of light. There is a really high vibration here, it's really fast. It's filling me up, I feel it. I can't hear anything but I feel. I

feel like I am getting bigger and bigger…Now I'm coming out of it and I still feel it because it's coming with me. I have so much light now! I'm going inside of it again… It says I can come here whenever I want.
Dr. G: Ask this energy who it is.
S: It says it's the River of Life. I said it doesn't look like a river. It's laughing. It says that it's my father and my mother, and the father and mother of everything. It says you can feel it too, and it just is. It says, "I am all there is."

I was speechless. My experiment worked. Moreover, Sophia was able to hear what The Source, God was saying.
Dr. G: What would be important for people to know?
S: It says that people need to open up. They seem to have built this hat on their head, like a lid that closes them. It says, "Just take the lid off! And the energy will come, the vibration, the connection!" But people don't want to let the lid go. They want to control. They don't understand the simple things. The energy is all there is. Everything is energy. Everything is love. It's all good and love. It says, "I am here and I will always be here. So come! I am everywhere around you. You feel me every day, you feel me every night." It says, "Touch the ground, touch the grass, touch the trees and you will feel me." It says that we need a lot of words, even though we really only need one. It says that love and creation are the same. I don't understand…

Sophia didn't understand that the word The Source was referring to, the only one needed was *love*. She was not familiar with the concept of positive energy being the energy of love, the energy that creates everything. It's at the base of everything in existence. Creation is love.
S: It says that I *am* this energy and everyone needs to understand that they *are* the same. They *are* this energy too. It says that even if people don't come, it will come to them. So everything is one. It says if you listen, you can hear its music, and it never stops playing… My Guides are calling me… They want to go, to leave me by myself so I can have my space. I feel very good, I feel complete… There is a lot of purple light around me, purple clouds… I came out of it. I'm taking all the people that welcomed me to this energy, to this light… I'm looking up to this gold and dark purple light, and it's falling on me and on them. It feels amazing! It makes me feel that I know that people need it. They need it so much. I would like to bring the whole world to this energy, to this light!

It seemed that Sophia had invited those welcoming spiritual energies from the River of Life to join her in the energy of The Source.

S: I can see green light too. The green light is surrounding the other people... This energy doesn't have beginning or end. When you go inside, you can go as deep as you can. It seems like it doesn't have boundaries. It's everywhere! It looks like a spiral of light, but it doesn't divide anything. It's changing its color. I see green, orange, dark purple and golden light. It's really shiny. The center is whiter and is spinning. I think I'm below the center because I can look up and it's spinning. It seems as if it's made out of tiny clouds of light. It's constantly and very slowly changing colors. Whenever I move, the energy goes through me. I feel as though I'm part of it. I'm going to the edge again. It's really gold... golden streams of light, so many of them. They look like transparent strings of energy with golden sparks that go up and down, but I don't know what the strings are. It says, "That's what I'm made out of."

I suggested that Sophia ask what this energy, beyond her perception, really is.

S: It says it is life. I feel like I've asked this before but I don't think I understood. It looks like it's a place where you come and go, or at least you stay here for a while. Or you can stay here forever, and even when you're gone, a part of you is still here...

Although Sophia didn't seem to understand what she was conveying, she was beautifully describing the process of souls' birth from Chi Energy, and the reuniting with God when souls reach that elevated state of consciousness. She had also explained that even souls who have not yet reached God's levels of vibration are free to visit whenever they choose.

S: I wish you could come here and feel it! It's so amazing! But I think it's time to go. It's making a bubble around me. It's beautiful! From outside, this energy looks like a round column of light, and I can't see where it starts or where it ends. It's white and gold, and it looks more intense in the middle. It's really shiny, and the inside looks like it's constantly moving up and down. It has so many transparent strings that are alive inside, with what appear to be sparkles going up and down inside the strings. You know when you look at fireworks and the colored sparkles fall down? The sparkles look just like that, but going up and down in the strings. And there are purple clouds of light that keep moving around this column of light. They are almost transparent but I can still see them. (The Masters later explained that those purple clouds of light were highly evolved souls who were close to, or on Chi Energy's levels of vibration.) I'm by myself now. I don't see the souls I brought in. They are probably inside. I'm like a bubble now. I'm wrapped up in its energy and I feel good. I feel protected. Now I'm floating backwards as if I would be lying on my back. I'm still looking at the column and I'm moving slowly away but without going in a specific direction. I see the universe, it's really peaceful. It's dark but not scary. I see stars like in the night sky. I am glowing light, and I just am here. I'm moving slowly, it's very relaxing. I hear that "Up here nothing ever goes to sleep. Nothing is changing."

The Masters later explained that the message Sophia received that "Up here nothing ever goes to sleep" suggests that consciousness never sleeps. It's always aware at its highest level of awareness—the higher self level—of everything that is going on. "Nothing is changing" suggests that Chi Energy will always be everywhere. Chi Energy, God is omnipresent and eternal.

SOPHIA'S INSIGHTS

S: Wow! What an incredible experience! Before I opened my eyes, I couldn't tell which of my arms was the left, and which was the right. At one point I felt tingling sensations all over my body. Before that, I felt tingling in this area (Sophia pointed to the middle of her forehead, to her third eye) and in my arms and hands. I felt like I was floating.
Dr. G: You expected to see a tree, didn't you?
S: Yes! I was very surprised to see this column full of light that had those transparent strings with flickers going up and down. From far away it just looked shiny, and when I got inside, it didn't feel like there were any divisions. It felt as if I went through the strings. Inside, there is no beginning and no end. You don't feel your body. You don't feel boundaries. You just feel the energy as a tingling sensation and you feel full of love. When I left, I was wrapped in that energy. It was in me and around me. It was really amazing! The energy said that everybody can go there but the challenge comes from the human ego that fights the information. You can have this type of experience only if you let go and don't expect anything.
Dr. G: Did you feel that there were others like you inside?
S: I felt but I didn't see any others like me. However, you could invite others, family and friends because some part of you is here and some part of you is there. If you want them to be there then they *are* there. So I invited the ones who welcomed me, my family. And I heard the energy laughing. It said that we complicate everything.
Dr. G: Who do you think this energy was?
S: I think it's the energy that creates everything, that is all around us. It's everywhere. It's just hard to imagine, as people, when you have all these physical things around you.

Dr. G: I told you to go to the Tree of Life but I mentally asked the Guides to take you to The Source of Life.

S: (Sophia began laughing.) Oh, I see. When I think of God, in my mind I see a person. Of course, now I understand… It makes sense. The problem is that people think God punishes you, but It really doesn't. People made that up to keep other people under their control. God is not like people think. It's really full of love. It has no criticism. It's the energy that creates everything. It's infinite, pure love… It's really amazing! I feel really wonderful!

It's remarkable how similar Sophia's description of The Source was to those given by the Masters, Mia and Julia. The details they have provided contribute to an increasingly clearer image of who and what God actually is.

THE FATE OF PLANET EARTH

As I returned to my conversation with Mia and the Spiritual Master, I asked about the fate of our planet.

SM: There is the possibility of advancement to a higher dimension of vibration for planet Earth and humanity. The planet will either advance to a superior dimensional level, remain on the existing level, or fall to a lower dimensional level. And if you're currently in the third dimension, you can either elevate to the fourth where your illnesses and worries will diminish, or you can descend to the second dimension, where you probably know how things are. It all depends on the energies that fluctuate through people. If people manage to let go of negativity, to not allow it to pollute the purity of their souls, then not only will they personally evolve energetically and spiritually, but the planet will evolve to a higher energetic level as well. Planet Earth's fate depends solely on humanity.

Dr. G: How will it be like here, on Earth, if the planet evolves at a higher dimensional level?

SM: When the planet elevates to a higher level, it will be much easier for every person to connect with Home and with us. Many of your so-called pains and illnesses will disappear because the low vibration energies that cause them will not be able to reach the new, higher vibrational level of the planet. Viruses, bacteria and diseases will cease to exist. Life expectancy will increase and science will be very advanced. Planet Earth's energy was very positive, vibrating on a high level when it was created and also during the time of the blossoming civilizations from the beginning of mankind.

Dr. G: Did the planet start to descend vibrationally after a while?

SM: We have remained in our planes of existence, and the planet lowered its vibration. As a result, the low vibration energies started to appear, and along with them illnesses, pains and suffering. Before that, humans lived a very, very long life.

Dr. G: How will life on Earth be if the planet falls to a lower dimensional plane?

SM: If Earth decreases to a lower dimensional plane it will be much more difficult for us to get in contact with you. Basically, the trust in yourself, in divinity, in us—the Guides—and in protective, angelic energies will disappear. Everything will be more chaotic. There will be more calamities, more illnesses and more pain. Technology will continue to exist but not advanced enough. However, in any case don't think that the planet will disappear. We will never disappear, nor planet Earth. We, the positive forces, desire for the Earth's level of vibration to be higher, for the planet to be closer to us; for you to have easier access to us and Chi Energy. As you can imagine, the low vibration forces are trying to somehow keep the planet on the current level, or even bring it to a lower level, to make it easier for them to access it. They don't want you to ask yourselves who you are, to wake up and become aware of your abilities because if you do that, you will vibrate so high as souls that they can no longer reach and influence you. And if the planet vibrates on a higher energetic level, the majority of the low vibration energies that create diseases and calamities will not be able to elevate themselves to that increased vibrational level. Those who will, will be transformed into positive energies. The challenge you're facing is to stop the ignorance of not allowing the truth to get to you because in your life there is a lot of routine and too little truth. You have to open your minds and understand that what is at Home is far beyond the fear-based indoctrination that has been perpetuated for so many hundreds of years. What will happen to planet Earth depends on humanity, on each one of you, and what kind of energy you make room for within your souls. The fate of planet Earth is in your hands. It remains within the power of each one of you whether or not easier paths to access divinity will be opened to you.

WHERE DOES THE INCREASED NUMBER OF SOULS COME FROM?

Dr. G: Many people wonder where all these souls are coming from, since the Earth's population was smaller for so long, and it has increased so much lately.

SM: One of the reasons is that so many souls who have returned Home from their human lives wanted to return to Earth to evolve vibrationally in order to more quickly reunite with Chi Energy. At the same time, many evolved souls who work on elevating Earth's level of vibration have chosen to divide their energy and reincarnate into a large number of people. Moreover, the confrontation between the negative and positive energies has reached a high intensity. The highest evolved souls are engaged in this, and they are helping humanity both in physical and nonphysical form to elevate the planet, to rediscover the higher dimensional plane that Earth was once on.

WHAT ELSE IS IMPORTANT FOR US TO KNOW?

SM: It's important for all of you to understand what moderation is. You often lose yourselves in material desires and forget that you also need spiritual nourishment. Apply moderation in everything you do. Find the balance! Try to not be hungry but not overeat either. Try to not be cold but not too hot either; try to not have too much but not too little either. Learn and practice moderation in absolutely everything you do.
Dr. G: What would you like not to forget if you reincarnated as a human being?
SM: That I'm there to give love, that's what I would like not to forget. And honestly, I would reincarnate into a poor, humble person.
Dr. G: What else is important for us to understand?
SM: That we, all the positive forces of the universe, wish for you— those of us incarnated—to have feelings of unconditional love and compassion toward one another. We want you to have faith in the creative force of The Source of Life—Chi Energy—and to know that you are not alone; that we are always with you. We desire for you to overcome the barriers of your dimension in order to connect with the wisdom that is accessible to every one of you. We would like you to awaken your souls and remember who you really are and why you are on Earth, and to take control over your life that each of you is creating. It's also important to remember to climb the stairs of life one by one. Everything will come to you at the right time, don't rush. Don't try to jump two or three steps at a time to get to the top. Your life, with your conflicts, with your ability to sense, feel or perceive is very delicate. It is, from a certain perspective, a perfection of beauty.
We, the ones at Home, would like to be able to protect you so that you don't feel pain and disappointment. But it's beyond our power because we cannot decide for you. On the other hand, every single disappointment you feel in life opens another universe, another reality or version of your life to you, and gives you the possibility of making

new decisions that can elevate you on your spiritual path. Learn to be patient because every step is very important for understanding the course of this life and to not distance yourself from the path you have chosen to follow. Nevertheless, we are with you when you accept us, and even when you don't accept us we are still with you.

MIA'S EVOLUTION

Dr. G: How do you see Mia at the end of these sessions?
SM: She is evolved and she is much more confident in herself. She doesn't see people with critical eyes anymore, and that's because of the experiences she is living with you when she makes these trips Home. She is now truly a source of positivity for those she comes in contact with.
Dr. G: I can't express my gratitude in words to thank you for sharing your wisdom with us.
SM: You are very welcome. We love you all. We will talk again soon.

MIA' S REVELATIONS

Mia described her trip Home when she came back to her conscious state of awareness.
M: It was very pleasant, calming and relaxing. I went near the Tree of Life. From a distance, it looks like an immense tree with many branches, with a dense crown and millions of sparkles or impulses of energy passing through each branch. It also has branches that hang down like vines, like a weeping willow. The color is superb and intense, and changes according to the impulses that pass through it. When you get close to it, you hear whispers and murmurs of many voices, as if every sparkle tells a story. The Tree is huge. I was curious to touch it but there was nothing to touch. It was as though my hand passed right through it. When I go Home I go mentally, not physically. I can imagine that I have arms and body but I don't see myself. I wanted to touch the Tree, but I realized "what do I think I'm supposed to be able to touch" because even *I* don't exist there with physicality. And that's why I create my body in my imagination. You can create whatever you want there. If you want to imagine a palace, you can but what's interesting is that when you get Home and you're in the spirit state, you don't have thoughts of material things. You don't desire a house or a Ferrari. I never had desires of this nature in that universe. What you feel is simply a wonderful and constant state of calmness, which is very difficult to describe in words. Nothing of the physical

realm interests you, and you don't have a care in the world. You can relax or do whatever you want, and you don't even realize whether a little or a lot of time has gone by because time doesn't exist there. At Home everything is superb. It's sublime! There, you don't think of anything bad. You feel truly at home, and you *know* that nothing bad can happen to you. You feel so protected, and you want to stay there all the time. Sometimes I don't want to come back but I realize that Home is my refuge where I can find peaceful moments. I feel blessed because I can go there anytime and also be here and have this physical life.

Since I've been speaking with you and we have done these sessions, it's as if a new philosophy has appeared in my life: that *we* are in control of ourselves and our bodies, and nothing can happen to us that is not in the control of our consciousness. And that's why I'm no longer afraid. I feel wonderful! I feel happy and I feel in love with life. A year ago I felt so depressed that it physically hurt. It hurt to be alive. It was like physical pain. It felt as if I couldn't breathe, that I could not take it anymore. It hurt to be in the body. But not anymore! I feel absolutely amazing now!

THE END—A NEW BEGINNING

So here is where our stories end and yours begin.

Mia, the young woman who was overwhelmed by severe depression and anxiety and was ready to take her life, now lives a balanced, healthy and happy life. During her amazing journeys beyond the Light she managed to discover the magnificent universe of our infinite Home. She learned what love can really do and became aware of the amazing abilities she possesses of bringing forth the wisdom of the universal mind, the knowledge found at the base of all knowledge. We had access to this knowledge many times throughout history, but for some reason we forgot about, misinterpreted or even denied its truthfulness over and over again. But one way or another, this eternal wisdom keeps finding its way back to us. This time it found its way back through Mia and this book.

Mia also discovered that she can access the Spiritual Masters as well as God—The Creator of life—and that she herself is a wonderful and powerful soul, as we all are. When we wash the grimy layer of negativity that covers our light, what we discover far exceeds anything we could ever expect or imagine.

Ben, the university professor who had struggled with severe depression and anxiety for many years, not only discovered that he had been part of an amazing movement that profoundly elevated the consciousness of mankind, but also came to understand beyond words—through feelings—what it meant to be washed over by divine light and love.

Julia, the interior designer who embarked on a journey of self-discovery, never imagined that her life purpose would be revealed to her by God Himself. She discovered that not only could she easily access and explore the splendor of the universe of Home as well as her former lifetimes, but that she could talk to The Creator, as I'm sure we all can. It's just that we never thought a direct conversation with God is possible, or that we could be worthy of communicating with God.

Sophia, the lady who uncovered a fascinating side of herself she never knew existed, shed light on what it means to function as a Spiritual Guide. She discovered the road back to Home, and experienced the brilliant energy of love that creates everything in existence—the Mother and Father of all there is: God, Chi Energy, The Source of Life.

They all learned that everything in existence is an extension of the brilliance of consciousness, of spirit and of love.

I feel that my journey of exploring the mysteries of consciousness is just at the beginning. I have asked the universe to help me grow spiritually, to elevate my life to better serve others, to understand the secrets of health and healing and to live in exciting times, and the universe has far exceeded my hopes and dreams! It took me Home with each of my clients, and through this book I wanted to take you along with me. I wanted to encourage you to function from the perspective of your true, unconditionally loving self—the positively-oriented part of your mind—and not from the perspective of your illusory, critical, negatively-oriented self—the ego that creates pain and suffering. I desired to help you let go of the beliefs that you are small, that you are insignificant, that you are a victim of circumstances, that nothing you think, say or do matters or changes anything. I wanted to show you what happens when you align yourself with your true nature, and allow the power of the love within you to be the driving force that leads your life. I wanted to empower you to be more of who you truly are—a powerful and loving God—and less of an imperfect Human.

We are all much more powerful, wise and complex than we think we are. No matter what part of the world we live in, what our current life circumstances are or how wealthy we are in this lifetime, our unconditional love will always be our strongest and most valuable asset. The best things about us are the things that cannot be bought, the things that nobody can take away from us: our ability to love, to forgive and to create. It is within our power to "overwhelm" each other with love, kindness and positivity.

We are all pure love. We are eternal beauty. We are greatness in human form. We are immortal Gods walking on this amazingly beautiful planet, and this whole magical world truly is at our fingertips.

About the Author

A researcher of the subconscious mind and human consciousness, Dr. Elena Gabor holds certifications in Hypnotherapy, Medical Hypnotherapy and HypnoCoaching and is a Certified Hypnosis Instructor. In 1995, she received her license as a Medical Doctor of Stomatology in Europe (the equivalent of the Doctor of Dental Medicine in the U. S.) and later specialized in General Stomatology. After ten years of working as a Medical Doctor of Stomatology, Dr. Gabor has redirected her practice toward medical hypnotherapy and alternative health.

Dr. Gabor has developed pioneering techniques for the exploration of the subconscious and superconscious levels of the mind, helping her hypnotherapy clients connect with their higher levels of awareness. She also guides them beyond their incarnations to their eternal home where souls live their timeless lives, connect with the universal mind and have direct experience with Divinity. The health and spiritual growth benefits of using these techniques are remarkable.

Dr. Gabor maintains private practices in Santa Monica, Los Angeles and Pasadena, California, as well as in Europe (Romania) helping thousands of people overcome their life and health challenges, and explore their immortality.

In addition to working with individual clients, she conducts experiential workshops and hypnotherapy certification programs.

Dr. Gabor has also created a series of audio recordings (Mp3s and CDs) in which she uses guided imagery, hypnosis, spiritual regression, meditation and visualization techniques for healing, spiritual growth and the exploration of immortality.

Dr. Gabor is currently writing the sequel, which features her client Mia and the unprecedented discoveries about human consciousness that were revealed during the continuation of their exploration of the subconscious universe. It also follows up on the other three cases described in the book *Home at the Tree of Life.* Furthermore, the sequel presents additional cases of healing and spiritual exploration, expanding the topic on subconscious science.

For more information or if you wish to share with Dr. Gabor your questions, experiences or how her book has helped you, please contact her at:

E-mail: drelenagabor@yahoo.com
Website: www.drgabor.com

About the Author